ANATOMY OF AN ESSAY

INSTRUCTIONS AND READINGS

Second Edition

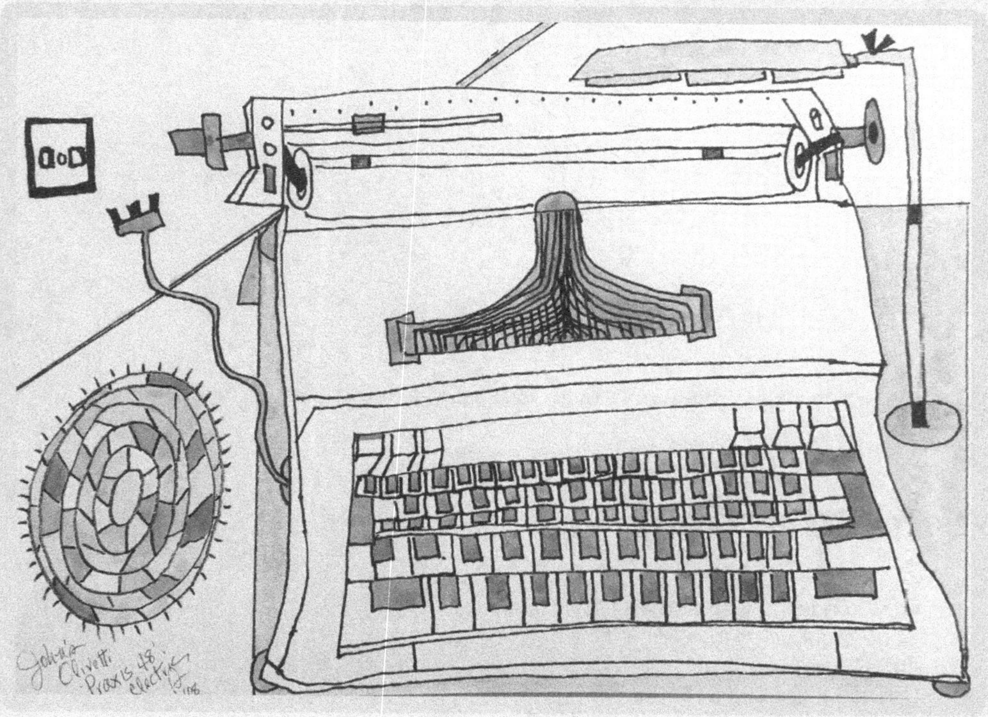

Tina D. Eliopulos and Todd Moffett

Kendall Hunt
publishing company

Cover and section-opener art: © Sandra C. Schultz (deceased), by Anne C. Schultz

www.kendallhunt.com
Send all inquiries to:
4050 Westmark Drive
Dubuque, IA 52004-1840

Copyright © 2019, 2023 by Kendall Hunt Publishing Company

ISBN 979-8-7657-4127-6

All rights reserved. No part of this publication may be reproduced, stored in a retrieval system, or transmitted, in any form or by any means, electronic, mechanical, photocopying, recording, or otherwise, without the prior written permission of the copyright owner.

Published in the United States of America

Dedications

To our students, whose thousands of interactions with us brought forth the ideas you see here.

Sandy Christy Schultz's artwork appears with the permission of her daughter Anne. In addition to her work as an artist, Sandy traveled many roads, devoured literature, wrote nonfiction and fiction, supported environmental projects, and gave friendship to all, including the editors of this text. A graduation gift from her father, the 1954 Olivetti Lettera 22 typewriter featured on the back cover and in the chapter headings of *Anatomy of an Essay* was Sandy's companion for over fifty years. On it, she crafted numerous creative pieces, including, in January of 1997, "Ode to the Olivetti," where she calls her companion her "true friend" and expresses her gratitude: "[T]hank you for not giving suggestions, advice, / where to go for help; / I could just let you put it down like I thought it."

Contents

A Note about Spelling .... *ix*

Chapter 1: Thesis 1
    The Gettysburg Address by Abraham Lincoln   11
    "Taming Silence" by DeAnna Beachley   12
    "I Was Young, Had Hair, and Went to War" by H. Lee Barnes   15
    "Is Carbonated Water Just as Healthy as Still Water?"
        by Christina Caron   19
    Discussion Questions for Chapter 1   22

Chapter 2: Development and Support 25
    "Being Good" by Frankie Mac   33
    "Black Halo" by Christine Boyka Kluge   37
    "So This Is Freedom" by S. L. Kelly   38
    "Black and White and Blue All Over" by Lisa Bailey   41
    "Drowning" by Violet E. Baldwin   44
    "Body Ritual among the Nacirema" by Horace Miner   47
    "O Christmas Tree" by Jack Simmons   54
    "Love in a Time of Terror" by Barry Lopez   56
    Discussion Questions for Chapter 2   65

Chapter 3: Organization 71
    Excerpt from *On Tyranny* by Timothy Snyder: Chapter 11,
        "Investigate"   84
    "Two Ways of Seeing a River" by Mark Twain   88

"Consider It Joy" by S. L. Kelly   90

"RuPaul's Effects on Gender Expression through Drag Culture" by Brooke Workman   95

"Morbid? No—*Coco* Is the Latest Children's Film with a Crucial Life Lesson" by Lucinda Everett   99

"Why Are Americans Afraid of Dragons?" by Ursula K. Le Guin   102

Discussion Questions for Chapter 3   109

Chapter 4: Mechanics 113

"To Scratch, Claw, or Grope Clumsily or Frantically" by Roxane Gay   123

Excerpt from *On Tyranny* by Timothy Snyder: Chapter 17, "Listen for Dangerous Words"   136

Excerpts from *Eats, Shoots & Leaves* by Lynne Truss: From "Introduction: The Seventh Sense"   138

"In Orbit" by Dariel Suarez   144

Discussion Questions for Chapter 4   154

Exercises—Set One   156

Exercises—Set Two   157

Chapter 5: Strategies for Advanced Essays and for Research 161

Sample Essay: "Jane Err" by Kassity Higgins   181

Sample Essay: "A Flawed Law" by Michele Olson   187

Chapter 6: The Literature Essay 195

"The Cask of Amontillado" by Edgar Allan Poe   219

"The Story of an Hour" by Kate Chopin   226

"Brothers" by Sherwood Anderson   229

"The Suitcase" by Meron Hadero   238

"Border Lines" by Alberto Ríos 250
"Mending Wall" by Robert Frost 251
"Inventing New Bodies" by Christine Boyka Kluge 253
"Black Pearl" by Christine Boyka Kluge 254
"The World Is Too Much with Us"
 by William Wordsworth 255
"Leaving Forever" by Denise Levertov 256
Sample Essay: "*Othello*: Three Deaths and a Promotion"
 by Kassity Higgins 257
Sample Essay: "Father Earth, the Tyrant" by Joshua Dycus 263
Discussion Questions for Chapter 6 272

Glossary of Important Terms *277*

A Note about Spelling

Some of the readings in this book were originally produced or published in the United Kingdom, which has spelling rules different from those in the United States. Please note that you will see British spellings in those readings.

Chapter 1
Thesis

Introduction

The act of writing conjures different emotions in each of us. For some, writing provides an outlet to express our convictions and ideas; for others, it induces the same fear felt when stalling our car in the middle lane of a six-lane interstate; and yet for others, writing is the pesky fly interrupting the perfect picnic—if we deal with it, we can return to the fun stuff. Our relationship with writing is connected to our early educational experience: we loved our fifth-grade English teacher, who made all assignments FUN, so we love to write; or we hated our fifth-grade English teacher, who made every assignment a time-sucking, tedious, tormenting task right before recess, so we hate it. But whether you love it, hate it, or are just bothered by it, you still have to write. And you already are doing it—probably multiple times a day like when you're writing an email to a coworker; blogging about your Disneyland trip; reviewing a restaurant on *Yelp*; texting about home designs you repinned on *Pinterest*; documenting a lab experiment in organic biology; Tweeting about tweeting (no idea what happens there); or penning (yes, with an actual ink pen) a letter to a loved one serving in the military. Humans write. We have to. We have a desire to communicate, and writing has been a medium we have used for centuries. If you cannot communicate, you cannot survive. The Sumerians knew this, and *thousands* of years later, we still do, too.

While in college, most of you will endure (and live to tell about it on *Rate My Professors*) at least one composition course. Others, depending on your major, will navigate two or three. But every college student will have to *write* in eighty percent of their classes (thank you, math class, for that twenty percent of fun). So it's time to take a deep breath, steady yourself, and commit to the writing process, especially the creation of the essay, your academic ally.

Freshman and sophomore composition courses sharpen the writing skills you developed in middle and high school, regardless of how many years removed from them you are or how you feel about those experiences. College writing emphasizes your ability to present your thoughts cogently. The primary vehicle of thought in composition courses is the essay, defined by twentieth-century critic and theorist Northrop Frye as "a literary composition on a single subject; usually short, in prose, and nonexhaustive." Tack onto Frye's definition that our word *essay* is derived from the French word *essai*, meaning "an attempt," and beginning writers should understand their purpose for writing an essay: to make an *attempt* at teaching, persuading, or informing their readers (their audience) of *their stance* on an issue—the topic of their essay—while providing some level of entertainment. The essay is sometimes ranked with poetry, fiction, and drama as a fourth literary genre. It's important. But it distinguishes itself from those other forms because it's a work of nonfiction—it may contain *real-life* anecdotes and narrative moments—and it's rooted in fact and TRUTH. Don't refer to your essays as short stories; they are not. Take a creative writing course if you want to write fiction. In composition courses, you are writing your own truth and about the truth of others.

In order to write the essay, you must understand the components of the essay itself: **thesis, development and support, organization,** and **mechanics**. As you work with each of these tools, your essay writing will improve and grow. This textbook instructs you how to use them and offers writing samples from professional and student writers that effectively—not necessarily perfectly—represent them. The components of an essay can also be considered a rubric—not sure who likes this word more, Gen Z's or academics—to evaluate writing. In other words, as you write, build your essay with these four components in mind because your instructor will evaluate your work based upon your competency in using them.

The *Grammarly* website credits Albert Einstein as saying, "A person who never made a mistake never tried anything new." As you read through this textbook's selections and work through its exercises and discussion questions, remember the famous physicist's words. These writers are exploring and experimenting with language and ideas to enrich their own lives and those of their readers. Their work may be the product of two or two hundred drafts. They may have given up on an idea only to dig it out of the trash and redo it. They persisted because they value writing. You too will write and rewrite and rewrite again. You too will learn from your mistakes and your successes. You too will write with purpose. Now go do it.

Writing the Thesis

An explicit **thesis** is a single (that means ONE) sentence that appears in the introductory paragraph of the essay. Its position in the paragraph is entirely up to the writer. It does not need to be the first or last sentence of the paragraph, but it certainly can be. Its placement must be meaningful—it controls what comes before and after it. The thesis sets forth a purpose by naming the essay's issue, conveying the writer's stance about the issue, and implying the work's intended audience. The thesis thus connects the writer, the issue, and the audience, the most important relationships in communication.

If implicit, the thesis still connects writer, issue, and audience, but it is not presented in a single sentence. Often, the thesis will be conveyed with a rhetorical device such as posing a question at the start of the essay and using the essay's content to answer it. In the majority of lower-division writing assignments, the thesis should be explicit unless the assignment dictates otherwise.

Whatever form it takes, the thesis is the brain of all essay content. Without one, your audience is lost. And if your audience is lost, it will abandon you. Your audience wants to learn from you, so your goal as a communicator is to demonstrate purpose. Writing is all about purpose—you must construct each essay with the intent to teach, inform, entertain, or persuade your audience. Consequently, creating a clear thesis is the writer's first task because when it's done correctly, you have taken a major step toward effective composition.

To create a thesis, you must understand the assignment. For example, if your English instructor asks you to write a two-page informative essay about nutrition, you know three essential things: your

Chapter 1: Thesis

purpose—to *inform* your audience—the **length** by which you have to achieve this task—*two pages*—and your assigned **topic**—*nutrition*. You must then narrow the assigned topic to a suitable issue, one that you can cover competently in the given length. To do so, you must employ a prewriting strategy. You CANNOT create a thesis if you have not completed one or more of the many types of prewriting or invention. Many of you already have a toolbox of prewriting skills. Some of you are comfortable with mapping, brainstorming, clustering, free writing, listing, outlining, etc. Each of these strategies has its own merits. Typically, the best choice is the one that allows you to get the most ideas freely onto the page—to purge your brain of any information that you possess about the assigned topic. Remember, when you are prewriting, there are really no wrong answers. You do not need to tinker with mechanics, organization, and development and support. If you feel comfortable prewriting on the computer, that's fine, but prewriting is intended to be a doodling mess, so why not take pen or pencil to paper and see what you can create? To illustrate, here is a cluster about nutrition:

Source: Tina Eliopulos and Todd Moffett

Chapter 1: Thesis

Once you complete your prewriting, you may want to let it sit before you study it and determine your level of comfort with the information in front of you. Such reflection may cause you to redo the prewriting or to plunge right into the next step, writing out a "working" thesis. Yes, your thesis is going to start doing the heavy lifting and earning its title as the essay's brain. Calling the thesis "working" means that you can revise it as you move through the drafting process. For example, if the topic calls for research, then you may need to modify the thesis to accommodate the material you gather. Another reason to change your thesis may have to do with changing your intended audience or rethinking your own stance for the essay. Whatever the reason, don't feel the need to marry yourself to your thesis until the final stages of the drafting process—building paragraphs, reorganizing ideas, etc.

But before we see the bigger picture, let's set our sights on creating the working thesis. One starting point is the **thesis triangle**, also called a communication situation graphic, also called several other names, but all with the same intent of visually showing you the relationship between the writer, the issue, and the audience. With this in mind, we return to our brainstorm to sort through the many ideas that appear on it and consider which ones are appropriate for a two-page informative essay. After thinking about how miserable you were on your last juice cleanse and how tired you grew of eating fish on the Mediterranean diet, you decide you'd like to write about granola. Who doesn't like granola? But what do you really know about granola other than you like it? When you have asked yourself this basic set of questions, then you realize your assignment is calling upon you to research your topic. (Later in this book, you will learn about more concrete and specific college-level approaches to research.) After spending an hour or so learning about granola, you feel ready to craft a thesis triangle. Here it goes:

Chapter 1: Thesis

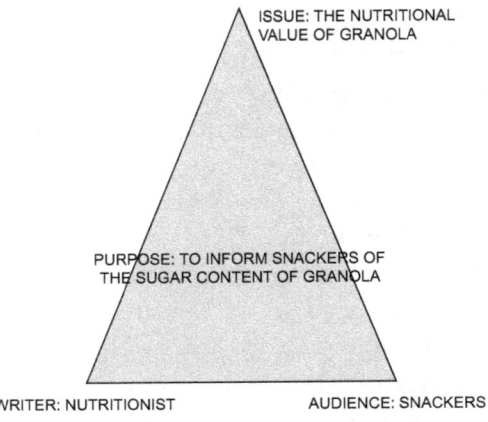

Source: Tina Eliopulos and Todd Moffett

If you want, you can add more details about the writer, issue, and audience to the triangle above to give yourself a better sense of each. For instance, for the writer, you might bullet-point that she is a mother with young kids, that she is alarmed by the sugar content of many processed foods, and that she deals with patients who suffer from diabetes and who struggle to maintain healthy blood sugar levels. For the issue, you might bullet-point that granolas are a grain product, but that those grains have natural sugars, and that granolas may contain as much as ten grams of processed sugar per serving. For the audience, you might add that they are unaware of the processed sugar content but that they are concerned about their health and that they are looking for nutritious snacking options.

Now, with this working thesis in hand, you can begin drafting your two-page informative essay on granola. Even though you have identified your writer persona as a nutritionist, that does not mean you have actually become one in the writing of the thesis triangle. The *writer*, obviously, is You. But You as the writer can adopt any number of personas, serious or not, to present yourself to your audience. You have many roles to fill in your life, and you can work as one of them when you become the writer. With this example in mind—the writer as nutritionist—you will use research from experts in food science to develop and support your thesis.

Likewise, your eventual audience may reach beyond snackers—really, who doesn't like to snack?—and benefit them. All essays have a wider audience, but you should always write with a *specific* audience in mind, well defined and interested in what you have to say about the issue. You want your essay content to address an audience that has a clear stake in what you have to say—a specific need for the information that you provide. Keep in mind that the wider audience is **never** the "general public"—that is, everyone. You **never** want to be considered the general writer. You want to be considered a writer with a unique and informed voice—and you want to extend the same courtesy to your reader.

Writing the Lead

Your essay's introductory paragraph will have more to it than just your thesis. In the rest of the introduction, you should engage your audience's interest so that they won't put down your essay after reading one sentence and sniff, "Boring!" In the newspaper business (yes, yes, who reads newspapers anymore? But still . . .), the introduction is known as the **lead** (or **lede**), and its very purpose is to keep the audience reading an article for more than five seconds. That's right! It takes readers—including, one might add, English professors—only five seconds to decide whether to continue reading an article. Be aware of yourself the next time you read a gamer's blog or an entertainment zine to see how long it takes *you* to decide.

For the lead, you may choose from among several strategies. Here are six of the most common: *direct statement, anecdote, surprise, description, mood, problem.*

> *Direct Statement:* The direct statement assumes that the topic you are discussing has enough appeal to stand on its own. The very first sentence of your essay, therefore, presents your topic without any attempt to burnish it.
>
> *Anecdote:* The anecdote is a very brief story (between fifty and one hundred words) that illustrates the topic you have chosen. The anecdote can be drawn from your own personal experience,

from that of a friend or relative, or from a general store of shared experience (the first day of school, for example).

Surprise: A surprising detail about your topic, one that your audience has not considered, gives your topic a shock value that creates a desire to read more. Readers will naturally want to know the source of their surprise, a need you should address at some point in the essay.

Description: A physical description based upon the five senses, especially if your paper topic is about a person, place, or thing, gives the reader a sensory impression that will carry through the rest of the essay.

Mood: A mood is an emotional atmosphere you create. Used in conjunction with description or anecdote, the mood can soothe, arouse, amuse, anger, charm, or create any emotional response that you feel will best set the tone for your essay.

Problem: The problem—a puzzle or a conflict you set before the reader—creates its own easy-to-follow storyline because the paper should inevitably present a cause of, a result of, or a solution for the problem. Like the surprise, the problem creates an expectation within the reader upon which you must deliver.

Here are some examples of these leads in action. The issue covered in each is steroids.

Direct Statement: Unsupervised steroid use can destroy your body—just as it did to Ken Caminiti, Lyle Alzado, and Rich Piana.

Anecdote: Starting when he was fifteen, Joe resorted to steroids because he was afraid of losing his spot on the varsity football team. Twice a week, his older teammate Ron would come to his house and shoot him in the buttocks with a hypodermic needle he had stolen from his mother, a registered nurse. Unfortunately, Ron one day missed the muscle and instead hit a nerve with the needle. The resulting damage nearly caused Joe to lose a leg.

Surprise: When men start using steroids, the first growth they might see is bigger breasts.

Description: Joe's thighs and buttocks have a patchwork of scars and bruises—like those of a junkie—from the needles he has used to inject himself.

Mood: Joe punched his fists through the wall and yelled at his wife for not having dinner ready promptly at six o'clock. After she ran from him and locked herself in their bedroom, he took a sledgehammer to the door. Only when the screaming of his terrified children snapped him out of his rage did he realize that his steroid use was turning him into a monster.

Problem: When Joe woke one day with pain in his back, he discovered that his skin had broken out into horrifying rashes.

Whichever lead you try, remember that it must help you clearly establish your thesis—the issue, audience, writer, and purpose of the essay. You will note that in some of the examples above, the issue is already stated in the lead itself. Once you have used your lead, make sure to present your thesis in a way that draws upon the energy (and follows the direction) your lead has established.

Thesis Writing Exercises

Consider the two alternative thesis triangles below. One presents an instructive thesis, teaching the audience about snack choices better than granola, and the other a persuasive thesis, telling the audience that granola is not as nutritional as snackers may believe. After studying both triangles, take another look at our original brainstorm—or create a completely new one—and craft four of your own thesis triangles, each representing one of the four distinct essay purposes: to inform, to teach, to entertain, and to persuade.

Chapter 1: Thesis

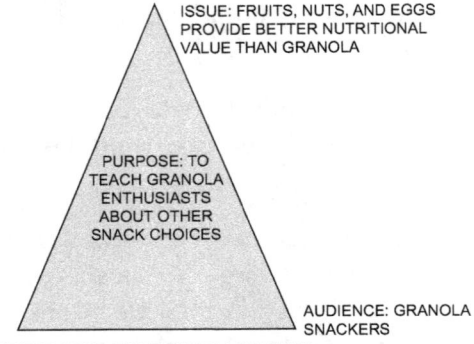

Working Thesis: Oranges, almonds, and eggs make better snack choices than granola bars.

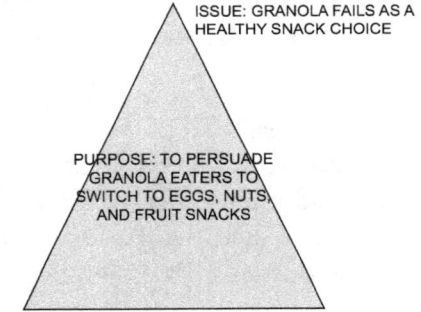

Working Thesis: Because of granola's processed sugars and empty calories, it fails to provide the necessary nutrients of other snacks such as oranges, almonds, and eggs.

Source: Tina Eliopulos and Todd Moffett

The Gettysburg Address
by Abraham Lincoln

Four score and seven years ago our fathers brought forth on this continent, a new nation, conceived in Liberty, and dedicated to the proposition that all men are created equal.

Now we are engaged in a great civil war, testing whether that nation, or any nation so conceived and so dedicated, can long endure. We are met on a great battle-field of that war. We have come to dedicate a portion of that field, as a final resting place for those who here gave their lives that that nation might live. It is altogether fitting and proper that we should do this.

But, in a larger sense, we can not dedicate—we can not consecrate—we can not hallow—this ground. The brave men, living and dead, who struggled here, have consecrated it, far above our poor power to add or detract. The world will little note, nor long remember what we say here, but it can never forget what they did here. It is for us the living, rather, to be dedicated here to the unfinished work which they who fought here have thus far so nobly advanced. It is rather for us to be here dedicated to the great task remaining before us—that from these honored dead we take increased devotion to that cause for which they gave the last full measure of devotion—that we here highly resolve that these dead shall not have died in vain—that this nation, under God, shall have a new birth of freedom—and that government of the people, by the people, for the people, shall not perish from the earth.

Source: The Gettysburg Address, 1863

Chapter 1: Thesis

Taming Silence
by DeAnna Beachley

Your old life was a frantic running from silence.
—Rumi

May. 1989. I got into my car, put UB40's *Labour of Love* in the tape deck. Other cassettes waited in a case on the seat beside me. There were few radio stations in the empty spaces on I-40 the 1,949 miles between Flagstaff, AZ, and Youngstown, OH. I glanced at myself in the rearview mirror, eyes haunted. I couldn't look at myself for too long. Preferred the middle distance.

My 1984 Honda two-door hatchback stuffed with thrift shop finds and books in every space. I didn't need a map because I had traveled this route three times already, but I kept one handy. I liked the comfort of that slightly worn map. I had delayed my departure as long as I could. I knew a confrontation awaited. I knew that it had ended with Steve, but the final break had yet to happen.

I was singing along to "Many Rivers to Cross," not even an hour out of Flag when I stopped at a gas station/diner to get a bowl of soup and a sandwich. After I ate, I went to change tapes and the cassette stuck. It wouldn't play. It wouldn't eject. *Son of a bitch*, I yelled to the tape deck, the map. *Shit*, to the clothing-filled garbage bags in the back. Frantic glance of my face in the mirror.

I couldn't listen to the radio. Nothing to keep me company but the car tires on the road and my thoughts. I watched the semis pass me on the highway, saw the turn-off to the Painted Desert, paid attention to how many miles to go before I got to Gallup.

Silence.

All that loud silence, the pressure in my ears. To think about what I didn't want to think about. To confront how I felt about Steve. How I put the relationship on a pedestal. Was I with him because he was nice to me in German class?

Eject.

Copyright © by DeAnna Beachley. Reprinted by permission.

Chapter 1: Thesis

I now saw the lava beds near Grants. The rough surfaces reminded me of all I had avoided, how everything roiled underneath. All molten.

Silence.

I had kept myself busy with research and papers that spring semester, stuffed down thoughts about my trip over winter break, afraid of what those thoughts would yield. How he showed up at the airport with his friend Fritz to pick me up. That should have been my first sign. Or that little shrug when he explained the black eye from a drunken fight where a gun was pulled. Or the times when I phoned him to talk throughout October and November, and he was not home. Or, or, or.

Eject.

To maintain distance from my thoughts, to avoid the silence, I made noise. I sang old church camp songs ("Camp Bethel Pep," "Make New Friends but Keep the Old"), 4-H songs I learned in fourth grade while living in Virginia (*There was a little chigger, I'm going crazy*). Parts of hymns I remembered ("Blessed Assurance," "Just As I Am"). I recalled those fearless moments, how I jumped willingly into lakes, and pools filled with cold Appalachian water. I thought of my parents, how my dad stopped talking to me when I moved in with Steve. Wondered how that relationship could be repaired, worried that it wouldn't. Would my friends return my calls after months of hearing nothing?

The New Mexico high desert gave over to the Texas panhandle and Amarillo. Occasionally, I'd press eject, to see if this time the player would release the tape, but it never did. I'd take a glance at the map: *Guide me. Help me find myself.*

Oklahoma never seemed to end, the road flat and straight, plains stretched for miles. Exhausted the song lyrics I remembered, tired of repeating them, I settled in to have a conversation. I cried. I yelled, *You bastard*, to the image of him in my head. I kept talking as those miles unfolded. Told myself I was living in the fantasy I had created in the daily letters I sent him. A boy and a girl remodeled an old schoolhouse, filled it with light, art, and antiques. They spent the spring walking freshly plowed fields looking for arrowheads. They found a painting at a thrift shop that ends up being worth thousands of dollars. Knew I had changed. I hiked the Grand Canyon twice that year. I had lost twenty-five pounds and bought myself a new leather skirt to celebrate. I delivered my first paper at a conference. I still couldn't look at myself too closely in the mirror.

The map there to remind how close I was to home, which would soon no longer be home.

The rolling hills of Missouri, Illinois, Indiana, and then finally, Ohio. My stomach ached from bad coffee and nerves, I practiced what I needed to say to him. Let the silence sink into my cells as I pulled into the driveway. Took a deep breath, gave myself one last look in the rearview mirror, *You can do this.* Opened the car door.

Chapter 1: Thesis

I Was Young, Had Hair, and Went to War
by H. Lee Barnes

I read too many stories of small lives in search of understanding something so vague it hardly seems a problem, if indeed it exists at all, and I wonder why these writers don't have messier lives or at least messier minds. Are their lives and minds as sterile as their prose is clean? What experience do they hit the water with when the fire is at their backs? The fact of experience may not stir a smooth, easy psychofictive drama that leads to a nice, neat epiphany, but experiences, especially those worth having, are rarely smooth and rarely internal. They are rather internalized, become perhaps obsessions.

I was young, had hair, and went to war. No experience since has been as forceful or as immediate or genuine. Thirty years later it is an after ring, an irritant, a vibration that gives tone to everything I write, but there is one moment that slips irresistibly into my consciousness. The moment lives by itself, forms and recasts itself in the fiction, nonfiction, and poetry I've written. In part, this is it:

> I stand on a mound atop my camp, Tra Bong, a bare swell of red earth, cut by trenches and surrounded by three barriers of barbed wire. Monsoon clouds stalk landward up the fertile valley, which in sunlight is emerald and shimmering with rice paddies where water lies so still you can walk the berms and see trees and sky reflected precisely on the surface. But now everything is leaden, and colorless except the red clay, which slurries in the trenches like molten rust. I watch one hundred Vietnamese soldiers march away from the camp led by four Americans, one my captain, two my friends, Brownie and Jacobson, and the last Riffschnelder, who is due to rotate out of the country in weeks. Him I barely know. There are reasons I cannot write this image out of my life, try though I may. First, all of the Americans died. Second, I was supposed to go on the operation and Brown died in my place. Third, it was an ill-advised mission. Fourth, I saw

---

Copyright © by H. Lee Barnes. Reprinted by permission.

a beetle crawl out of a bullet hole in Jacobson's forehead. Fifth, Captain Fewell's body was never recovered, but his head was discovered months later in a Buddhist pagoda where he'd been decapitated. I along with a handful of others survived to try and make sense of our buddies' deaths and to speculate, I especially, on that most profound and most dreadful of questions: Why me? (Or, if you prefer: Why not me?)

All experience orders up opposing questions, and roughly the same lame answers, and despite the impact of this particular experience, more than fifteen years lapsed before I began writing about Vietnam. The first manuscript, a novel, went through a round of rejections, some complimentary, most standard, before I wrote away from that subject. Twelve years would pass before Vietnam again found space in my writing. When it did, it became the force behind a novel manuscript, a novella, seven short stories and an ongoing string of poems, all written in two years. Obsession.

Of course I didn't realize it was an obsession until Alberto Ríos, who teaches graduate writing at ASU, told me of a seminar he conducts called "Obsessions." The concept is to take a particular image, work it and rework it for an entire semester, following whatever direction it takes. The method, even as he described it to me, resounded with truth, for as a way to develop an honest dialogue with experience, the writer must, I think, be a bit obsessed. This, it seems, is approximately what I've experienced in writing about Vietnam. It isn't the fact or the truth of the experience I wish to capture, but the intensity and effect. Poe was right on this count: The writer should write toward effect. Roderick Usher, crushed under the weight of his house, took the full force of it in front of his friend's eyes. In my story "Gunning for Ho" Bruce Stoner used explosives and a television camera to negate the problem of distance. The narrators (survivors) are compelled to tell the story. The plots are (quite by accident) parallel but the experiences that impel the stories are dissimilar and thus the details are quite different. Each experience has its own frequency. I don't know what inspired Poe, but I drew upon the experience of climbing mountains into Laos, of being in the Tra Bong Valley, of seeing friends die, of witnessing and engaging in youthful macho behavior. Plot limits stories; experience limits the writer but creates a uniqueness of vision.

In both "Gunning for Ho" and "Cat in the Cage" I use the image of a prisoner carried in a bamboo cage. This was an actual condition some captured Americans, particularly pilots and Special Forces troopers, endured. Though I never experienced it, I was indoctrinated to the possibility of suffering such mistreatment if captured. I, by being in proximity to where such things happened, experienced the fright. I best relate this to a woman I know who suffers nightmares about rape, all manner of violations. I'll not venture into the psychology of her phobia, but I know with certainty she has experienced the terror of rape. Must a woman be raped to feel the fear or imagine the indignities involved?

Along with the actual and imagined experience, my writing includes use of the collective experience, which includes history and social setting. This is the hard part of writing stories about Vietnam; here is where gender and age, where bias and assumption, where "other" experiences and myths and stereotypes emerge. I know from rejections that accompany my Vietnam stories (and there are many) that women generally, particularly young women, can't enter into the narratives. The stories, simply put, meter out too high on the testosterone scale—men, Vietnam, death. The collective experience of women readers from my generation seems rooted in antiwar marches or loss of family or friends and the women's movement (and those are their stories); the younger ones' reactions are likely linked to *Rambo* and bad-movie dates with pimply-cheeked kids who were raised watching cartoon warriors (and those are their stories). Women and men alike associate Vietnam with My Lai, napalm, heroin addiction and racism. It's so easy to view it from these perspectives, to give it your own slant. (In fact My Lai was an aberration, but atrocities committed by the Viet Cong and North Vietnamese on Montagnard and South Vietnamese were commonplace and part of a political strategy.)

Recently I read of a Navy corpsman who served with the Marines at Hue. He'd crawled out into enemy fire to carry wounded Marines to safety or to administer aid and gather ammunition.

Though wounded several times, he'd continued to go out and had saved several Marines. He was so badly shot up that he was thought to be dead and was set aside with the dead while the wounded were evacuated. Somehow he lived through his wounds and drifted into obscurity. Over twenty-five years later he was recognized by one of the Marines who'd witnessed his courage on that violent day. Others came forward to testify to this man's selfless acts of courage. Thirty years after the battle, he was awarded the Congressional Medal of Honor. This speaks of old-fashioned heroism, but in a way speaks also of the collective experience I mentioned, the one that is somehow counter to the greater consciousness of the literary establishment. The corpsman's story isn't one day at Hue or a ceremony during which the president of the United States drapes a medal over a hero's neck; it is the thousands of days in between and the tomorrow he faces.

I like the splash and the ripples that move the boat, the sudden surprise when a fish jumps unexpectedly. I feed off what is incomprehensible. I want a continuing dialogue with the boy who stood atop that mound of red clay and watched his friends march down a valley to their deaths. He raises the questions that start the process (for these are my stories).

Is Carbonated Water Just as Healthy as Still Water?
by Christina Caron

Unsweetened carbonated water is a better choice than soda or fruit juice. But don't overdo it, experts say.

There's still water, and then there's what my four-year-old calls "spicy water," better known as seltzer or sparkling water. Crisp, bubbly and effervescent, carbonated water has become a daily ritual for many and a growing segment of the beverage industry, with yearly sales now topping $4 billion in the United States.

For those who crave it, carbonated water offers a sensory experience that flat water cannot: There's the satisfying snap as you pull back the tab on the can. The sound of the fizz as you unscrew the bottle cap to pour yourself a glass. The tingly sensation as the beverage hits your tongue, sometimes with a hint of "natural" flavor.

Still water is great for hydration, "but you would be surprised at the number of people who don't like the taste and are unwilling to drink it," said Anne Linge, a registered dietitian-nutritionist at the University of Washington Medical Center in Seattle. "Adding carbonation may make it more acceptable."

More acceptable, perhaps, but also just as healthy?

Nutritionists agree that carbonated water (a category that includes seltzer water, which is artificially carbonated, and naturally sparkling water) is just as hydrating as regular water; however, tap water has the added benefit of fluoride, which helps prevent tooth decay.

"If you are using fluoridated water for brushing your teeth, cooking and some of your hydration, you can also include sparkling water in your diet," Linge said. And if you use tap water to make your own carbonated water at home, then your bubbly water already has fluoride in it.

But keep in mind that carbonated water is more acidic in our mouths than flat water.

From *The New York Times*, September 14, 2021 by Christina Caron. Copyright © 2021 The New York Times. All rights reserved. Used under license.

Bubbly water contains carbon dioxide, which is converted to carbonic acid when it mingles with saliva, lowering the pH level of your mouth. The pH scale indicates whether a solution is more acidic (lower pH) or alkaline (higher pH). Drinks with a lower pH can be erosive to teeth, making them more susceptible to cavities; however, unsweetened carbonated water is not nearly as erosive as soda or fruit juice, according to a 2016 study published in the *Journal of the American Dental Association*.

Some carbonated water brands include ingredients like citric acid for taste, which can raise the acidity level. Adding your own slices of lemon or lime would have a similar effect. And because the ingredient list will often say "natural flavor," it is hard to know exactly what was added.

Research on carbonated water and its effect on the teeth is sparse. But according to Dr. Brittany Seymour, an associate professor at the Harvard School of Dental Medicine and a spokeswoman for the American Dental Association, "It would take quite a lot of consumption throughout the day to have damaging effects similar to what we'd see with fruit juice or soda."

The bottom line: Because carbonated water still has the potential to be erosive, think of it as a once-a-day treat rather than your main source of water, Seymour said.

"If you want to have two or three sparkling waters a day, perhaps pair them with a meal," she added.

When you eat, your mouth produces additional saliva, which can help neutralize acids on the surface of your teeth.

If you prefer drinking it alone, without food—Seymour usually drinks unsweetened seltzer while cooking dinner—use a straw to help the water bypass your teeth. In general, try not to sip it for more than an hour. Drinking carbonated water over a long time period prolongs the amount of time that your teeth are exposed to acidity.

If you love fizzy water and like to drink it multiple times a day, without meals, consider brushing your teeth with a fluoride toothpaste afterward to stave off tooth decay. Just make sure to wait at least thirty minutes after your last drink, Seymour said.

Chapter 1: Thesis

Why? The acidity of the carbonated water softens the enamel of your teeth. Taking a break gives your enamel a chance to re-mineralize and return to its normal hardened state, which is the ideal surface for brushing because it can better tolerate abrasives, she added.

If you have kids who also like to indulge in bubbly water, "I would say in general it's fine," Seymour said. But, she added, "I wouldn't do it every day with my daughter." Ideally, parents should encourage their children to drink still, fluoridated water to guard against cavities, she said, and reserve the sparkling water for special occasions.

Carbonated beverages can also contribute to gas and bloating, but the degree varies from person to person.

"When you swallow carbonation, it has to come out somewhere, so you either belch it out or it's passed through flatulence," said Courtney Schuchmann, a registered dietitian at University of Chicago Medicine who specializes in gastrointestinal health. "If you're someone who already has issues with gas and bloating, it can cause more symptoms for you."

Carbonation can also make acid reflux worse and have a "filling effect," which may diminish your appetite by creating distention in your belly, she added.

Regardless of what type of water is preferred, Schuchmann said she typically counsels her clients to drink about half their body weight in ounces, assuming they have a normal body mass index. Those fluids can also include coffee, tea and the water in fruits and vegetables. But there is no hard and fast rule about how much water to drink each day, she added, because it depends on many factors, including your body size, activity level, environment, medical conditions and so on.

Something else to keep in mind: Many people assume club soda and seltzer water are interchangeable. However, club soda usually has sodium.

"For someone watching their blood pressure, that is something to take into consideration," Schuchmann said. "It depends on what the rest of your diet looks like and how much sodium is coming from other sources."

Discussion Questions for Chapter 1

1. Create a thesis triangle for each essay in this chapter. Clearly, the writer of each is the author of the piece, but see if you can discern something about the writer's stance, background, or persona. Identify the issue and three details about that issue. Identify the audience and determine the audience's stake in and opinion toward the issue. Write down each author's purpose and thesis sentence. If the thesis sentence is implied, then write one using your own words. Once you have completed the thesis triangle, determine if you feel the writers achieved their purposes.

For Abraham Lincoln

1. Lincoln's Gettysburg Address is a famous speech. How do Lincoln's words represent his place in American history? Did his actions as a president match the message of his words? Why or why not? Think of other famous speeches and measure the words of the speech against the actions of the speaker.
2. Lincoln makes use of what are known as figures of speech, an idea explained more completely in chapter two and in the glossary at the back of this reader. What figures can you find in his speech?
3. Identify another speech, song, poem, painting, or sculpture that commemorates a historic moment. Name its creator, intended audience, and subject matter. What devices did its creator use to convey its purpose? How does it uphold or honor that moment? Has it evolved beyond its original intent?

For DeAnna Beachley

1. Beachley, in her opening paragraphs, uses one of the leads to engage her audience. Which lead, and how does it play out in the rest of her essay?
2. Throughout her essay, Beachley reacts to a cassette tape that is stuck in her car's player. Why is the tape important to the journey she is making? What does the tape seem to symbolize about her own life? Beachley also refers to a map multiple

times in the essay. What does the map symbolize about her? How has technology changed the way we carry memories? (You can read more about symbolism in chapter six.)

For H. Lee Barnes

1. Barnes and Lincoln seem to address audiences with widely different attitudes about the issues they have raised. On the one hand, Barnes seems to be addressing an audience that is hostile toward (or at least ignorant of) the experience of Vietnam War veterans. On the other hand, Lincoln is addressing an audience sympathetic toward the soldiers who died for the Union in the Civil War. What strategies do the authors use to engage with these audiences? Write out your own stance on the issues that the authors address.
2. An important idea Barnes addresses seems to be obsession, a concept he learned while studying creative writing. Barnes's obsession is spurred by an image from Vietnam. That image, which Barnes still carries with him, has served as a catalyst for much of his writing. What is the image? What is an experience that holds such significance in your life? Think of one that carries the intensity and effect that Barnes mentions. How have you grown or been affected by it?
3. Compare and contrast the tone taken by Beachley and Barnes toward the personal experiences described in their essays. How has each writer been shaped by their experiences?

For Christina Caron

1. Christina Caron poses a question as the title of her piece. Does she ever answer it? If so, where? And what side of the issue does she seem to support?
2. What exactly is Caron's purpose for writing? Why do you think she began her lead with a reference to her four-year-old's name for sparkling water?
3. Bottled water is a large and lucrative industry. Does this industry benefit or exploit consumers? Explain your answer.

Chapter 2
Development and Support

Writing is much like growing up. As we age, we learn from our mistakes—we repeat what works well for us and we discard what fails us. Likewise, as writers, we turn to patterns of writing that have proven to help us communicate our ideas to others.

We call these patterns **development and support**. The composition instructor defines development and support as the means used by a writer to elaborate, explain, or prove the essay's thesis. Development and support is as important to a writer as evidence is to an attorney. Imagine a lawyer attempting to win over a jury without proof. It just does not happen. Similarly, once a writer has crafted a working thesis, she must begin to gather the necessary development and support. Sometimes in the prewriting or invention stage, you will brainstorm ideas that will actually be part of the development and support you will use in the essay. So look closely at that cluster or that triangle or that free write again. Now you will use those ideas with intent.

There are several ways of developing a thesis:

Description
Narration
Example
Process
Comparison and Contrast
Analogy
Cause and Effect
Classification and Division
Definition
Argumentation

25

Chapter 2: Development and Support

We start with **description**, perhaps the most important, because the other modes named above rely on this skill, and all types of writing—personal, academic, creative, vocational, professional—require it. Description allows readers to understand a subject through their senses: sight, sound, taste, touch, and smell. For example, if you are eating at a sushi restaurant for the first time, you may need some assistance to navigate the menu. You've never tried unagi before, but your friends have, so you ask them, "What does it taste like?" You probably will not agree to try it just because they reply, "It's good." *Good* is one of those abstract words that means something different to each of us. You need concrete details. So when your friends say, "It has a strong salty flavor and firm texture that is balanced very nicely by the sweet sauce in which it's prepared," the description now appeals to your senses, and you are more willing to try this new food even when you find out that unagi is eel. (Another treatment of concrete versus abstract language appears in the discussion of poetry in chapter six.)

While description focuses on sensations, **narration** relies on a sequence of events. For example, your experience with unagi could evolve into a series of episodes setting out how your friends took you to the sushi bar, how you saw unagi on the menu, how you first tasted it, and how it became your favorite food. Your introduction to such an essay might be as follows: "Many twenty-one-year-olds mark their legal age with a drink at the bar, but I chose a different path. I went to a bar and met unagi. Now, I spend each year celebrating my birthday with an eel." Narration thus can share a personal experience by relating the actions taken by the people involved, the purpose being to point out how one of those actions changed the life of the person telling the story. The order of events in a narration is often chronological—but not always. Sometimes a flashback—an action taken at an earlier time—may break the order. Sometimes the writer may relate the events out of order to create surprise, suspense, or some other effect.

An essay using description or narration will contain multiple **examples**, which in their own right are an essential method of development. An example is a specific instance of a general idea and is usually signaled by a transition such as *for example, for instance*, or *to illustrate*. Say your essay's purpose is to explore historic vacation spots. You may want to illustrate them according to their geographic locations: "Each region in the United States has several historic landmarks to visit. For example, in the west, tourists flock to California's gold country to recall the riches discovered there in 1848 and reflect on the grit and ingenuity of the early western settlers. Similarly, while visiting Pennsylvania, many gather to view the Liberty Bell and marvel at the Founding Fathers' role in securing America's freedom." Examples can be stacked or isolated within the essay's body paragraphs. What's important is to make sure the examples support the thesis and the paragraph idea and are interpreted accordingly.

Another form of development, **process**, is quite popular. Think about the thousands of instructional videos found on the internet. Many of these are *directional processes*—processes designed to teach you how to follow the steps yourself—such as how to build a rocking chair, how to make a meringue, how to install an air filter in a fish tank, or how to apply mascara. Similarly, you might find books at your local bookstore on how to deal with grief, how to play fantasy baseball, how to mine a database using SQL, or how to start your own online business. The subject matter is as diverse as the readers who seek them out. On the other hand, an *informational process* tells us not how to do something but how something came about. Thus, accounts of how humans landed on the Moon, how the alphabet formed, how bees make honey, and how the Vegas Golden Knights won the Western Conference of the NHL in 2018 are informational processes. Either type of process needs to be enriched by examples that underscore the concise steps. If telling your audience how to schedule a trip, for example, you might list a process such as this one: "When planning your vacation to New York City, the first thing you must do is consider which of the city's landmarks fit your interests, then you must save money to enjoy each of them, and then you must contact your travel agent to secure the most budget-friendly rates for airfare and hotel."

Comparison and contrast, like process, is a thinking strategy that we do every day. Should I wear slacks or shorts? Should I travel surface roads or the freeway? Should I splurge on dinner out or make a peanut butter and jelly sandwich? Underlying questions like these are comparisons of how one might look in pants versus shorts, how long it might take to travel one route or the other, or how much better a pie from Metro Pizza might taste than the sandwich. Developing our ideas with comparison and contrast comes quite naturally, but we still need to identify some points of distinction when we attempt to do the same task in writing.

To compare, we find similarities. Thus, if we compare Fatburger to Shake Shack, we find that they both have a basic menu of burgers, fries, and shakes; loyal customers; and burgers with an appealing taste. To contrast, on the other hand, we find differences. For instance, Fatburger and Shake Shack use different toppings and seasonings on their burgers, size their burger patties differently, and offer different sides and drinks: Fatburger sells onion rings, but Shake Shack will turn a shake into a malt. Frequently, our purpose when comparing or contrasting is to make a choice. Our reason for comparing Fatburger and Shake Shack thus might be to pick one or the other as our next burger option: "Though Fatburger has tastier burgers, Shake Shack offers malts and crispier fries and thus makes a better overall meal."

An **analogy**, like a comparison, looks for similarities between two (or more) items. However, a comparison looks for similarities between two items that are somewhat alike. If you are looking for likenesses between the Toyota Camry and the Honda Accord, for example, you are making a comparison between two cars—two like objects. An analogy, on the other hand, makes a comparison between two unlike objects. To illustrate, a comparison of a Toyota Camry and molten lava is an analogy. The writer, assuming the reader has a stronger understanding of one of the two objects, creates an analogy to explain one object through the other.

The analogy sometimes starts with a figure of speech known as a *simile*. The basic pattern of the simile creates likeness: "A ___ is like a ___." If you put two unlike objects—or an abstraction and a concrete word—in the blanks, you begin the process of creating an analogy. In the case of our example above, you would have started with something like this: "A Toyota Camry is like molten lava." You can create others such as "Love is like a rose," or "Poetry is like a bird in flight." To develop the analogy completely, however, you will then need to explain and describe exactly how your two chosen terms are alike.

Instead of a simile, you may also start an analogy with a figure known as a *metaphor*. The basic pattern of the metaphor establishes not just likeness but equality: "A ____ is a ____." We can take one of the similes we started above and turn it into a metaphor like so: "A Toyota Camry is molten lava." The association is stronger with the metaphor than with the simile because you are saying that the two objects are not just similar but the same. The trick to creating metaphors (and similes) is understanding that some trait of one of the objects is being transferred to the other. To develop the analogy further, you must clearly identify and describe that trait so that your reader will see why you are making the comparison. In this case, you can describe for the reader how fast molten lava moves or what it looks like. With that knowledge, the reader can better understand some aspects of the Toyota Camry.

Cause and effect is a pattern of development often required in classes other than English. A biology teacher may ask, for example, how radiation affects skin cells. An automotive instructor might ask why a car's engine is sputtering rather than purring. A dental hygienist may explain how plaque may cause gums to recede if it is not properly removed. A cause is the reason behind an action taken, a choice made, or a circumstance that exists. An effect, on the other hand, is the result of an action taken, the outcome of a choice, or the impact of a circumstance. For example, in her article "Morbid? No—*Coco* Is the Latest Children's Film with a Crucial Life Lesson," journalist Lucinda Everett discusses how several Disney films affect the children who view them. Everett makes a poignant case for the lessons to be learned from the film *Up*: "It charts every punishing blow of adult life from losing a baby to money troubles to repeatedly putting your dreams on hold."

Classification and division are patterns of development that examine classes, categories, or components. On the one hand, classification splits a large group into two or more smaller groups, each with a distinct feature shared by its members; on the other, division splits one item into its elements, ingredients, or parts. For instance, after my one thousand experiences of eating sushi in the Las Vegas Valley, I can classify the many restaurants as traditional, contemporary, or fusion. Or I can focus on one restaurant—say, Osaka—and divide its version of the unagi roll into its pieces: eel, rice, nori, cucumber, and unagi sauce.

Definition, like division, isolates a subject and describes its unique characteristics. You can look up the word in the dictionary if you do not know its denotative meaning, but when you are developing a definition in your own essay, instructors will want you to create your own. To do so, use this frame: A ____ is a ____ that ____. In the first blank, put the *term* to be defined. In the second, put the *class* to which the term belongs. In the third, put the *differentiation*: what makes the term different from other items in its class. A definition based on this model might look like so: "A <u>bicycle</u> is a <u>mode of transportation</u> that <u>requires human propulsion</u>." In many courses, you may be asked to write an extended definition: creating a simple definition based on the frame above but then lengthening your answer with other methods of development. Extending the bicycle example above, a student may go on to describe a certain style of bike, or classify types of bikes, or compare racing bikes to commuter bikes, or determine the health effects of bike riding.

An **argument** (or an appeal to *logos*) is a chain of reasoning such as is found in *induction* or *deduction*, or is a *body of proofs* gathered from research. Induction studies a pattern of similar events that leads to a general hypothesis:

1. When I drove my first Ford Mustang, it had great acceleration.
2. When I drove my second Ford Mustang, it, too, had great acceleration.
3. When I drove my third Ford Mustang, yet again it had great acceleration.

4. Therefore, it's likely that if I drive another Ford Mustang, it will have great acceleration.

Deduction moves from general truths to specific examples and often takes the form of a *syllogism*, with a major premise, a minor premise, and a conclusion:

Major premise: All dogs are mammals.
Minor premise: Winnie is a dog.
Conclusion: Therefore, Winnie is a mammal.

The syllogism follows a formula: Members of group A (dogs) are assigned a quality B (mammals); individual C (Winnie) is a member of group A (dogs); therefore, individual C (Winnie) also has quality B (mammal).

If you're writing an assignment that calls for research, then you must provide a body of proofs, many of which may come in the form of statistics, research data, and quotations. These proofs must present evidence from experts in the field or from other credible sources whose authority will bolster your own standing as a writer and add strength to your voice. Statistics, research data, and quotations will require that you investigate outside sources, preferably your course textbooks or materials available in your school library. More information on how to incorporate and document materials taken from primary and secondary sources appears in chapters three, five, and six. Here's an example of an argument supported by expert knowledge and data: "Research done by the Psychology Institute of Harvard University reveals that four out of five adult Americans take vacations to relieve stress. This finding rings true to Gina, a AAA travel agent in Las Vegas, who recently made plans for the following clients: Stephanie booked a week-long stay at a spa in Palm Springs, California, to escape her chaotic job as a receptionist at a major law firm; Rowdy sought hiking information for Estes Park in Colorado to recover from a family death; and Blossom booked a flight to Cannes, France, to attend the film festival and get away from her sixty-hour work weeks."

Chapter 2: Development and Support

Development and support should be tailored to meet the needs of the audience to whom you are writing. For example, if your audience is a group of businessmen and you want to convince them that a different managerial strategy will save their corporation money, then you will probably want to provide a statistical model for your own strategy and an analysis of the effects your proposed change will cause. Personal experiences in the form of a narrative may not have the information your audience needs. On the other hand, if you are speaking to some ten-year-olds at a summer camp about drug abuse, you will want to keep your ideas and explanations simple. You won't want to cite hard statistics to support a cause-and-effect analysis but rather tell them what happened to your nine-year-old brother when the police found him carrying a joint in his back pocket. A narrative of personal experiences in this case would work better.

Development and support can help you if you are stuck for an idea. Consider trying a type of development and support you haven't used yet in the paper. If you've been using several personal examples and have exhausted your knowledge about the topic, you might think about doing some research in the library or maybe looking at the chain of causes and effects that is connected with your issue. Each new means of development and support that you use can add a paragraph (or even more) to your paper.

It is important, however, that you read your essay prompt or test question closely before you begin writing your response. Instructors may specifically allow, require, or prohibit certain modes of development and support depending on the assignment.

When you make a point or state an argument in your paper, you should always ask yourself, "Why?"—Why is this so? Why is this important? Why does this have an effect on my issue? Asking yourself "Why?" will force you to answer "Because," and this answer will in turn force you to rethink your issue using the types of development and support you have at your disposal.

The writers of the essays that follow incorporate a variety of patterns of development, each hoping to prove a point.

Being Good
by Frankie Mac

"Are you *good* at anything?"

"...What?"

The question startled me. I was sitting at my desk in my sixth-grade classroom hovering over a disgruntled-looking art project. My knuckles whitened as I nervously gripped the glue stick in my hand. Where did this come from? The poser of the question was Daphne, a girl whom I'd known since kindergarten, and who'd since then been my personal Regina George. A cloud of frustration filled my lungs and stomach. What I couldn't admit to myself in that moment was that I didn't have an answer.

"I'm good at school."

Daphne and her posse began snickering and muttering to themselves. *How pathetic.* Daphne had the singing pipes of Celine Dion. Her right-hand girl Shelly was a star soccer player who invited people over to her house just so they could see her medals. Lisa drew sketches that were so detailed and beautiful that our art teacher constantly accused her of tracing. Everybody in my grade had a *thing*. What was I good at?

And so, the odyssey began.

That year, I joined a Greek dance troupe upon the strict wishes of my well-meaning, but overbearing mother. I enjoyed going to practice. I made good friends of a similar cultural background. But when it came time for choosing someone to do a spotlight performance or sing a solo during a folksong for one of the more complicated dances, I was always overlooked, even though I was one of only two girls in the troupe. After one among my plethora of rejections, my dance instructor pulled me aside and told me that maybe I should settle for the background.

Then, in eighth grade, I tried out for the school track team. My PE coach told me that I was fast, and that I should consider giving one of the long-distance runs a shot, despite the fact that the only

© Frankie Mac

sport I'd ever participated in was witty banter. By some Christmas miracle, I actually made the team, which, to me, was a success in itself. However, when it came down to our first and only meet, I came in last in my race. I'll never forget the look of disappointment on my teammates' faces, and the slimy feeling of my hand as I was given a participation ribbon.

Amid all of this mediocrity and failure, part of me started to wonder what the point of all this was. Why was the need for the knowledge of being good at something, especially as a middle schooler, so dire? But my other half, the stronger of the two, told the first one to shut up.

Finally, high school arrived, as well as a world of possibility. As orientation came to a close, I had a lot to consider. I didn't want my high school experience to mimic the one I'd had in junior high: go to school, go home, do schoolwork, sleep, repeat. That monotonous routine wasn't going to prove that bitch from sixth grade wrong. It was time to let go.

I looked over all my options. I figured sports were totally off the table, since I couldn't go through that condescending humiliation again. My conservative Catholic high school clearly wouldn't offer Greek folk dancing. But I figured I'd stick to the arts. In my mind, they felt like the safest bet. That narrowed my search down to two potential fates: ceramics and theater. But since I wasn't one who enjoyed getting my hands dirty in a literal sense, the latter it was.

Theater came to me as a surprisingly exciting prospect. In the fifth grade, my parents and I had gone to see the musical *Wicked* in LA, and afterward, I had demanded that we play the original Broadway soundtrack in our car for months. The idea that I could be the next Elphaba—strong and free and the center of attention—or any other character I could imagine, was too seductive for me to handle.

And so, during the second week of school, I signed up for the Fall Farce. The audition would take place on my fifteenth birthday.

Upon arrival, a dark-haired girl with a nervous smile and a stick up her ass handed me an audition side.

"You'll be waiting in the black box," she said.

"Cool."

Chapter 2: Development and Support

When I entered the cramped, cluttered space, I thought there'd been some sort of mistake. It was absolute hormonal mayhem. Guys were rolling around doing acrobatics hindered by gravity. Girls were in the corner talking and singing to themselves, occasionally getting aggressive in a Jekyll/Hyde manner. The volume in the room reached an all-time high, and my nerves kicked in. Preparing for the worst, I popped a squat in isolation.

"Frankie," I heard above the chaos, twenty minutes later. It was the dark-haired girl poking her head in the door.

"Yeah?"

"They're ready for you."

The dimly lit theater had a welcoming blue and brown color scheme. I thought I was alone standing on the stage until I squinted out into the audience. Three people were sitting in the front row. One was a student—a tall dude with a big nose and glasses who I was almost certain was in my math class. The second was a serious, elegant woman in her mid-twenties donning all black. Then, there was the third, Yvonna Francisco-Enriquez. She had a figure and a face as imposing as her name. Although she seemed a little kooky in a brightly patterned paisley dress and clogs, there was something terrifyingly omniscient behind her gaze.

"Frankie Mac . . ." she pondered, looking at a sheet in front of her, "What a fantastic name."

I gulped. "Thank you."

"Freshman, huh?"

"Yeah."

"Well . . . let's see what you've got."

I read. The whole time, all three observers roared with a laughter harder than a canned audience in a sitcom. At first, I thought they were laughing out of cruelty, the sort of enjoyment I'd been so used to. I finished.

"Was that okay?"

They looked at each other.

". . . Get the others in here."

Like a trained dog, the boy with the glasses ran out of his seat and exited the theater. When he returned, all the other auditioners who had been in the black box were at his heels.

"All right, people," boomed Yvonna, "This is Frankie Mac. Watch and learn."

With a smug grin that only someone who knows show business can give, she turned to me.

"Do it again."

I obeyed. It was the same response. With every line I spoke, chuckles burst through the house. The something—the feeling I'd sensed squirming in the pit of my stomach since my entry into high school—suddenly morphed into a fuzzy ball of light. I was trying to stay in character, but I soon found myself beaming with joy.

The same ball of light years later led me to participate in South Coast Repertory Theater's Acting Intensive Program. When the program began, I didn't feel anxiety. Proving myself was no longer a concern because I knew what I was good at. Then, one day, I was sitting in my Training for the Audition class, where we were adding "special skills" to our theatrical résumés.

I stared at mine blankly.

"Joy," I asked my instructor, "what constitutes as a special skill?"

She chuckled. "Anything that isn't acting, obviously."

Silence fell between us. As I wracked my brain, desperate for an idea, Joy said five words that branded into my memory.

"What are you good at?"

In that moment, something clicked. Unlike what Daphne tried to teach me many years ago, life isn't for the one-trick ponies. It's for the people who take a leap of faith—for those who go out for the track team or the dance troupe, despite the awareness that they might fail. But those people don't stop trying once their niche is found. That's why I won't be good at something. I will be good at many things for the rest of my life.

Black Halo
by Christine Boyka Kluge

Like an arrow, your mind flies through the bull's-eye at the center of the camera's view finder. You aim it through your pupils, out through that tiny circle, into the framed world. You invest that focused landscape with all that makes you human: your longing, your love, all of your dark thorns and sapphires. Hold your hands steady, extended toward its beauty. Make it true. Press the button.

When you develop your photographs, examine each one under a microscope. You'll see which parts of you entered that captive scene. There are your fingerprints, lodged in the bark of the oak. They form a path leading into the lightning-split heartwood. The reflections in your eyes are now sparks on the nickel-sized pond. Your dappled complexion freckles the grass at water's edge; the grass curves like windblown hair beneath the weight of your past exhalation.

Concentrate again. Explore the labyrinth inside your skull, groping for tendrils that unfurl through the optic nerve, for the leaf that tints your blood with chlorophyll. Search for whatever leaped backward, inside your head, from that rectangle of light and shadow. Find what threaded into your mind through the black halo, as the shutter clicked.

Black Halo first appeared in *Stirring the Mirror*, the author's collection from Bitter Oleander Pr Copyright © by Christine Boyka Kluge. Reprinted by permission of the author.

So This Is Freedom
by S. L. Kelly

When I decided to learn to ride a motorcycle, I had two goals in mind: learn to ride and ride as far as you can! I did not make the connection between riding and freedom until I found myself in the middle of the Nevada desert.

My riding story began in September of 2016 when I purchased a 1999 Honda Nighthawk from *Craigslist*. It was the first step in my journey toward achieving a long-forgotten dream. When I was about ten years old, one afternoon, my older sister and I were busy creating our futures. While she opted for two kids, an economy car, and a house, I announced, "When I grow up, I'm gonna buy a motorcycle and ride all over the world!" That memory suddenly came flooding back thirty years later, when I found myself in the middle of an MSF course in the parking lot of a community college.

I rode my starter bike for ten months, practicing the skills I learned in the MSF course on the streets of Sin City. In July 2017, I purchased my first "big" bike, a 2016 Kawasaki Versys 650LT in candy metallic orange. I named her Virginia. She spoke to me about her ability to go anywhere—freedom. I liked that.

To me, freedom means the ability to "come and go as you please" or to "live without limits" or restrictions of any kind. These definitions barely scratch the surface of the concept, a notion I would come to realize once I got Virginia up to highway speed on my first ride through the desert.

The Nevada desert is both stunning and mesmerizing. While visually beautiful and frightening, there are many stories about strange things that happen in the desert, alien landings, holes filled with the bodies of wily gangsters and spiritual awakenings. The desert is certainly alive. Amid the tall rocks, black mountains, and cacti, though, I had my first real experience with freedom.

At 65 miles an hour, I was cruising along relishing the fact that I had made a great choice in a motorcycle for my riding style and my

---

"So This Is Freedom," first appeared in the anthology, *Women Who Ride: Rebel Souls, Golden Hearts, and Iron Horses*, edited by Sarah Andreas, 2018. Reprinted with permission of the author.

Chapter 2: Development and Support

future riding aspirations. I felt blessed. Virginia and I were becoming fast friends. She was eating up the curves. The windscreen was doing its job, and although I had begun to feel a little numbness in my throttle hand, I felt good. While taking in the scenery, my mind was busy taking in road conditions, my speed, fuel consumption, and the 70-degree weather. In short, I was doing the "work" of riding and doing my best to "enjoy the ride."

A strange feeling overwhelmed me. This was new. As a rider, I understand the danger that is ever-present on a motorcycle. I understand that few people accept the risk that comes with riding. I had accepted that risk with full knowledge of what could happen. I do this every time I get on my bike. This wasn't a feeling of fear or anxiety. I was no longer worried about my being able to "keep up," maneuvering curves, my speed or the amount of fuel left in my tank. As I glanced around me at the scenery, I suddenly realized that what I was feeling was free.

Riding through the desert among the rocks, I was not afraid. I did not feel lonely, abandoned, or near the brink of certain death. I felt a connection to my bike; it is so much more than just a means of conveyance. I felt a sense of camaraderie with my fellow riders, those in my small group and those I happily waved the lowered "peace" sign to as they passed on the other side of the road. We were all in this together, having the same experience. For a few moments, the world existed, but it existed of my will. I felt that I could change the trajectory of my future with a simple turn down a new road or byway. I could see the road ahead, with its ups and downs, lying straight and curved before me, and on that bike, I felt that I could handle any situation that came my way. Optimism. Freedom.

My thoughts were transported back in time. While the future was ahead of me, I thought about my past and the pasts of women like me. I thought about the trepidation with which I had accepted the challenge of learning to ride a motorcycle. I thought about the many women who were not allowed the privilege of living their dreams. Riding through the desert that day was transcendent. I embodied the spirit of my ancestors, and they were pushing me forward. What did they dream as enslaved Negro women? Would they have accepted the same challenge that I had? What might they have achieved if they had been given the opportunity? Everything. Freedom.

That Saturday afternoon in the desert, I learned a new definition of freedom. Freedom is following your passion. Having the desire and determination to follow your dreams at all costs. The *feeling* of freedom is riding a motorcycle. I get it now. Fifteen months ago, I bought a motorcycle and learned to ride it. Because I can.

Black and White and Blue All Over
by Lisa Bailey

Not everyone learns about their legendary mistakes while standing in line at the grocery store, but if a piano is going to land on a community newspaper publisher, that's exactly where it will happen.

"Can you believe they put that photo in there?"

The guy in front of me slapped a copy of my newspaper against the checkstand. It was fairly early in the morning; after delivering all my newsstand, I'd just dropped the kids off at school—and I'd come back to the grocery store to pick up a couple of gallons of milk.

"Oh, I know," the checker said, her hands busy swiping the guy's beef jerky over her scanner. "Nobody can believe it."

I didn't recognize the guy. The checker fussed over bagging his half-case of Bud Light and potato chips. *Probably a hunter*, I thought.

"What's wrong with the photo?" I asked the guy, quickly, before the checker noticed me and could tell him who I was. I tried not to wince as he angrily jammed the copy of my newspaper back onto the checkstand. He left the paper hanging, cockeyed, over the edge of the counter.

"I mean, there's just common decency, isn't there?" he muttered. "Who else but a newspaper would put a picture of a dismembered hand on the friggin' front page?"

Who else but a newspaper, indeed? By the time the infamous hand photo was printed, I *was* the newspaper. Equal parts honest and nosy, I sported such an abysmal level of self-esteem that I was convinced that working eighty hours a week—*every* week—was exactly what I deserved. I was also just stupid enough to believe that I had a shot at redemption every week, too—which shackled me so firmly to my black-and-white mistress that the two of us became indistinguishable.

The schizophrenic ability of a good journalist to remain invisible in public but fearless in print might have served me well on an

---

Copyright © Lisa Bailey. Reprinted by permission.

anonymous big-city beat, but in a small town . . . well, people cannot be blamed for thinking that I was completely crazy.

Those people showed up to holler at me on my front porch, since the newspaper office was in our house. I knew all of them. I knew the tearful ones who showed up clutching notebook-paper obituaries. I knew the city councilmember who sent me drunken emails every Saturday night—he'd cruelly point out all the mistakes I'd made in the paper that week before hinting that he wanted to sleep with me.

"I've never seen anyone with such an easily-triggered sense of justice, Goldilocks," he sneered in one email.

Since the business was continually strapped for cash, I had to take accident pictures. (A front-page wreck photo in a small town is a guaranteed sellout.) I became a wizard at finding access to blocked scenes—plowing my old Taurus through the weeds on canal roads if necessary. It wasn't uncommon for me to beat the ambulance.

But the hand photo was taken at a double fatality that featured easy parking. The victims had ended up in the parking lot of an ag chemical company just east of Royal City, and I felt like I was cheating when I pulled up—it was almost too easy, like going to the mall.

I remember shooting a little mangled red and white Coleman cooler that was lying next to the car as the blanket-covered bodies of the two women were loaded.

The women's lunch—tinfoil-wrapped tamales—had spilled out of the cooler and onto the gravel of the parking lot. Everything was splattered with blood. I couldn't stop thinking about how they'd probably grabbed a few things from the fridge right before they'd left for work—in a hurry, laughing maybe—never knowing it would be one of the last things they ever did.

Although I was used to cops making inappropriate jokes at fatalities, when a trooper rolled his eyes about the "whole famdamily" (while nodding toward the silent relatives of the dead women), I barely managed a polite smile.

Over a dozen people stood and watched the bloody sedan—not wailing, not crying, just staring. They rimmed the edge of the WSP-required fifty-foot fatality buffer like a guardrail. The EMTs

Chapter 2: Development and Support 43

had half-heartedly flung disposable blue sheeting over the back door of the mangled sedan for privacy as they had worked to remove the bodies of the two women. I noticed they'd even left their discarded nitrile gloves lying around: a sign of frustration they'd lost both the victims.

I came home, still thinking about the tamales on the bloodstained gravel, and threw up in the utility sink in my laundry room. Then I Photoshopped the pictures of the crushed car, sharpening the focus, and—as advised by our press—I changed the photos into black and white so they would "dot up" better.

And that was how a bright blue nitrile glove thrown on the shattered back window of a Honda became a dismembered hand.

The newspaper went under last year, after the recession choked off the last of our dying ad revenue. All I have is a stack of silent morgue books now, big, awkward library-bound things stacked in my downstairs pantry along with cans of kidney beans and extra paper towels. I used to pay the bindery in Walla Walla every year to make us a tidy book of our back issues, and I always wondered what the binders thought as they lined up a whole year of our news to sew together. Not that it matters now.

It doesn't seem like those silent morgue books should be able to contain my raucous eight years of being a newspaper. But isn't the past always muffled by the ash of history as it sifts down on all of us? Sifting and sifting, until even someone who had to know everything can forget, until even the most high-contrast black-and-white memories start to gray and blur, until even a rubber glove in the back of a wrecked car can look like it's waving goodbye.

Drowning
by Violet E. Baldwin

Nobody really remembers what life was like when they were a toddler. All memories before age five seem to fuse into one grand flashback. Like shifting shadows, the slightest details of my childhood vacations are vague; however, when I was no more than three years old, I experienced an unforgettable sensation that was forever etched into my memory. It was the day I almost drowned in the radiant blue sea.

My great-grandfather grew up on the white sand beaches of Puerto Rico, with the sun beating down on his face and the cool water rushing over his feet as he trotted his Paso Fino horses along the bright blue shoreline. For his eightieth birthday, he wanted us to go back to that place he once loved. He wanted my family to experience the beauty of the chrysanthemum sunset over the pastel blue waters. He wanted to show us how the colors mixed and made an alluring portrait on the waterfront.

That part, however, I do not remember. I do not remember the smell of sea salt every morning as we woke up on the beach, nor the color of the ripe bananas growing outside the creaking white house we had rented for the week. I do not remember the sweet taste of water from a fuzzy green coconut as it trickled down my throat or the chirp of the coqui singing outside my window. I was only three.

It was a quiet morning in the hefty white building in which the many hallways and the doors seemed never ending to the minuscule toddler roaming about. The birds would sing just outside the towering, cream-colored door housing a brass oblong handle. I sat with my family at breakfast eager to play in the froth of the waves and feel the beads of sand between my petite toes. I scarfed down the unimportant breakfast and chugged my Ovaltine chocolate milk concoction patiently yearning for the moment I could feel the cool ocean breeze on my face and the warmth of the sand on my feet.

©Violet E. Baldwin

That moment finally arrived. We made our way down to the shore I was fidgety and impatient throughout the lengthy walk among the trees reminding me of green army men preparing for battle. I felt the crisp breeze on the tips of my ears. My nose tickled as the salty sea air hit me directly in the face. My father picked me up and proceeded to hoist me into the air. My mother, aunts, and grandparents settled in on the sand.

My mother set my then-infant brother on the sand beside her. He gleefully shoveled piles of the golden, honeysuckle-colored sand into his mouth. My aunts took to the waves on their surfboards, tackling each tower of water head on. My dad's warm hand held mine as we raced toward the waves crashing on the shore. He held me by my waist and hurled me over the blueberry waves which crashed and produced a foam colored like the moon. I laughed as the tomfoolery seemed to last forever. I was having the time of my life.

Without warning everything seemed to shift. My father was no longer waist deep in the water. His legs kicked frantically as he treaded the water. The waves seemed to grow; they were trying to swallow us whole. Soon all that was above the waterline was our heads bobbing in the waves. My dad held me up and kept me afloat; he tried not to panic so as to keep me calm. I knew something was wrong.

On shore my mother was in a frantic state of emergency, signaling to my aunts who were too far away to hear the screams over the crashing of the waves. My grandparents joined in, but their efforts were not effective. It was at that moment my grandfather made the choice to swim out in an attempt to save us. He powered out there with all his adrenaline pumping, but when his toes no longer gripped the sand on the bottom, he was stuck as well. We all swam there, treading water, my grandpa now holding me so my father could focus his energy on keeping himself alive.

There is a feeling that a three-year-old should never have to feel, the feeling of helplessness. I saw it in my grandfather's eyes as he held me above the waves. I turned to my dad who was slowly giving in to the hateful deep waters. I then realized that this was it; as a three-year-old I had to understand that we were all about to give in to the greedy tide that had pulled us out to sea.

In this moment we saw my aunt paddling her long surfboard toward us; she reached us just before we let go. With the last bit of strength my grandpa had, he lifted me onto the board, then himself. My dad held onto the board, his energy drained. She pulled us back to shore. We crawled along the sand which had never felt so pleasant before. That day the ocean was not able to defeat me. I didn't give in to the harsh forces that attempted to drag us down.

A three-year-old child's life is brimming with hope and possibility. When something takes place to shift that paradigm, the effects can be devastating. Nearly losing my life in the ocean was one of those moments. The vivid memories would pursue me for years, never allowing me to forget the day I could have lost my life to the harsh reality of ignorance in an unknown environment.

Body Ritual among the Nacirema
by Horace Miner

The anthropologist has become so familiar with the diversity of ways in which different peoples behave in similar situations that he is not apt to be surprised by even the most exotic customs. In fact, if all of the logically possible combinations of behavior have not been found somewhere in the world, he is apt to suspect that they must be present in some yet undescribed tribe. This point has, in fact, been expressed with respect to clan organization by Murdock (1949:71). In this light, the magical beliefs and practices of the Nacirema present such unusual aspects that it seems desirable to describe them as an example of the extremes to which human behavior can go.

Professor Linton first brought the ritual of the Nacirema to the attention of anthropologists twenty years ago (1936:326), but the culture of this people is still very poorly understood. They are a North American group living in the territory between the Canadian Cree, the Yaqui and Tarahumare of Mexico, and the Carib and Arawak of the Antilles. Little is known of their origin, although tradition states that they came from the east. According to Nacirema mythology, their nation was originated by a culture hero, Notgnihsaw, who is otherwise known for two great feats of strength—the throwing of a piece of wampum across the river Pa-To-Mac and the chopping down of a cherry tree in which the Spirit of Truth resided.

Nacirema culture is characterized by a highly developed market economy which has evolved in a rich natural habitat. While much of the people's time is devoted to economic pursuits, a large part of the fruits of these labors and a considerable portion of the day are spent in ritual activity. The focus of this activity is the human body, the appearance and health of which loom as a dominant concern in the ethos of the people. While such a concern is certainly not unusual, its ceremonial aspects and associated philosophy are unique.

The fundamental belief underlying the whole system appears to be that the human body is ugly and that its natural tendency is to

---

"Body Ritual among the Nacirema" by Horace Miner, originally published in *American Anthropologist*, June 1956, pp. 503–507.

debility and disease. Incarcerated in such a body, man's only hope is to avert these characteristics through the use of the powerful influences of ritual and ceremony. Every household has one or more shrines devoted to this purpose. The more powerful individuals in the society have several shrines in their houses and, in fact, the opulence of a house is often referred to in terms of the number of such ritual centers it possesses. Most houses are of wattle and daub construction, but the shrine rooms of the more wealthy are walled with stone. Poorer families imitate the rich by applying pottery plaques to their shrine walls.

While each family has at least one such shrine, the rituals associated with it are not family ceremonies but are private and secret. The rites are normally only discussed with children, and then only during the period when they are being initiated into these mysteries. I was able, however, to establish sufficient rapport with the natives to examine these shrines and to have the rituals described to me.

The focal point of the shrine is a box or chest that is built into the wall. In this chest are kept the many charms and magical potions without which no native believes he could live. These preparations are secured from a variety of specialized practitioners. The most powerful of these are the medicine men, whose assistance must be rewarded with substantial gifts. However, the medicine men do not provide the curative potions for their clients, but decide what the ingredients should be and then write them down in an ancient and secret language. This writing is understood only by the medicine men and by the herbalists who, for another gift, provide the required charm.

The charm is not disposed of after it has served its purpose, but it is placed in the charm-box of the household shrine. As these magical materials are specific for certain ills, and the real or imagined maladies of the people are many, the charm-box is usually full to overflowing. The magical packets are so numerous that people forget what their purposes were and fear to use them again. While the natives are very vague on this point, we can only assume that the idea in retaining all the old magical materials is that their presence in the charm-box,

Chapter 2: Development and Support

before which the body rituals are conducted, will in some way protect the worshipper.

Beneath the charm-box is a small font. Each day every member of the family, in succession, enters the shrine room, bows his head before the charm-box, mingles different sorts of holy water in the font, and proceeds with a brief rite of ablution. The holy waters are secured from the Water Temple of the community, where the priests conduct elaborate ceremonies to make the liquid ritually pure.

In the hierarchy of magical practitioners, and below the medicine men in prestige, are specialists whose designation is best translated "holy-mouth-men." The Nacirema have an almost pathological horror of and fascination with the mouth, the condition of which is believed to have a supernatural influence on all social relationships. Were it not for the rituals of the mouth, they believe that their teeth would fall out, their gums bleed, their jaws shrink, their friends desert them, and their lovers reject them. They also believe that a strong relationship exists between oral and moral characteristics. For example, there is a ritual ablution of the mouth for children which is supposed to improve their moral fiber.

The daily body ritual performed by everyone includes a mouth-rite. Despite the fact that these people are so punctilious about care of the mouth, this rite involves a practice that strikes the uninitiated stranger as revolting. It was reported to me that the ritual consists of inserting a small bundle of hog hairs into the mouth, along with certain magical powders, and then moving the bundle in a highly formalized series of gestures.

In addition to the private mouth-rite, the people seek out a holy-mouth-man once or twice a year. These practitioners have an impressive set of paraphernalia, consisting of a variety of augers, awls, probes, and prods. The use of these objects in the exorcism of the evils of the mouth involves almost unbelievable ritual torture of the client. The holy-mouth-man opens the client's mouth and, using the above mentioned tools, enlarges any holes that decay may have created in the teeth. Magical materials are put into these holes. If there are no naturally occurring holes in the teeth, large sections of one or more teeth are gouged out so that the supernatural substance can be applied. In the client's view, the purpose of these ministrations is to arrest decay and to draw friends. The extremely sacred and traditional character of the rite is evident in the fact that the natives return to the holy-mouth-men year after year, despite the fact that their teeth continue to decay.

It is to be hoped that, when a thorough study of the Nacirema is made, there will be careful inquiry into the personality structure of these people. One has but to watch the gleam in the eye of a holy-mouth-man, as he jabs an awl into an exposed nerve, to suspect that a certain amount of sadism is involved. If this can be established, a very interesting pattern emerges, for most of the population shows definite masochistic tendencies. It was to these that Professor Linton referred in discussing a distinctive part of the daily body ritual that is performed only by men. This part of the rite involves scraping and lacerating the surface of the face with a sharp instrument. Special women's rites are performed only four times during each lunar month, but what they lack in frequency is made up in barbarity. As part of this ceremony, women bake their heads in small ovens for about an hour. The theoretically interesting point is that what seems to be a preponderantly masochistic people have developed sadistic specialists.

The medicine men have an imposing temple, or *latipso*, in every community of any size. The more elaborate ceremonies required to treat very sick patients can only be performed at this temple. These ceremonies involve not only the thaumaturge but a permanent group of vestal maidens who move sedately about the temple chambers in distinctive costume and headdress.

The *latipso* ceremonies are so harsh that it is phenomenal that a fair proportion of the really sick natives who enter the temple ever recover. Small children whose indoctrination is still incomplete have been known to resist attempts to take them to the temple because "that is where you go to die." Despite this fact, sick adults are not only willing but eager to undergo the protracted ritual purification, if they can afford to do so. No matter how ill the supplicant or how grave the emergency, the guardians of many temples will not admit a client if he cannot give a rich gift to the custodian. Even after one has gained

Chapter 2: Development and Support

admission and survived the ceremonies, the guardians will not permit the neophyte to leave until he makes still another gift.

The supplicant entering the temple is first stripped of all his or her clothes. In every-day life the Nacirema avoids exposure of his body and its natural functions. Bathing and excretory acts are performed only in the secrecy of the household shrine, where they are ritualized as part of the body-rites. Psychological shock results from the fact that body secrecy is suddenly lost upon entry into the *latipso*. A man, whose own wife has never seen him in an excretory act, suddenly finds himself naked and assisted by a vestal maiden while he performs his natural functions into a sacred vessel. This sort of ceremonial treatment is necessitated by the fact that the excreta are used by a diviner to ascertain the course and nature of the client's sickness. Female clients, on the other hand, find their naked bodies are subjected to the scrutiny, manipulation, and prodding of the medicine men.

Few supplicants in the temple are well enough to do anything but lie on their hard beds. The daily ceremonies, like the rites of the holy-mouth-men, involve discomfort and torture. With ritual precision, the vestals awaken their miserable charges each dawn and roll them about on their beds of pain while performing ablutions, in the formal movements of which the maidens are highly trained. At other times, they insert magic wands in the supplicant's mouth or force him to eat substances that are supposed to be healing. From time to time, the medicine men come to their clients and jab magically treated needles into their flesh. The fact that these temple ceremonies may not cure, and may even kill the neophyte, in no way decreases the people's faith in the medicine men.

There remains one other kind of practitioner, known as a "listener." This witch-doctor has the power to exorcise the devils that lodge in the heads of people who have been bewitched. The Nacirema believe that parents bewitch their own children. Mothers are particularly suspected of putting a curse on children while teaching them the secret body rituals. The counter-magic of the witch-doctor is unusual in its lack of ritual. The patient simply tells the "listener" all his troubles and fears, beginning with the earliest difficulties he can remember. The memory displayed by the Nacirema in these exorcism sessions is truly remarkable. It is not uncommon for the patient to bemoan the rejection he felt upon being weaned as a babe, and a few individuals even see their troubles going back to the traumatic effects of their own birth.

In conclusion, mention must be made of certain practices which have their base in native esthetics but which depend upon the pervasive aversion to the natural body and its functions. There are ritual fasts to make fat people thin and ceremonial feasts to make thin people fat. Still other rites are used to make women's breasts larger if they are small, and smaller if they are large. General dissatisfaction with breast shape is symbolized in the fact that the ideal form is virtually outside the range of human variation. A few women afflicted with almost inhuman hypermammary development are so idolized that they make a handsome living by simply going from village to village and permitting the natives to stare at them for a fee.

Reference has already been made to the fact that excretory functions are ritualized, routinized, and relegated to secrecy. Natural reproductive functions are similarly distorted. Intercourse is taboo as a topic and scheduled as an act. Efforts are made to avoid pregnancy by the use of magical materials or by limiting intercourse to certain phases of the moon. Conception is actually very infrequent. When pregnant, women dress so as to hide their condition. Parturition takes place in secret, without friends or relatives to assist, and the majority of women do not nurse their infants.

Our review of the ritual life of the Nacirema has certainly shown them to be a magic-ridden people. It is hard to understand how they have managed to exist so long under the burdens that they have imposed upon themselves. But even such exotic customs as these take on real meaning when they are viewed with the insight provided by Malinowski when he wrote (1948:70):

> Looking from far and above, from our high places of safety in the developed civilization, it is easy to see all the crudity and irrelevance of magic. But without its power and guidance early man could not have mastered his practical difficulties as he has

done, nor could man have advanced to the higher stages of civilization.

References Cited

Linton, Ralph. *The Study of Man.* New York: D. Appleton-Century Co., 1936.

Malinowski, Bronislaw. *Magic, Science, and Religion.* Glencoe: The Free Press, 1948.

Murdock, George P. *Social Structure.* New York: The Macmillan Co., 1949.

O Christmas Tree
by Jack Simmons

Every day, every time I walk into my bedroom, I am greeted with the sight of a very festive tree. There was a period in my life when I would have thought this was unusual; after all, Christmas ended over two months ago, and I was never someone that possessed any meaningful amount of holiday spirit in the first place. This tree is a three-and-a-half-foot plastic shrub with plastic lightbulbs glued to every plastic branch, and yet somehow it sheds needles and makes a constant mess like a real Douglas fir. It holds no ornaments save for one lone Santa Claus that wears a sombrero, plays a guitar, and dances on wiggly little legs. Sometimes, sitting at my desk, I turn to look at this tree and contemplate what a strange war it's waging upon the rest of this room's design scheme. Then, I smile, remembering that it's actually the most important piece of furniture that I own.

It was November of 2018 and my long-distance girlfriend was coming to visit me in Las Vegas for the first time ever. I had been living alone for about a year until then, and after all that time, my home was still a bleak, utilitarian space that lacked anything like the art, accents, and family photographs that most people use to decorate theirs. I looked around one day, and all at once, the inspiration struck me to do whatever I could to prevent myself from exuding the vibe of a cold-hearted psychopath. I found my salvation, a cheap two-pack of plug-in Christmas trees, at the local Target. Movies often represent the act of fetching one of these trees as an onerous struggle, played for laughs with physical comedy, so I was pleased to be able to wheel mine right out of the store with a standard-issue shopping cart. My girlfriend was fond of Christmas, and I was fond of her, so it really did seem like the perfect way to bring a little hominess to the home that she was about to use as the template to judge my mental and emotional normalcy.

That visit was a big success if you were wondering, but Christmas passed and so too did my need for festive cheer. I retired the tree to a

© Jack Simmons

hallway closet, brought it back out the next year, retired it again, and brought it back once more. It was only then, in 2020, that I began to fully appreciate the value of my purchase. My desk is positioned opposite of a large window in my bedroom that spends a majority of each day in the direct line of the sun. The screen glare that comes of this is unmanageable, so I have no choice but to pull down and leave down the blackout shades every day, skulking through life in darkness like a modern-day Boo Radley. For that reason, I found a surprise need for the soft, indirect light that only the feeble bulbs of this Christmas tree could supply, and when January came around, I couldn't bear to give that up. Now it's March of 2021, and it's still protecting me from stubbed toes.

Remember Sombrero Santa? My girlfriend and I bought him this year in La Jolla, California, at a gift shop in a charming tourist trap they call Old Town. Our other ornaments, which we removed and boxed away shortly after Christmas in accordance with seasonal orthodoxy, were bought at Walmart when we realized in a panic that we were crazy to have no ornaments to hang on our own tree. This absurd new Santa, in spite of his tacky and ambiguously offensive appearance, represents a much bigger adventure of his own. He has inspired our plan to continue purchasing ornaments to commemorate all of the wonderful events of our lives together, and better yet, we intend to leave them up year-round in complete indifference to whatever the current holiday might be. It's romantic, it's sweet, and it's making me far more sentimental than I ever thought possible. The idea of this tree one day being covered in ornaments that each has its own story to tell makes me a happy man. Sombrero Santa will not dance alone for much longer.

Every day, the Christmas tree in my bedroom confirms its status as my favorite object in the room. I work from home and spend most of my time at my desk, so I can say without exaggerating that this silly plant is the light of my life, literally and metaphorically. That being said, I will not hesitate to toss it out with the trash when I find a better tree that doesn't shed. I made its twin from the original two-pack disappear when there wasn't room for it, and I will be more than happy to do it again.

Love in a Time of Terror
by Barry Lopez

This world is just a little place, just the red in the sky, before the sun rises, so let us keep fast hold of hands, that when the birds begin, none of us be missing.
—Emily Dickinson, in a letter, 1860

Some years before things went bad, I arrived in an Aboriginal settlement called Willowra, in Australia's Northern Territory. A small village, it's haphazardly situated on the east bank of the Lander River, a dry watercourse. (I'd driven into the area several days before with a small team of restoration biologists. They were intent on reintroducing a small marsupial in the vicinity, the rufous hare-wallaby [*Lagorchestes hirsutus*, or *mala* in the local language]. The animal had been eliminated locally by feral house cats, domestic pets left behind decades before by white settlers.) When I arrived in Willowra, I was introduced to several Warlpiri people by a friend of mine, an anthropologist named Petronella Vaarzon-Morel. She'd been working for some years around Willowra and when the biologists dropped me off—that work now completed—she helped move me into a residence in the settlement, a guesthouse where she had been living. Petra then returned to her home in Alice Springs and I was on my own.

Before she left, Petra had pointed out numerous places in the countryside nearby that I should neither approach nor show any interest in. These were mostly innocuous-looking spots to my eye—rocks, trees, small sand hills—but they were important elements in the Dreamtime narratives that form the foundation of Warlpiri identity. Many of these sites were close to the Lander. When I asked my hosts, then, if I might walk out into the desert a few miles, in the direction that I was indicating, and then return along roughly the same track, the man I was speaking to pointed in a slightly different direction and said simply, "Maybe better."

Reprinted by permission of SLL/Sterling Lord Literistic, Inc. Copyright © 2020 by Barry Holstun Lopez.

Chapter 2: Development and Support

I set off that afternoon on a walk north and west of the village, across a rolling spinifex plain that stretched away to hills on the horizon in almost every direction. The flow of the bland, uniform colors of the countryside was only broken up by an occasional tree or a copse of trees.

This universe of traditional Warlpiri land was completely new to me. I had no anxiety, however, about getting lost out there. At a distance of several miles, the settlement and the Lander, with its tall gallery forest of gum trees growing along its banks, remained prominent, in a land that displayed to my cultural eyes no other real prominences.

It was midday when I left so if I happened to walk too far to the west (on what would soon be a moonless night in June) darkness might conceivably force me to lie down and wait for dawn. (I could easily have strayed unawares into some broad, shallow depression on that plain, from which all horizons would appear identical.) But getting lost seemed most unlikely. Starlight alone, in this sparsely populated country lying on the southern border of another, much more stark, challenging, and enormous desert, the Tanami, would be enough to guide me home.

My goal that day was intimacy—the tactile, olfactory, visual, and sonic details of what, to most people in my culture, would appear to be a wasteland. This simple technique of awareness had long been my way to open a conversation with any unfamiliar landscape. Who are you? I would ask. How do I say your name? May I sit down? Should I go now? Over the years I'd found this way of approaching whatever was new to me consistently useful: establish mutual trust, become vulnerable to the place, then hope for some reciprocity and perhaps even intimacy. You might choose to handle an encounter with a stranger you wanted to get to know better in the same way. Each person, I think, finds their own way into an unknown world like this spinifex plain; we're all by definition naive about the new, but unless you intend to end up alone in your life, it seems to me you must find some way in a new place—or with a new person—to break free of the notion that you can be certain of what or whom you've actually encountered. You must, at the very least, establish a truce with realities not your own, whether you're speaking about the innate truth and aura of a landscape or a person.

I've felt for a long time that the great political questions of our time—about violent prejudice, global climate change, venal greed, fear of the Other—could be addressed in illuminating ways by considering models in the natural world. Some consider it unsophisticated to explore the nonhuman world for clues to solving human dilemmas, and wisdom's oldest tool, metaphor, is often regarded with wariness, or even suspicion in my culture. But abandoning metaphor entirely only paves the way to the rigidity of fundamentalism. To my way of thinking, to prefer to live a metaphorical life—that is, to think abstract problems through on several planes at the same time, to stay alert for symbolic and allegorical meanings, to appreciate the utility of nuance—as opposed to living a literal life, where most things mean in only one way, is the norm among traditional people like the Warlpiri, in my experience. In listening to negotiations, for example, between representatives of industrialized societies and representatives of traditional societies, it has always seemed to me that the latter presentation is meant to be more open to interpretation (in order not to become trapped in literalness), while the former presentation too often defaults to logic and "impressive" data sets, but, again, perhaps this is only me.

The goal in these conversations, from a traditional point of view, is to put off for a good while arriving at any conclusion, to continue to follow, instead, several avenues of approach until a door no one had initially seen suddenly opens. My own culture—I don't mean to be overly critical here—tends to assume that while such conversations should remain respectful, the outcome had to conform to what my culture considers "reality."

My point here is that walking off into what was for me anonymous territory, one winter afternoon in north-central Australia, was not so much an exercise in trying to improve myself as a naturalist as it was an effort to divest myself of the familiar categories and hierarchies that otherwise might guide my thoughts and impressions of the place.

I wanted to open myself up as fully as I could to the possibility of loving this place, in some way; but to approach that goal, I had

Chapter 2: Development and Support 59

first to come to know it. As is sometimes the case with other types of acquaintanceships, to suddenly love without really knowing is to opt for romance, not commitment and obligation.

The evening before I went off to explore the desert around Willowra, I finished a book called *The Last of the Nomads* by William John Peasley, published in 1983. Peasley recounts here a journey he made into the Gibson Desert in Western Australia with four other white men in the winter of 1977. They were accompanied by an Aboriginal man named Mudjon. The group was looking for two Mandildjara people believed to be the last of the Mandildjara living in the bush. Mudjon, a Mandildjara elder living at the time in a settlement on the western edge of the Gibson called Wiluna, had known for decades both of the people they were searching for—a hunter, Warri Kyango, and his wife, Yatungka Kyango. These two had refused to "come in" to Wiluna with the last of the Mandildjara people during a prolonged drought in the seventies. Mudjon respected their effort to continue living a traditional life under these very formidable circumstances but he feared that at their ages—Warri was sixty-nine, Yatungka sixty-one—they were getting too old to make their way successfully in the outback without the help of other, younger people.

The search for this couple, across hundreds of square miles of parched, trackless country, interrupted in various places by areas of barren sand hills, culminated with the party's finding the couple, together with their dingos, at a place called Ngarinarri. (The dingos helped them hunt and huddled up close with them on cold nights to share their warmth.) A few palmfuls of muddy water every day from a seep, and a small store of fruit from a nearby stand of quandong trees, was all that was sustaining them. Warri was injured and sick, and they were both emaciated.

An argument later ensued in Wiluna and then spread far and wide about the insistence of the rescue party that the couple travel with them back to Wiluna instead of leaving them there to die at Ngarinarri, which it seemed they preferred to "civilized" life in Wiluna.

I wasn't party to this, of course, so can offer no judgment, but this is an old story, characterizing many encounters over the years between "civilized" and traditional styles of living in the Australian bush. Like many readers, I brooded over the fate of these people for days after reading the book. (They both passed away within a year of their arrival in Wiluna, despite the availability there of food, water, and medical treatment.) This is a story of injustice, of course, and also a tragedy that virtually anyone can understand. What really stuck in my mind, though, was how love dramatized this narrative, a narrative as profound in its way as the other narrative, the one about colonial indifference and enduring harm.

Because Warri and Yatungka were both born into the same moiety among the Mandildjara, they were prevented by social custom from marrying. When they defied this custom and married anyway, their lives from then on, after their formal banishment, became far more difficult. They knew if they attempted to return to the society of their own people, they risked being physically punished. So they chose a life on their own. Even when they learned, years later, that they had been forgiven, and that their Mandildjara culture was unraveling further in the face of colonial intrusion, and even though they learned that a terrible period of widespread drought had brought most all of the "desert tribes" into white settlements like Wiluna, they continued to choose their marriage and their intimately known traditional country.

Warri and Yatungka looked after each other over all that time, and they took care of their beloved country according to the prescriptions and proscriptions in the Dreamtime stories, observing their obligations to it. They also knew, I have to think, that the watering places their people had traditionally depended on for generations had now withered and dried up or, in the case of the animals they regularly hunted, their food had simply departed the country. And yet they refused to succumb, even at what you might call the point of their natural end. It would be arrogant and certainly perilous to subscribe to any theory of what the two of them might have been thinking at the end, at Ngarinarri. What stood out for me as obvious, however, was their fierce allegiance—to their Mandildjara country and to each other. Death in this case was not for them tragic but inevitable, onerous but acceptable; and death in this place was preferable to lives lived out in Wiluna.

Chapter 2: Development and Support

But, of course, again, this is not for me to determine.

The day I walked out into the desert in the direction I was pointed I was intent on immersing myself in the vastness of something I didn't know. I carried in my backpack a few books about recognizing and preparing "bush tucker," the desert plants and small creatures that could sustain Aboriginal people; a dependable bird book; and some notes about marsupials and poisonous snakes. In terms of what governed the line of my footsteps, my many changes of direction, my pauses, my squattings down, it was primarily my desire to pursue immersion—letting the place overwhelm me. Drifting through my mind all the while, however, was the story of Warri and Yatungka, or at least the version of it that was written up and that I had read.

At some point late that day, I came upon several dozen acres of land more truly empty than the desert landscape I'd been walking through for hours. It consisted of an expanse of bare ground and coarse sand with shattered bits of dark volcanic rock scattered about. I walked as carefully here as I might have through an abandoned cemetery. Silence rose from every corner of the place, and the utter lack of life here drew heavily on my heart. As I walked on, I saw no track of any animal, no windblown leaf from a mulga tree, no dormant seed waiting for rain. Other images of bleakness came to mind: bomb-shattered rubble that buried the streets of Kabul; a small island in Cumberland Sound, a part of Baffin Island in Nunavut, Canada, where dozens of large whale skeletons lay inert in acres of tawny sea grass rolling in the wind like horses' manes; the remains of a nineteenth-century whaling station; tiers of empty sleeping platforms, each bunk designed to hold four men, rising to the ceiling in a derelict barracks at Birkenau, where every night exhausted men lay in darkness, waiting to be carted off in wheelbarrows to the nearby ovens and burned on the day they could no longer wield their tools.

I had halted with these images pushing through my mind and in the moment was toeing a stone the size of my fist when another thought burst in, that most of the trouble that afflicts human beings in their lives can be traced to the failure to love.

*

Chapter 2: Development and Support

In the summer of 1979, I traveled to an Eskimo village in the central Brooks Range in Alaska called Anaktuvuk Pass. My friend Bob Stephenson had a sod home in this settlement of 110 Nunamiut people, and in the days following our arrival we spent many hours listening to stories about local animals: wolverines and snowy owls, red foxes and caribou. The Nunamiut were enthusiastically interested in their lives, as were we. We spent a few days too hunting for active wolf dens in the upper reaches of the Anaktuvuk River. Then we flew several hundred miles west to the drainage of the Utukok River. Bob was a large-mammal biologist with the Alaska Department of Fish and Game, and the department maintained a temporary summer camp there on the middle Utukok, where field biologists could regularly observe tundra grizzlies, caribou, wolves, gyrfalcons, wolverines, and other creatures during the summer months. Bob and I stayed a few days with them and then helicoptered south to a place in the De Long Mountains farther up the Utukok called Ilignorak Ridge. We camped there for a week, watching a wolf den across the river from us—five adults and five pups.

Whenever I'm asked what I love, I think of the aggregate of relationships in that place that summer. Twenty-four hours of sunshine every day at 68° northern latitude. Cloudless skies, save for fair-weather cumulus. Light breezes. No schedule for our work but our own. Large animals present to us at almost every moment of the day. And, this far north of the treeline, looking through a gin-clear atmosphere with forty-power spotting scopes, we enjoyed unobstructed views of their behavior, even when they were two or three miles away. I had daily conversations with Bob about the varied and unpredictable behavior of wild animals (or, as I later came to think of them, free animals, those still undisturbed by human interference). We reminisced about other trips we'd made together in the years before this, on the upper Yukon River and out to St. Lawrence Island, in the northern Bering Sea.

The mood in our camp was serene, unhurried. We were excited about being alive, about our growing friendship, about this opportunity to watch free animals in good weather, and about the timelessness of our simple daily existence. I loved the intensity of our vigil. Every day we watched what was for us—probably for anyone—the most spectacular things: wolves chasing caribou; a grizzly trying to break into the wolf den, being fought off by a single young wolf; thirty caribou galloping through shallow water in the Utukok, backed by the late evening sun, thousands of flung diamonds sparkling in the air around them; an arctic fox sitting its haunches ten yards from the tent, watching us intently for twenty minutes.

When we returned to base camp, we enjoyed meals with the other scientists and talked endlessly with them about incidents of intriguing behavior among the animals we all watched every day. One afternoon someone brought in a mammoth tusk she had dug out of a gravel bank close by. Somehow, we no longer felt we were living in the century from which we had arrived.

During those days we all resided at the heart of incomprehensible privilege.

Evidence of the failure to love is everywhere around us. To contemplate what it is to love today brings us up against reefs of darkness and walls of despair. If we are to manage the havoc—ocean acidification, corporate malfeasance and government corruption, endless war—we have to reimagine what it means to live lives that matter, or we will only continue to push on with the unwarranted hope that things will work out. We need to step into a deeper conversation about enchantment and agape, and to actively explore a greater capacity to love other humans. The old ideas—the crushing immorality of maintaining the nation-state, the life-destroying belief that to care for others is to be weak, and that to be generous is to be foolish—can have no future with us.

It is more important now to be in love than to be in power. It is more important to bring E. O. Wilson's biophilia into our daily conversations than it is to remain compliant in a time of extinction, ethnic cleansing, and rising seas. It is more important to live for the possibilities that lie ahead than to die in despair over what has been lost.

Only an ignoramus can imagine now that pollinating insects, migratory birds, and pelagic fish can depart our company and that we will survive because we know how to make tools. Only the misled can insist that heaven awaits the righteous while they watch the fires on Earth consume the only heaven we have ever known.

The day of illumination I had in the spinifex plain west of Willowra, about a world generated by the failure to love, which was itself kindled by the story of the lovers Warri and Yatungka, grew out of my certain knowledge that, years before, I had experienced what it meant to love, on those summer days with friends in the Brooks Range. The experience delivered me into the central project of my adult life as a writer, which is to know and love what we have been given, and to urge others to do the same.

In this trembling moment, with light armor under several flags rolling across northern Syria, with civilians beaten to death in the streets of Occupied Palestine, with fires roaring across the vineyards of California, and forests being felled to ensure more space for development, with student loans from profiteers breaking the backs of the young, and with Niagaras of water falling into the oceans from every sector of Greenland, in this moment, is it still possible to face the gathering darkness, and say to the physical Earth, and to all its creatures, including ourselves, fiercely and without embarrassment, I love you, and to embrace fearlessly the burning world?

Discussion Questions for Chapter 2

For Frankie Mac

1. Most of us have experienced a Daphne (or a Donald) in our lives. Describe yours. Did your Daphne make you strive to be better, or did she prevent you from achieving your goals? Describe a few specific moments from your experience with this individual. Looking back on them, how do you wish you could change those moments? If you feel you reacted in an effective way, explain why.
2. In addition to description, what other types of development does Mac employ? How do these types serve the thesis? Write out the essay's thesis first, and then list five examples that validate it.
3. What are you "good at"? Describe it. Do you share this ability with others? How has this ability shaped your sense of yourself?

For Christine Boyka Kluge

1. Kluge is writing a prose poem, and she uses some figures of speech (see the figures named earlier in this chapter and in the glossary) to develop the content. Which does she use, and where does she use them?
2. Kluge uses second-person ("you") pronouns throughout the poem. To whom is she speaking? She also makes use of the imperative mood, which signifies a command or a request. Write out an example of when she uses this mood. Why does she use it?
3. What situation is Kluge discussing in this poem? In what ways is it similar to the situation set out in Bailey's essay "Black and White and Blue All Over"?
4. What exactly is the "black halo" Kluge references at the end of the piece? Why do you think she uses that image as her title?

For S. L. Kelly

1. Kelly creates a causal chain within her essay. It begins with her childhood conversation with her sister about their dreams and ends with the essay's final sentence. List the effects between those two declarations in her life. How does each connect to the other?
2. What assumptions do you make about those who participate in a particular hobby or vocation? Identify one or two hobbies or activities and write out your assumptions. What are these assumptions based on? How does Kelly challenge assumptions about riding a motorcycle? What are the differences in how Kelly and Kluge capture the activities described in their pieces?
3. Kelly's essay defines freedom. Paraphrase (that means use your own words) her definition. How does her technique for defining her key term contrast with that used by Mac in her essay to define what it means to "be good" at something?
4. What does freedom mean to you? Identify a hobby, avocation, or activity that you enjoy that symbolizes your pursuit (and realization) of freedom.

For Lisa Bailey

1. Bailey divides the essay into four sections (the extra line breaks signal the sections). What is the main point raised by each of the four sections? Why do you think the section breaks occur where they do?
2. Bailey uses multiple types of development to validate her implied thesis. First, in your own words, write out the essay's purpose, and then identify four types of development used in the piece. How does each effectively serve the thesis? If you were Bailey's publisher when this piece went to print, what other details would you have encouraged her to add to the story?

3. Both Mac and Bailey frame their essays with an image. What are these images, and how do they help the writers achieve their purposes? How do the meanings of these images change from when they are first introduced in the essays?
4. In your own words, describe how Bailey feels about her profession versus how her community feels about it. How do these views counter and serve one another?
5. Identify a photo or an image whose content you did not understand upon first looking at it. What did you initially see? Then describe its truth after you looked at it more fully. What meaning did it gain?

For Violet E. Baldwin

1. Compare and contrast the methods used by Baldwin and Mac to confront situations that once intimidated them. What tone does each writer take in her essay, and how do their tones affect your understanding of the significance of these situations for them?
2. Name something that once prompted or that still elicits fear in you. Describe the cause (if known) of this fear. What are some techniques that you employ to ease the fear?
3. Write out four sensory details that Baldwin uses to convey her subject matter. What important facts about her, her environment, and her family do these details convey to the reader?
4. Baldwin presents a concise thesis. Write it out, and then create a thesis triangle that presents the essay's writer, issue, audience, and purpose. Based on your reading of the essay, add three details about the writer, the issue, and the audience.

For Horace Miner

1. Miner's essay has long been considered a satire both of American hygiene practices and of the field of anthropology. What exactly is a satire? Which hygienic practices are being satirized? How are anthropologists being satirized?

2. Miner seems to say that the rituals of the Nacirema indicate "definite masochistic tendencies" (paragraph 12). Which rituals in particular reveal these tendencies? Is he right in his evaluation? Having experienced Nacirema rituals for yourself, are there others you could add to the list?
3. Miner seems to be creating a classification system for medical practitioners in his report. Who is being classified, and what are the categories by which he classifies them?

For Jack Simmons

1. Simmons is trying to explain the importance of a supposedly insignificant item in his life. What is that item, and why does it truly hold significance for him? Think of an item in your life that, if a stranger were to see it, might appear to be insignificant. What is that item, and what significance does it hold for you?
2. Simmons also seems to hold an ironic or contradictory feeling toward the item. Where does he express this feeling? Why do you think he holds it?
3. Which of the development strategies does Simmons make use of? What organizational plan does he use to arrange them?
4. How does Simmons's personality reveal itself in the essay? Look closely at his persona and his tone.

For Barry Lopez

1. "Love in a Time of Terror" is a piece with allusions to conflicts between indigenous and colonial cultures. Are these issues important to you or to a region with which you are familiar? If so, why?
2. Lopez intersperses present-time action (things that he's doing) with recollections of historical events, past experiences, and stories from scientists and other explorers. Why does he do this? What would his writing be like if he had simply described what he himself was doing?

3. Identify a specific seemingly barren landscape. If any, what people once lived on it? Why did they leave? What intrigues you about this place? What truths does it hold?
4. To which senses does Lopez appeal most strongly in his descriptions? Why did he choose to appeal to those senses?
5. How do Lopez, a naturalist, and Miner, an anthropologist, compare and contrast in their treatment of conveying a people's history? What techniques do they use? Compare and contrast how the personas they create affect their essays' purposes.
6. When Lopez writes, "[W]e have to reimagine what it means to live lives that matter, or we will only continue to push on with the unwarranted hope that things will work out," what is he asking his readers to do?

Chapter 3
Organization

"Get your stuff together!" Have you heard those words before? Typically, that command addresses some level of chaos in our midst. Although some thrive in a less than organized environment, most do not. Hence, the many *YouTube* channels geared to get you, your closet, your family, your pet, your garage, your spice rack, etc., organized. And if you cannot do it on your own with the help of a show's advice, you can hire a life coach who may begin with a seemingly simple message—get rid of the clutter in your life: If you do, your mind and body will thank you. Well, consider your composition instructor your writing's life coach. And the first thing your instructor will advise you to do with your essay is to organize it. If the essay's content is not organized, it will read like an unwelcome word salad.

As we draft, rewrite, and revise, we must keep in mind the several levels of organization that operate within a paper at once:

Word by word
Sentence by sentence
Paragraph by paragraph
Overall for paper

Word by Word

Word-by-word organization is sometimes referred to as *syntax* and is usually covered when discussing mechanics. Word-by-word organization is important because the positions of the words can determine the meaning of a sentence. For instance:

I almost killed seventy people.
I killed almost seventy people.

These two sentences have the same words in them, but by shifting two of the words, we give them very different meanings.

Word-by-word organization is also affected by grammatical structures, such as passive and active verb formations, questions, commands, and dependent and independent clauses. These structures can show the relative importance of the ideas in a sentence or establish a sequence. Look at these three sentences:

The ball was hit by Tom before it broke the window.
Tom hit the ball before it broke the window.
Before it broke the window, Tom hit the ball.

When you put something at the end of a sentence—or in the last slot of a clause—you are giving it a special stress, called **end focus**, that you want your readers to notice. These three sentences are saying the same thing, but each is stressing something different about what happens by placing the end focus on a different pair of words. You can actually hear the stresses if you read the sentences aloud. The first sentence, written in passive voice, puts primary stress on *window* and secondary stress on *Tom*. The second sentence, written in active voice, puts primary stress on *window* and secondary stress on *ball*. The third sentence, written in active voice but with the dependent clause coming first, reverses the order of the events; also, the primary stress is on *ball* and secondary stress is on *window*.

There are other ways of altering word order to manipulate end focus. For example, if you have the sentence *A giant black dog is sitting on the doorstep*, the natural end focus is on *doorstep* since it comes at the end of the sentence. But the most interesting detail in the sentence is the dog, as signaled by the adjectives loaded in front of the word. To give the dog proper stress, we can move it to a place of more prominence with a ***there*-transformation**:

There is a giant black dog sitting on the doorstep.

Now when you read the sentence aloud, the stress falls on *giant black dog*. What we've done is removed that phrase from the subject position it held in the original sentence, stuck the word *There* (an expletive) in its place, and shifted it behind the verb *is*, thus giving it the final slot in the clause. We can also use a transformation called the ***it*-cleft**:

It's a giant black dog that is sitting on the doorstep.

Again, when you read the sentence aloud, the stress falls on *giant black dog*. We did the same thing here as we did in the *there*-transformation: moved the phrase out of the subject position, filled the subject slot with an expletive (*It*), and put the phrase into a slot behind the verb *is*. We might instead try a transformation called the ***what*-cleft**:

What's sitting on the doorstep is a giant black dog.

Here, the phrase *a giant black dog* falls at the very end of the sentence for maximum stress. We can do something similar with a transformation called the **participle shift**:

Sitting on the doorstep is a giant black dog.

Or with a **preposition shift**:

On the doorstep is sitting a giant black dog.

With these last three transformations, you are not only giving *giant black dog* extra stress by using end focus but also building anticipation. The shift in syntax alerts your reader that something special, or surprising, or shocking is coming at the end of the sentence, and the reader will expect a payoff to reward her patience. Consider these sentence pairs:

Hearing snarls and howls so loud that they could raise the dead, Tom opened the door. A giant black dog was sitting on the doorstep.

Hearing snarls and howls so loud that they could raise the dead, Tom opened the door. Sitting on the doorstep was a giant black dog.

We've changed the verb tenses, but still, the second sentence pair, by holding *a giant black dog* until the very end, should cause you more anticipation before you finally learn what is snarling and howling so loudly.

Sentence by Sentence

Sentence-by-sentence organization usually follows some sort of sequence, usually either of time or space. That means when we are telling a story, one event usually follows another event; when telling a friend how to change an oil filter, you tell her what steps she must take from first to last in order to do the job. Each sentence should set forth a step in that process.

Sentence-by-sentence organization can also be determined by the purpose of the sentences within a paragraph. You've probably been told that a paragraph in an essay should begin with some sort of topic sentence and end with a conclusion, with some sentences of explanation or development in between:

> Topic sentence (with transition)
> Narrow down
> Quotation (or example, description, etc.)
> Explanation
> Conclusion

Two paragraphs based on that model might look like this:

> A typical paragraph begins with a topic sentence that sets forward the point to be discussed. The point is narrowed down to a specific instance of development and support in the next sentence—or, if a quotation from an outside source will be used to support the point, then this sentence introduces the source of the quotation; as Maxine Hairston and John J. Ruszkiewicz tell

their readers, "You have to select [quotations] purposefully, introduce them intelligently, and tailor them to fit your own language" (626). After using a quotation or providing an example, you might explain how the example supports the point you're making. If your point needs no further explanation, you can conclude the paragraph with this sentence and move on to your next point.

Often, the first sentence of a paragraph will serve as a transition. In that case, you need to signal your reader with one of the transition words, by repeating a key word, or by using a synonym for a key word from a previous paragraph. The transition word does not have to appear at the front of the first sentence, but it needs to be present so that you establish the relationship between the paragraphs and signal to your reader whether you are continuing with a previous idea or introducing a new one. This transition shows the reader the direction of your paragraph and avoids confusion. Once the point of the second paragraph is explained adequately, then it too can be concluded, and you can move on to the next paragraph.

Scrambling the sentence order of these paragraphs would confuse their meaning because the sentences fulfill specific duties within the paragraphs: to introduce the main idea, to elaborate on the idea, and to finish with the idea while preparing the reader for the next paragraph. Sentence-by-sentence organization works in conjunction with the essay's purpose. The model above is especially important for presenting research and evidence. The chapters on the research essay and the literature essay will address how the model works for those types of essays.

Sentence-by-sentence organization is also strongly governed by a feature called the **known-new contract**. This feature works together with the end focus principle of word order and is important for establishing cohesion in a series of sentences. The contract is as follows: The writer puts information that is already known to the reader at the front of a sentence, and she puts information that is new to the reader at the end of the sentence, where it gains emphasis from end focus. The contract is the reason why, in the sentences with

Chapter 3: Organization

Tom opening the door above, *a giant black dog* works better at the end position, because the detail about the dog is new information and deserves special placement. It also brings cohesion to the two sample paragraphs illustrating the five-step model above. Let's look at the first of those paragraphs again, this time with the known information underlined and the new information in bold:

> A typical <u>paragraph</u> begins with **a topic sentence that sets forward the point to be discussed**. The <u>point</u> is narrowed down **to a specific instance of development and support in the next sentence**—or, if a <u>quotation from an outside source</u> will be used **to support the point**, then <u>this sentence</u> introduces **the source of the quotation**; as Maxine Hairston and John J. Ruszkiewicz tell their readers, "You have to select [quotations] purposefully, introduce them intelligently, and tailor them to fit your own language" (626). After using a quotation or providing an example, <u>you</u> might explain **how the example supports the point you're making**. If your <u>point</u> needs **no further explanation,** <u>you</u> can conclude **the paragraph with this sentence and move on to your next point**.

In the first sentence, the word *paragraph* is known information because it was introduced beforehand ("Two paragraphs based on that model . . ."). In the next sentence, the word *point* is known information because it was introduced in the previous one. The phrase *quotation from an outside source* is known information because quotations are a form of development and support, the idea introduced as new in the previous sentence. This pattern of placing information you've already covered in the subject slot of your following sentences is behind the idea of **cohesion** mentioned above. If you open a sentence with new information—information you have not yet made known—you will confuse your reader, who will wonder where this information is coming from. By starting your sentences with known information, you create a pleasing flow between them. Your sentences, however, must also be governed by **coherence**—one unifying principle—as emphasized in the next level of organization.

Paragraph by Paragraph

Paragraph-by-paragraph organization is also determined by purpose. Each paragraph should illuminate one idea, and you should move on to another paragraph when you introduce a new idea or change directions with the old one. For example, if your history instructor has asked you to discuss the causes of the Civil War, then each body paragraph should address a particular cause. Likewise, if your culinary professor has asked you to write the recipe for making meringue, then each paragraph should set out a step in the process. And again, if for a sociology survey you are tasked with classifying high school cliques, then each paragraph should describe a different group.

The paragraphs so far in this chapter have followed this thinking: After the paragraph introducing the four levels of organization, each paragraph since has focused on one of those levels; paragraph breaks have indicated each new level or a fresh idea about the current level. Sometimes an idea will take more than one paragraph to develop— an idea might take you in one direction, then another. But all of the paragraphs relating to the same central idea should link together to keep that idea unified.

One way to link paragraphs and sentences is to use **transitions**. Transitions are like road and street signs: They provide us with directions so that we can arrive at our proper destination. Imagine driving through an unfamiliar city with no street signs—At which corner do I turn? Am I traveling east or west? Where is the nearest freeway?— and you will understand the difficulty of reading a paper without clear transitions. There are two main ways of providing transitions. The first is by using transitional words and phrases. For this method, keep this list of transition words and phrases handy:

Time Order and Sequence: first, first of all, for one thing, one way, second (or secondly), the third reason, another, another way, also, next, and, in addition, moreover, furthermore, then, after, before, while, meanwhile, now, during, later (on).

Spatial: above, across, after, around, behind, below, beside, in front (back) of, near, next (to), over, under(neath), toward the start (end) of, at the start (back) of, to the left (right) of, on top of, on the bottom of.

Similarity or Equality: similarly, similar to, analogous to, likewise, in like manner, in accordance with, in a similar (the same) way (fashion, manner), correspondingly, equally, identically, in equal manner (fashion), just as, parallel to.

Change of Direction: although, alternatively, but, however, yet, while, in contrast, despite, still, on the other hand, otherwise, on the contrary.

Illustration: for example, for instance, as an illustration, to illustrate, particularly, specifically, such as, like.

Conclusion: therefore, consequently, thus, then, as a result, in summary, to conclude, last (most) of all, in the end, finally.

By using one of the transitional words or phrases in the first sentence of your paragraphs, you signal to your reader the sequence of your thoughts and connect the ideas you are developing.

The second method of making transitions is to repeat a key word or idea (or a synonym or a pronoun substituting for that idea) from a previous paragraph in the first sentence of the new paragraph. The first sentence of this paragraph repeated the word *transitions*; the repetition signaled that this paragraph was related to the previous one because it was talking about the same topic. It also used the word *second* (a transitional word) to let you know that it was moving on to the next type of transition. You must remind your reader what direction you are taking and which of your ideas are related, or else your reader will feel as though you have left her stranded in that unfamiliar city. Clear transitions provide signs for your reader to follow.

Overall for Paper

Overall-for-paper organization incorporates all of the levels mentioned above, but one important consideration will guide how you order your ideas within a paper: Your ideas must make as much impact upon your reader as possible. Three common ways of organizing your paper for effect are by chronology, by relative importance, and by subordination-coordination.

Chronology

If you are reporting a series of events, describing a process, or writing about a topic that involves a sequence, then the most natural way to organize your paper would be by chronology. Violet E. Baldwin's essay "Drowning" follows this method to report on a near-tragic series of events that happened to her while vacationing with her relatives in Puerto Rico, from the moment she and her family went down to the shoreline, to the terrifying moments when she and her father were caught by the waves, to the final rescue by her aunt and their safe return to the beach.

Relative Importance

This method means saving "the best for last"; that is, saving your strongest argument or example or description for last and structuring your essay according to Aristotelian plot structure. Perhaps you've talked about the idea of plot and seen this picture:

This drawing might look like a mountain to you, and that might be a good way to remember it. The first, smaller peak is the **initial conflict**, which sets everything in motion. The long uphill toward the second peak is the **gradual rise in tension** or the **complication**. The top of the second peak is the **climax**. Baldwin's essay "Drowning" makes use of this method as well: She establishes the initial conflict in the opening paragraphs by foreshadowing the accident and by listing the sensory impressions she can no longer remember because of the terror she experienced later; the gradual rise in tension comes as she describes how the waves pull her and her father into deeper water, how her father struggles to keep her afloat, how her aunts cannot hear her family's cries, and how her grandfather swims out to help them. Her most startling and provocative details come last as she describes the helplessness in her grandfather's eyes, her father's losing battle with the undertow, and her realization that they are about to die. The climax—and a release of the built-up tension—comes when her aunt paddles over and saves them all with her surfboard. Used correctly, this type of organization can pull a reader through an essay by arousing and maintaining her interest.

Subordination-Coordination

Subordination-coordination is a method of grouping similar ideas. To use this method when writing your own papers, follow these four steps:

1. Make a complete list of the ideas, issues, topics, and/or arguments that you wish to discuss in your paper.
2. See if any items on the list are related. If they are, group them together (this is coordination) in a list. Above the list, write out the quality that relates the items in the list (this is subordination). Repeat this step until all of the items have been put into lists. For instance, if your list reads

    carrots bread pork
    cereal orange juice peas
    beef rice turnips milk

    you can align carrots, peas, and turnips under the heading *vegetables*; you can align pork and beef under the heading *meats*; you can align bread, cereal, and rice under the heading *grains*; you can align orange juice and milk under the heading *drinks*.

3. Find a "title" that describes the common feature(s) of all the lists (this is subordination again). For the example used in step two, you can align all of the lists under the title *foods* or *grocery list*.
4. Now redraw your lists—with the headings and title included—in an outline form:

Foods
I. Vegetables
   A. Carrots
   B. Peas
   C. Turnips
II. Meats
   A. Pork
   B. Beef
III. Grains
   A. Bread
   B. Cereal
   C. Rice
IV. Drinks
   A. Orange Juice
   B. Milk

You now have a blueprint for your paper. Your title becomes a thesis statement; your headings become sections within the paper; the items under each heading become the topics of individual paragraphs.

The overall organization of a paper can also be influenced by the type(s) of development and support you use to elaborate your thesis. For example, if you are describing an object, you may want to organize the details spatially: move from the top to the bottom of the object, or from the left side to the right, or from front to back. If a car is your object, that would mean starting with the roof and finishing with the underside, or going from the driver's side to the passenger's side, or going from the front bumper to the rear bumper. A description can also be organized by sensory impression: first, by how it looks; then, by how it sounds; then, by how it smells, and so on.

Here are some methods of development and support and the organization patterns that can be used with them:

Cause and Effect
   Centered around key event
   Chronological

Comparison and Contrast
   Alternating
   Continuous

Classification and Division
   Subordination-Coordination
   Best for last (Relative importance)

Description
   Chronological
   Spatial
   Sensory impression
   Best for last

Definition
   Definition/example/definition/example
   Definition/example/example . . .

Examples
   Chronological
   Subordination-Coordination
   Best for last

Process
   Chronological
   Spatial
   Simple to complex (start with easy steps and move toward more difficult ones)

Argument
   Alternating (supporting argument/opposing argument/supporting/opposing)
   Continuous (supporting/supporting/opposing/opposing)
   Specific to general (inductive)
   General to specific (deductive)

Best for last
Background information/opposing view/supporting arguments

Quotations/Citing Authorities/Statistics
Best for last
Subordination-Coordination

If it better serves your paper's purpose, you may choose more than one method for organizing your paper; these strategies are not mutually exclusive. The key point to remember when selecting your method, as stated above, is making an impact upon your reader. At all times, you must consider the effect you are trying to create on the audience.

You should also remember that the four levels of organization build upon one another; all four levels must work together to create the greatest impact upon your reader. However, you should wait to consider your paper's organization until you have finished a rough draft and are about to begin another. The ideas presented above will be easier to use when you have a first draft on the page.

Finally, keep the lessons of your writing life coach with you as you move beyond the academic environment. You may not write a formally organized description or a cause and effect or a comparison essay while on the job. But your boss will likely ask you to inventory a warehouse, or the doctor on duty will ask you to evaluate a patient's symptoms and discuss when they began and how they have changed, or a prospective buyer will ask you to explain the difference between the Toyotas on your car lot versus the Hondas across the street. At that moment, you may need your coach to remind you of the organization patterns you have learned in this chapter.

Works Cited

Hairston, Maxine, and John J. Ruszkiewicz. *The Scott, Foresman Handbook for Writers*. Scott, Foresman, 1988.

Chapter 3: Organization

Excerpt from *On Tyranny*
by Timothy Snyder

Chapter 11, "Investigate"

Figure things out for yourself. Spend more time with long articles. Subsidize investigative journalism by subscribing to print media. Realize that some of what is on the internet is there to harm you. Learn about sites that investigate propaganda campaigns (some of which come from abroad). Take responsibility for what you communicate with others.

"What is truth?" Sometimes people ask this question because they wish to do nothing. Generic cynicism makes us feel hip and alternative even as we slip along with our fellow citizens into a morass of indifference. It is your ability to discern facts that makes you an individual, and our collective trust in common knowledge that makes us a society. The individual who investigates is also the citizen who builds. The leader who dislikes the investigators is a potential tyrant.

During his campaign, the president claimed on a Russian propaganda outlet that American "media has been unbelievably dishonest." He banned many reporters from his rallies, and regularly elicited hatred of journalists from the public. Like the leaders of authoritarian regimes, he promised to suppress freedom of speech by laws that would prevent criticism. Like Hitler, the president used the word *lies* to mean statements of fact not to his liking, and presented journalism as a campaign against himself. The president was on friendlier terms with the internet, his source for erroneous information that he passed on to millions of people.

In 1971, contemplating the lies told in the United States about the Vietnam War, the political theorist Hannah Arendt took comfort in the inherent power of facts to overcome falsehoods in a free society: "Under normal circumstances the liar is defeated by reality, for which there is no substitute; no matter how large the tissue of falsehood

---

"Listen for Dangerous Words" and "Investigate" from *On Tyranny: Twenty Lessons from the Twentieth Century* by Timothy Snyder. Copyright © 2017 by Timothy Snyder. Used by permission of Tim Duggan Books, an imprint of the Crown Publishing Group, a division of Penguin Random House LLC. All rights reserved.

Chapter 3: Organization   85

that an experienced liar has to offer, it will never be large enough, even if he enlists the help of computers, to cover the immensity of factuality." The part about computers is no longer true. In the 2016 presidential election, the two-dimensional world of the internet was more important than the three-dimensional world of human contact. People going door-to-door to canvass encountered the surprised blinking of American citizens who realized that they would have to talk about politics with a flesh-and-blood human being rather than having their views affirmed by their Facebook feeds. Within the two-dimensional internet world, new collectivities have arisen, invisible by the light of day—tribes with distinct worldviews, beholden to manipulations. (And yes, there is a conspiracy that you can find online: It is the one to keep you online, looking for conspiracies.)

We need print journalists so that stories can develop on the page and in our minds. What does it mean, for example, that the president says that women belong "at home," that pregnancy is an "inconvenience," that mothers do not give "100 percent" at work, that women should be punished for having abortions, that women are "slobs," "pigs," or "dogs," and that it is permissible to sexually assault them? What does it mean that six of the president's companies have gone bankrupt, and that the president's enterprises have been financed by mysterious infusions of cash from entities in Russia and Kazakhstan? We can learn these things on various media. When we learn them from a screen, however, we tend to be drawn in by the logic of spectacle. When we learn of one scandal, it whets our appetite for the next. Once we subliminally accept that we are watching a reality show rather than thinking about real life, no image can actually hurt the president politically. Reality television must become more dramatic with each episode. If we found a video of the president performing Cossack dances while Vladimir Putin claps, we would probably just demand the same thing with the president wearing a bear suit and holding rubles in his mouth.

The better print journalists allow us to consider the meaning, for ourselves and our country, of what might otherwise seem to be isolated bits of information. But while anyone can repost an article, researching and writing is hard work that requires time and money.

Chapter 3: Organization

Before you deride the "mainstream media," note that it is no longer the mainstream. It is derision that is mainstream and easy, and actual journalism that is edgy and difficult. So try for yourself to write a proper article, involving work in the real world: traveling, interviewing, maintaining relationships with sources, researching in written records, verifying everything, writing and revising drafts, all on a tight and unforgiving schedule. If you find you like doing this, keep a blog. In the meantime, give credit to those who do all of that for a living. Journalists are not perfect, any more than people in other vocations are perfect. But the work of people who adhere to journalistic ethics is of a different quality than the work of those who do not.

We find it natural that we pay for a plumber or a mechanic, but demand our news for free. If we did not pay for plumbing or auto repair, we would not expect to drink water or drive cars. Why then should we form our political judgment on the basis of zero investment? We get what we pay for.

If we do pursue the facts, the internet gives us enviable power to convey them. The authorities cited here had nothing of the kind. Leszek Kolakowski, the great Polish philosopher and historian from whom this book takes its epigraph, lost his chair at Warsaw University for speaking out against the communist regime, and could not publish. The first quotation in this book, from Hannah Arendt, came from a pamphlet entitled "We Refugees," a miraculous achievement written by someone who had escaped a murderous Nazi regime. A brilliant mind like Victor Klemperer, much admired today, is remembered only because he stubbornly kept a hidden diary under Nazi rule. For him it was sustenance: "My diary was my balancing pole, without which I would have fallen down a thousand times." Václav Havel, the most important thinker among the communist dissidents of the 1970s, dedicated his most important essay, "The Power of the Powerless," to a philosopher who died shortly after interrogation by the Czechoslovak communist secret police. In communist Czechoslovakia, this pamphlet had to be circulated illegally, in a few copies, as what east Europeans at the time, following the Russian dissidents, called "samizdat."

"If the main pillar of the system is living a lie," wrote Havel, "then it is not surprising that the fundamental threat to it is living in truth."

Since in the age of the internet we are all publishers, each of us bears some private responsibility for the public's sense of truth. If we are serious about seeking the facts, we can each make a small revolution in the way the internet works. If you are verifying information for yourself, you will not send on fake news to others. If you choose to follow reporters whom you have reason to trust, you can also transmit what they have learned to others. If you retweet only the work of humans who have followed journalistic protocols, you are less likely to debase your brain interacting with bots and trolls.

We do not see the minds that we hurt when we publish falsehoods, but that does not mean we do no harm. Think of driving a car. We may not see the other driver, but we know not to run into his car. We know that the damage will be mutual. We protect the other person without seeing him, dozens of times every day. Likewise, although we may not see the other person in front of his or her computer, we have our share of responsibility for what he or she is reading there. If we can avoid doing violence to the minds of unseen others on the internet, others will learn to do the same. And then perhaps our internet traffic will cease to look like one great, bloody accident.

Two Ways of Seeing a River
by Mark Twain

Now when I had mastered the language of this water and had come to know every trifling feature that bordered the great river as familiarly as I know the letters of the alphabet, I had made a valuable acquisition. But I had lost something, too. I had lost something which could never be restored to me while I lived. All the grace, the beauty, the poetry, had gone out of the majestic river! I still kept in mind a certain wonderful sunset which I witnessed when steamboating was new to me. A broad expanse of the river was turned to blood; in the middle distance the red hue brightened into gold, through which a solitary log came floating, black and conspicuous; in one place a long, slanting mark lay sparkling upon the water; in another the surface was broken by boiling, tumbling rings that were as many-tinted as an opal; where the ruddy flush was faintest was a smooth spot that was covered with graceful circles and radiating lines, ever so delicately traced; the shore on our left was densely wooded, and the somber shadow that fell from this forest was broken in one place by a long, ruffled trail that shone like silver; and high above the forest wall a clean-stemmed dead tree waved a single leafy bough that glowed like a flame in the unobstructed splendor that was flowing from the sun. There were graceful curves, reflected images, woody heights, soft distances, and over the whole scene, far and near, the dissolving lights drifted steadily, enriching it every passing moment with new marvels of coloring.

I stood like one bewitched. I drank it in, in a speechless rapture. The world was new to me and I had never seen anything like this at home. But as I have said, a day came when I began to cease from noting the glories and the charms which the moon and the sun and the twilight wrought upon the river's face; another day came when I ceased altogether to note them. Then, if that sunset scene had been repeated, I should have looked upon it without rapture and should have commented upon it inwardly after this fashion: "This sun means

---

"Two Ways of Seeing a River" by Mark Twain, 1883.

that we are going to have a wind tomorrow; that floating log means that the river is rising, small thanks to it; that slanting mark on the water refers to a bluff reef which is going to kill somebody's steamboat one of these nights, if it keeps on stretching out like that; those tumbling 'boils' show a dissolving bar and a changing channel there; the lines and circles in the slick water over yonder are a warning that the troublesome place is shoaling up dangerously; that silver streak in the shadow of the forest is the 'break' from a new snag and he has located himself in the very best place he could have found to fish for steamboats; that tall dead tree, with a single living branch, is not going to last long, and then how is a body ever going to get through this blind place at night without the friendly old landmark?"

No, the romance and beauty were all gone from the river. All the value any feature of it had for me was the amount of usefulness it could furnish toward compassing the safe piloting of a steamboat. Since those days, I have pitied doctors from my heart. What does the lovely flush in a beauty's cheek mean to a doctor but a "break" that ripples above some deadly disease? Are not all her visible charms sown thick with what are to him the signs and symbols of hidden decay? Does he ever see her beauty at all, or doesn't he simply view her professionally and comment upon her unwholesome condition all to himself? And doesn't he sometimes wonder whether he has gained most or lost most by learning his trade?

Consider It Joy
by S. L. Kelly

Consider it all joy, my brethren, when you encounter various trials, knowing that the testing of your faith produces endurance. And let endurance have its perfect result, so that you may be perfect and complete, lacking in nothing.
 —James 1:2-4

A little more than a year ago, the Covid-19 pandemic caused the world to pause. In the beginning, it was hard to understand how to move forward. After the lockdown, it felt like a kind of global reset presented an opportunity to take stock of life and all that is essential to it. My experience in the pandemic culminated in a lesson in what it actually takes to face any trial in life, pandemic or otherwise. Trials come to make us stronger. It took a run-in with a plastic fuel switch to remind me.

My life was routine and safe, bedrock even. To shake things up, in 2017, I decided to buy a motorcycle in hopes of fulfilling a childhood dream of riding across country. I purchased a used Kawasaki Versys, a tall sport-touring motorcycle. I practiced riding for nine months, balancing the bike on my tiptoes at every stop. I saved money, purchased the necessary gear, and prepared for the trip. In July 2018, I rode that bike from Nevada to Florida and back. It was amazing. Fulfilling that challenge introduced a need to ride that has since become essential to my life. For me, riding is life, like breathing.

During the lockdown, I refrained from riding. The daily news reports of overworked first responders, overrun hospital emergency rooms, a lack of protective gear and an inadequate number of ventilators for coronavirus patients kept me home, grounded. I did not want to add to an already stressful situation essential workers were experiencing in ERs across the city. One accident could send me to the coronavirus hot zone of the local hospital. Like everyone else, I stayed home. I prayed.

"Consider It Joy," first appeared online on May 20, 2021, in the *Nevada Humanities' Heart to Heart* series, a collection of artistic works created by Nevadans during the COVID-19 pandemic. Reprinted by permission of the author.

Chapter 3: Organization

For a few months, working from home kept me busy and focused on completing daily goals. Still, the endless stream of news stories on the global fight against the virus fed my paranoia about what life might be post-pandemic. With each passing day, the walls began closing in on me. Work, news, worry, repeat. I needed an outlet. I needed to ride. This presented an issue. The prepaid maintenance package I had purchased when I bought my bike had expired and due to the virus, I had put off taking the bike in for service for as long as I could trying to avoid contact with people. It was simple: I needed my bike. If I was going to ride, then service was necessary, and it was up to me.

To prep, I gave the bike the once over. I checked my previous service records and my mileage, and I consulted a service manual for maintenance tips. I checked the oil reservoir window and saw what looked like stale black coffee. I needed to change the oil, flush and replace the coolant, replace the air filter, and to solve a visibility issue I had while riding at night, I wanted to replace my stock headlights with LEDs. I purchased the necessary supplies for the job and picked a morning to begin my project. I was excited, and a bit nervous. What if I screwed something up and the bike wouldn't start? How would I get it to the shop to get it repaired without a trailer? What if I did irreparable damage?

I started with the headlights. After watching several *YouTube* videos on how to convert a stock headlamp to an LED, I felt confident in my ability to perform this simple task. One thing all of the videos had in common was one caveat about a retainer clip that could pose a problem when installing the new bulb. Still, I felt I could handle it. Changing the first bulb proved to be no challenge. It took a few tries to replace the retainer clip, but it was not as tough as I had expected. The second bulb was a different story. When I attempted to replace the old bulb, I discovered that, unlike the left side, there was not enough space to maneuver my index finger inside the headlight assembly to replace the clip. I struggled for about thirty minutes. After several attempts, my fingers could take no more, so I gave up and tried a new method. This time, I disconnected the middle fairing from the front end of the bike to give myself room to work. With the middle

Chapter 3: Organization

fairing loose and supported by my left hand, I replaced the second LED with my right hand. When I finally set the last retainer clip into place, with sore index fingers, I was elated. "I got it!" All of the trouble it took just to get to this point was simply part of the process. Adapt. Adjust. Move forward.

After the bulb conversion, I was energized. I moved on to changing the oil and replacing the coolant with relative ease. These things were not altogether new to me. When I first decided to buy a motorcycle, I bought an older 250cc Honda on which to practice riding, and to learn how to perform basic maintenance, so changing the oil held no mystery. I leaned into the work with renewed vigor and spirit.

The trouble started in my attempt to disconnect a fuel switch to free the tank from the frame. The switch is plastic, and the ends of the two lines are married by a tab that must be released in order to disconnect the fuel line. Further complicating things was the fact that the switch is positioned between the tank and the frame in such a way that, again, if you have large hands, the chances of easily freeing the tab from the housing are minimal. Full stop. No matter how much I contorted my hands to release the tab, it would not budge. I struggled with it for about twenty minutes. A sinking feeling came over me. I had gone too far. What was I thinking? I stepped back and looked at my bike, naked and in pieces. Nuts, bolts, plastic pins and plastic fairings were scattered all over the garage floor. Afraid to move forward, I gave up. I felt like a fool.

When I was young, I can remember sitting in my father's garage watching him do his work. It is one of my most vivid images of him: he in his Key overalls, face shield down, with a gloved hand holding a welding torch, hard at work making money with magic. There was not a single thing that he could not build, or a job he didn't complete. To him, every task could be tackled "as long as you have the right tools and a little bit of know-how." In his world, this was the way to get things done. "Slow down. Think. There's got to be another way to release that switch."

Defeated, I begrudgingly put the bike back together, reassembling every nut, bolt, plastic retainer pins, fairings and all. I was embarrassed and ashamed of myself for foolishly going into territory in which I clearly didn't belong. I had gotten in over my head. I closed my garage door on my failure. In my head, I kept hearing my father's voice, "There's gotta be a way to release that clip." I was being haunted.

I went for a drive in my Jeep, Nate. When I got back home, forty-five minutes later, I walked right past my unfinished maintenance project without even looking at it. Normally, it is all I can do *not* to look at my bike whenever I am in the garage. It is common knowledge among bikers that the only thing a biker loves more than riding and talking about their bike is looking at it. I fell into my favorite chair in my living room, tormented by the fact that I was so easily defeated by a plastic fuel switch. This could not stand. I thought about it, and went back to the drawing board, *YouTube*! I looked up more videos on how to remove the gas tank on my make and model of bike. There had to be something that I was missing. There had to be a way to free that switch. I went back out to the garage and took the bike apart again. I had to finish the job. That gas tank was coming off one way or another.

On this second attempt, my fear of doing damage to the bike dissipated. I took control of the situation. I studied the repair manual instructional photos, and I watched another video on the process of removing the tank a few more times, rewinding as necessary, before I again attempted to disconnect the switch. This time, I slowed down. I allowed myself to breath while working my fingers into position to release the tab that would release the switch. After a few tries, the tab was released with little effort. It felt like the last nerve holding on to a loose tooth had finally given in, revealing the prettiest gap-toothed grin! With the switch loose, I slowly pulled the gas tank away from the frame and set it on the garage floor. With the tank off the bike, the skeleton of my machine was exposed, sparse. There is not a lot to a motorcycle. The technology that makes the bike go is minimal. A frame, an engine, a gas tank, wiring, battery, handlebars, seat and wheels. This is part of the beauty of the machine. Altogether, when properly maintained, these things produce magic.

With the tank off, I replaced the air filter and slowly put the bike back together. I wanted to make the moment last. There was no need to rush. I had to make sure that every piece was secure. I relished every second. The sense of accomplishment was overwhelming. I had done it. I completed my project on Valentine's Day, February 14, 2021.

The next day, I rode to lunch with a friend as a test run. On the I-15, we merged into traffic like corpuscles in the bloodstream, sailing past the Strip amid the Presidents' Day tourists heading west towards Los Angeles. Riding a motorcycle on a freeway is like a dance. You find the beat in order to enjoy the rhythm. Timed just right, you fly along to the melody of traffic, jockeying for the optimal position. With the wind in my face, and a slight grip on the throttle, I embraced the vibration and the steady pull of the engine, listening for any change in rhythm. The work was done. I smiled inside, thinking, "It's perfect. The magic is back."

As I ride my bike along streets slowly waking in the midst of shared trauma, I twist the throttle, change lanes, understanding all that is required to endure life in a pandemic is faith, "a few tools, and a little bit of know-how."

RuPaul's Effects on Gender Expression through Drag Culture
by Brooke Workman

Harmful stereotypes surrounding masculinity have had a chokehold on American society for years. They've created serious problems for men who may not feel comfortable conforming to the conventional ideas of what a man "should" be. Breaking through these stereotypes is an act of courage; however, even after this courage is found, it can still take a gender-nonconforming man a long time before he's fully comfortable living a life he wants and deserves. One such man who conquered this challenge is RuPaul Andre Charles—a well-rounded entertainer and the creator of *RuPaul's Drag Race*. *Drag Race* is a television show beloved not only by people who participate in or enjoy drag, but also by those who may not have previously understood the depth of drag culture. Through the notoriety that *Drag Race* has established over the last thirteen years, RuPaul has helped others rebel against archaic notions of masculinity and gender performativity, impacted society's acceptance of queer culture, and made a vital mark on queer history.

Traditional masculinity is comprised of certain unspoken rules. The biggest deviation from these rules is acting or presenting in a way that could be perceived as "feminine" or "gay." Prejudice of this nature represses a man's imagination in choosing how to express his gender. In "Why Are Americans Afraid of Dragons?," Ursula K. Le Guin discusses how imagination, and the training of it, is essential for the human mind. When one does not learn how to discipline their imagination, they tend to fear it (104). Therefore, if men are never given the societal freedom to imagine a new or different way to express their gender, people will continue to dread rejection of the gender binary. Trepidatious restraints on masculinity harm men who simply wish to use gender deviation as an expressive art form—an art form such as drag. Drag queens are people, usually men, who dress feminine in a bold and exaggerated way. Drag culture is centered

---

© Brooke Workman

around rebelling against fear of gender deviation, and RuPaul has given many people the opportunity to discover more about their gender as a part of this community. The drag community has no limitations to its creativity, and RuPaul himself has made huge strides in showing our misogynistic world that men are allowed to be feminine. However, these strides were not taken lightly, as many people are still very unaccepting of nontraditional gender performance. Mark Greene, senior editor for the Good Men Project, discusses how the rules of traditional masculinity are "enforced through shaming and bullying . . . the purpose of which is to force conformity to our dominant culture of masculinity and to perpetuate the exploitation, domination, and marginalization of women and people who are queer, genderqueer and transgender." Going against these rules and directly into the fire of shaming and bullying from society takes courage. That is why participating in drag is such a substantial risk to take. But when RuPaul continually tells his contestants and audience "If you can't love yourself, how in the hell you gonna love somebody else," that assumed risk—slowly but surely—begins to shrink.

With the success of his presence in the mainstream media, RuPaul has been able to give a discernable voice to the queer community. For instance, Honey Mahogany is a drag queen who gained popularity from her time on *RuPaul's Drag Race*, and she used her newfound fame wisely after leaving the show. She became a political activist, and when asked in an interview for *Vogue* how she entered politics, she said, "I was a social worker and I was working a lot with my community, the LGBTQ community, and seeing firsthand a lot of the displacement that was hurting folks. For some people it really was a matter of life and death" (qtd. in Wheeler). What motivated her to get involved, she said, was that she "learned through organizing that politics and policy were an incredibly important part of conservation and making systemic change" (qtd. in Wheeler). Not only has RuPaul reached the LGBTQIA+ community, but his work has been watched by people who previously have never been interested in drag or queer culture. This includes the younger generation. In *Anatomy of an Essay*, Lucinda Everett states, "Kids accept the society we present them, meaning films that normalize any and every expression of

Chapter 3: Organization 97

what it means to be human are a key tool in moving us towards a more inclusive society" (101). RuPaul has opened a discussion and given relevance to the topic of challenging gender performance. This means that when more people are inspired to speak up about their identity, new generations who are exposed to this topic will be more understanding and accepting. RuPaul has truly shown that the voice of one powerful person carries far and wide in elevating the voices of others.

Though society has been exposed to queer culture for centuries, it has not been widely accepted until the twenty-first century. During the late 1800s into the mid 1900s, law enforcement would target members of the LGBTQIA+ community. For example, "masquerade laws" would allow people to get arrested for crossdressing. Scholar William N. Eskridge, Jr., discusses how "by the beginning of the 20th century, gender inappropriateness . . . was increasingly considered a sickness and public offense" (qtd. in Ryan). These bigoted laws and attitudes are what ultimately led to the Stonewall riots. Though gender nonconformity was ultimately no longer considered a crime, it still was not smiled upon by the general public. This led to the prominence of ball culture within the drag community in the 1970s and later. People would organize fantastical soirées that celebrated queerness and gender nonconformity away from society's scrutiny. They would even include competitive performances during which drag queens would show off their most elaborate looks. Here, LGBTQIA+ performers and spectators were given a safe space where they were free to be themselves, especially since many were afraid to come out to their colleagues and blood relatives. Then, in 1993, RuPaul brought drag and ball culture into the limelight with the release of his album *Supermodel of the World*, followed by the premiere of *RuPaul's Drag Race* on VH1 sixteen years later. These pieces of media sequentially became powerful additions to queer history. They helped give society the tools to normalize queerness and gender nonconformity and inspired both contestants and viewers alike to publicly challenge gender norms.

Though the drag community isn't fully immune to homophobic backlash, it's undeniable that RuPaul has elevated a movement surrounding the appreciation and significance of queer culture. Because of this, we can consider him to have made a strong positive impact on our society. His success has inspired conversations about gender identity and helped debunk the myth that men must consistently appear masculine in order to be "real" men. His work has allowed more people to feel comfortable expressing their authentic selves to friends and family, and his presence in the media has given people broader exposure to drag—a creative outlet that would not have been legally or easily accessed in the eighteenth and nineteenth centuries. Because of RuPaul's charisma, uniqueness, nerve, and talent (and those he's projected it onto), we've made great strides in creating a more gender-expressive world.

Works Cited

Everett, Lucinda. "Morbid? No—*Coco* Is the Latest Children's Film with a Crucial Life Lesson." *Anatomy of an Essay: Instructions and Readings*, edited by Tina D. Eliopulos and Todd Moffett, Kendall Hunt Publishing, 2018, pp. 99–101.

Greene, Mark. "The History of 'The Man Box.'" *Medium*, 15 January 2019, remakingmanhood.medium.com/the-history-of-the-man-box-e6eed6d895c4.

Le Guin, Ursula K. "Why Are Americans Afraid of Dragons?" *Anatomy of an Essay: Instructions and Readings*, edited by Tina D. Eliopulos and Todd Moffett, Kendall Hunt Publishing, 2018, pp. 102–108.

Ryan, Hugh. "How Dressing in Drag Was Labeled a Crime in the 20th Century." *History*, 25 June 2019, www.history.com/news/stonewall-riots-lgbtq-drag-three-article-rule.

Wheeler, André-Naquian. "How *RuPaul's Drag Race* Prepared Honey Mahogany for a Career in Politics." *Vogue*, 30 June 2021, www.vogue.com/article/honey-mahogany-san-francisco-trans-democrat-interview.

Morbid? No—*Coco* Is the Latest Children's Film with a Crucial Life Lesson
by Lucinda Everett

Some say we're forcing children to face issues beyond their years. But films can help make them resilient, self-aware adults.

At the weekend Disney Pixar's new film, *Coco*, hit cinemas. It topped the UK box office and has already won a Golden Globe, so you can probably guess what it's about. Princesses, right? Or dinosaurs, maybe.

Nope. It's death: actual send-the-12-year-old-hero-to-the-afterlife-to-meet-his-dead-relatives-type death. Set during the Mexican *Día de Muertos* (Day of the Dead), when people remember their departed loved ones, its core message is that those we lose live on in our memories. Speaking of memory, there's also a character with senile dementia. Really kid-friendly stuff.

Children's films have always had life lessons at their heart. And while most of them have traditionally sat in the positive platitudes category—work hard, be brave, do the right thing—there have been some home truths over the years, too: people are cruel (the *Dumbo* lesson); you'll outgrow your childhood and its trappings (thanks, *Toy Story 2*).

But in recent years, as young people's lives have become more complex and challenging than ever before, kids' movies have stepped up, tackling increasingly tricky subjects. If there's something you're loth to talk to a child about, chances are there's a film that will do it for you.

Death is one tough subject that has always been common—even if not quite as central as it is in *Coco*. Disney's first heroine, Snow White, was an orphan, and they were soon offing loved ones on screen, starting with Bambi's mum. In fact, a 2014 *British Medical Journal* study found that, proportionally, main characters die on screen in more children's animated films than dramatic films for adults.

Copyright © Guardian News & Media Ltd 2018

By 1994, *The Lion King*'s Simba was experiencing real grief, and in *Toy Story 3* (2010) the heroes slid towards seemingly certain death, hand-in-hand, eyes closed, accepting. But they escaped: death was still a plot point. These days it *is* the plot.

If you're thinking life can be as painful as death, modern kids' films have got that covered too. Take the opening sequence of Pixar's *Up* (2009). You know, the one that shows you how dead you are inside by how long you can last without blubbing. It charts every punishing blow of adult life from losing a baby to money troubles to repeatedly putting your dreams on hold.

In the last decade, Disney films have also turned their gaze outwards, championing society's mistreated and marginalized. Disney's 2013 megahit *Frozen* was a feminist triumph, with two kick-ass female leads and a finale centered on sisterhood. It also briefly showed what many believe was Disney's first same-sex couple, complete with cute kids. And it opened a conversation about parental abuse. Not the overt torture of Disney's early wicked stepmothers, but a more insidious brand that saw Elsa's parents shame her for being different.

In 2015, Pixar's *Inside Out* tackled what is often the very trickiest subject for children to understand—their own feelings. Set inside the head of a young girl struggling with life, it personified her four key emotions, and concluded that it's actually totally fine to feel sad, something any child struggling with depression will find deeply reassuring.

And if that wasn't grown-up enough, 2016 saw Disney release *Zootropolis*, an anthropomorphic comedy with a hard-hitting message about racial inclusion—highly subversive given the xenophobic political rhetoric that was rife at the time.

Some may say we're forcing kids to face issues that are beyond their years—that we should go back to the old days where, aside from the odd bereavement, most troubles were solved with a little courage and a singsong. But times have changed, and the way children experience life has changed, too. There are new pressures, new fears, new opportunities, and the chance to mix with people whose identities and choices are, thankfully, being newly embraced by society.

Films are the perfect way for children to understand all this—not only via storylines that they can relate to but in a safe space where they can ask questions freely.

What's more, the common reference point that films provide means that answering those questions becomes easier for parents, and a more open and honest conversation can develop. Let's face it, most kids won't even bat an eyelid at the stuff adults worry will shock or confuse them. Kids accept the society we present to them, meaning films that normalize any and every expression of what it means to be human are a key tool in moving us towards a more inclusive society.

But perhaps most importantly of all, films can help kids cope better when life's struggles hit them for real. They've already experienced some of the associated emotions vicariously. They've seen how the characters handle the situation. Perhaps they've even thought about what they'd do in the same position. If modern kids' films can help the next generation grow into resilient, self-aware, inclusive adults, I say: keep them coming.

Why Are Americans Afraid of Dragons?
by Ursula K. Le Guin

This was to be a talk about fantasy. But I have not been feeling very fanciful lately, and could not decide what to say; so I have been going about picking people's brains for ideas. "What about fantasy? Tell me something about fantasy." And one friend of mine said, "All right, I'll tell you something fantastic. Ten years ago, I went to the children's room of the library of such-and-such a city, and asked for *The Hobbit*; and the librarian told me, 'Oh, we keep that only in the adult collection; we don't feel that escapism is good for children.'"

My friend and I had a good laugh and shudder over that, and we agreed that things have changed a great deal in these past ten years. That kind of moralistic censorship of works of fantasy is very uncommon now, in the children's libraries. But the fact that the children's libraries have become oases in the desert doesn't mean that there isn't still a desert. The point of view from which that librarian spoke still exists. She was merely reflecting, in perfect good faith, something that goes very deep in the American character: a moral disapproval of fantasy, a disapproval so intense, and often so aggressive, that I cannot help but see it as arising, fundamentally, from fear.

So: Why are Americans afraid of dragons?

Before I try to answer my question, let me say that it isn't only Americans who are afraid of dragons. I suspect that almost all very highly technological peoples are more or less antifantasy. There are several national literatures which, like ours, have had no tradition of adult fantasy for the past several hundred years: the French, for instance. But then you have the Germans, who have a good deal; and the English, who have it, and love it, and do it better than anyone else. So this fear of dragons is not merely a Western, or a technological, phenomenon. But I do not want to get into these vast historical questions; I will speak of modern Americans, the only people I know well enough to talk about.

Copyright © 1974 by Ursula K. Le Guin. First appeared in *PNLA Quarterly* 38 in 1974. Reprinted by permission of Curtis Brown, Ltd.

In wondering why Americans are afraid of dragons, I began to realize that a great many Americans are not only antifantasy, but altogether antifiction. We tend, as a people, to look upon all works of the imagination either as suspect, or as contemptible.

"My wife reads novels. I haven't got the time."

"I used to read that science fiction stuff when I was a teenager, but of course I don't now."

"Fairy stories are for kids. I live in the real world."

Who speaks so? Who is it that dismisses *War and Peace*, *The Time Machine*, and *A Midsummer Night's Dream* with this perfect self-assurance? It is, I fear, the man in the street—the hardworking, over-thirty American male—the men who run this country.

Such a rejection of the entire art of fiction is related to several American characteristics: our Puritanism, our work ethic, our profit-mindedness, and even our sexual mores.

To read *War and Peace* or *The Lord of the Rings* plainly is not "work"—you do it for pleasure. And if it cannot be justified as "educational" or as "self-improvement," then, in the Puritan value system, it can only be self-indulgence or escapism. For pleasure is not a value, to the Puritan; on the contrary, it is a sin.

Equally, in the businessman's value system, if an act does not bring in an immediate, tangible profit, it has no justification at all. Thus the only person who has an excuse to read Tolstoy or Tolkien is the English teacher, because he gets paid for it. But our businessman might allow himself to read a best-seller now and then: not because it is a good book, but because it is a best-seller—it is a success, it has made money. To the strangely mystical mind of the money-changer, this justifies its existence; and by reading it he may participate, a little, in the power and mana of its success. If this is not magic, by the way, I don't know what is.

The last element, the sexual one, is more complex. I hope I will not be understood as being sexist if I say that, within our culture, I believe that this antifiction attitude is basically a male one. The American boy and man is very commonly forced to define his maleness by rejecting certain traits, certain human gifts and potentialities, which our culture defines as "womanish" or "childish." And one of these traits or potentialities is, in cold sober fact, the absolutely essential human faculty of imagination.

Having got this far, I went quickly to the dictionary.

The *Shorter Oxford Dictionary* says: "Imagination. 1. The action of imagining, or forming a mental concept of what is not actually present to the senses; 2. The mental consideration of actions or events not yet in existence."

Very well; I certainly can let "absolutely essential human faculty" stand. But I must narrow the definition to fit our present subject. By "imagination," then, I personally mean the free play of the mind, both intellectual and sensory. By "play" I mean recreation, re-creation, the recombination of what is known into what is new. By "free" I mean that the action is done without an immediate object of profit—spontaneously. That does not mean, however, that there may not be a purpose behind the free play of the mind, a goal; and the goal may be a very serious object indeed. Children's imaginative play is clearly practice for the acts and emotions of adulthood; a child who did not play would not become mature. As for the free play of an adult mind, its result may be *War and Peace*, or the theory of relativity.

To be free, after all, is not to be undisciplined. I should say that the discipline of the imagination may in fact be the essential method or technique of both art and science. It is our Puritanism, insisting that discipline means repression or punishment, which confuses the subject. To discipline something, in the proper sense of the word, does not mean to repress it, but to train it—to encourage it to grow, and act, and be fruitful, whether it is a peach tree or a human mind.

I think that a great many American men have been taught just the opposite. They have learned to repress their imagination, to reject it as something childish or effeminate, unprofitable, and probably sinful.

They have learned to fear it. But they have never learned to discipline it at all.

Now, I doubt that the imagination can be suppressed. If you truly eradicated it in a child, he would grow up to be an eggplant. Like all our evil propensities, the imagination will out. But if it is rejected and despised, it will grow into wild and weedy shapes; it will be deformed. At its best, it will be mere ego-centered daydreaming;

at its worst, it will be wishful thinking, which is a very dangerous occupation when it is taken seriously. Where literature is concerned, in the old, truly Puritan days, the only permitted reading was the Bible. Nowadays, with our secular Puritanism, the man who refuses to read novels because it's unmanly to do so, or because they aren't true, will most likely end up watching bloody detective thrillers on the television, or reading hack Westerns or sports stories, or going in for pornography, from *Playboy* on down. It is his starved imagination, craving nourishment, that forces him to do so. But he can rationalize such entertainment by saying that it is realistic—after all, sex exists, and there are criminals, and there are baseball players, and there used to be cowboys—and also by saying that it is virile, by which he means that it doesn't interest most women.

That all these genres are sterile, hopelessly sterile, is a reassurance to him, rather than a defect. If they were genuinely realistic, which is to say genuinely imagined and imaginative, he would be afraid of them. Fake realism is the escapist literature of our time. And probably the ultimate escapist reading is that masterpiece of total unreality, the daily stock market report.

Now what about our man's wife? She probably wasn't required to squelch her private imagination in order to play her expected role in life, but she hasn't been trained to discipline it, either. She is allowed to read novels, and even fantasies. But, lacking training and encouragement, her fancy is likely to glom on to very sickly fodder, such things as soap operas, and "true romances," and nursy novels, and historico-sentimental novels, and all the rest of the baloney ground out to replace genuine imaginative works by the artistic sweatshops of a society that is profoundly distrustful of the uses of the imagination.

What, then, are the uses of the imagination?

You see, I think we have a terrible thing here: a hardworking, upright, responsible citizen, a full-grown, educated person, who is afraid of dragons, and afraid of hobbits, and scared to death of fairies. It's funny, but it's also terrible. Something has gone very wrong. I don't know what to do about it but to try and give an honest answer to that person's question, even though he often asks it in an aggressive and contemptuous tone of voice. "What's the good of it all?" he says. "Dragons and hobbits and little green men—what's the *use* of it?"

The truest answer, unfortunately, he won't even listen to. He won't hear it. The truest answer is, "The use of it is to give you pleasure and delight."

"I haven't got the time," he snaps, swallowing a Maalox pill for his ulcer and rushing off to the golf course.

So we try the next-to-truest answer. It probably won't go down much better, but it must be said: "The use of imaginative fiction is to deepen your understanding of your world, and your fellow men, and your own feelings, and your destiny."

To which I fear he will retort, "Look, I got a raise last year, and I'm giving my family the best of everything, we've got two cars and a color TV. I understand enough of the world!"

And he is right, unanswerably right, if that is what he wants, and all he wants.

The kind of thing you learn from reading about the problems of a hobbit who is trying to drop a magic ring into an imaginary volcano has very little to do with your social status, or material success, or income. Indeed, if there is any relationship, it is a negative one. There is an inverse correlation between fantasy and money. That is a law, known to economists as Le Guin's Law. If you want a striking example of Le Guin's Law, just give a lift to one of those people along the roads who own nothing but a backpack, a guitar, a fine head of hair, a smile, and a thumb. Time and again, you will find that these waifs have read *The Lord of the Rings*—some of them can practically recite it. But now take Aristotle Onassis, or J. Paul Getty: could you believe that those men ever had anything to do, at any age, under any circumstances, with a hobbit?

But, to carry my example a little further, and out of the realm of economics, did you ever notice how very gloomy Mr. Onassis and Mr. Getty and all those billionaires look in their photographs? They have this strange, pinched look, as if they were hungry. As if they were hungry for something, as if they had lost something and were trying to think where it could be, or perhaps what it could be, what it was they've lost.

Chapter 3: Organization

Could it be their childhood?

So I arrive at my personal defense of the uses of imagination, especially in fiction, and most especially in fairy tale, legend, fantasy, science fiction, and the rest of the lunatic fringe. I believe that maturity is not an outgrowing, but a growing up: that an adult is not a dead child, but a child who survived. I believe that all the best faculties of a mature human being exist in the child, and that if these faculties are encouraged in youth they will act well and wisely in the adult, but if they are repressed and denied in the child they will stunt and cripple the adult personality. And finally, I believe that one of the most deeply human, and humane, of these faculties is the power of imagination: so that it is our pleasant duty, as librarians, or teachers, or parents, or writers, or simply as grownups, to encourage that faculty of imagination in our children, to encourage it to grow freely, to flourish like the green bay tree, by giving it the best, absolutely the best and purest, nourishment that it can absorb. And never, under any circumstances, to squelch it, or sneer at it, or imply that it is childish, or unmanly, or untrue.

For fantasy is true, of course. It isn't factual, but it is true. Children know that. Adults know it too, and that is precisely why many of them are afraid of fantasy. They know that its truth challenges, even threatens, all that is false, all that is phony, unnecessary, and trivial in the life they have let themselves be forced into living. They are afraid of dragons, because they are afraid of freedom.

So I believe that we should trust our children. Normal children do not confuse reality and fantasy—they confuse them much less often than we adults do (as a certain great fantasist pointed out in a story called "The Emperor's New Clothes"). Children know perfectly well that unicorns aren't real, but they also know that books about unicorns, if they are good books, are true books. All too often, that's more than Mummy and Daddy know; for, in denying their childhood, the adults have denied half their knowledge, and are left with the sad, sterile little fact: "Unicorns aren't real." And that fact is one that never got anybody anywhere (except in the story "The Unicorn in the Garden," by another great fantasist, in which it is shown that a devotion to the unreality of unicorns may get you straight into the loony bin). It is by such statements as, "Once upon a time there was a dragon," or "In a hole in the ground there lived a hobbit"—it is by such beautiful non-facts that we fantastic human beings may arrive, in our peculiar fashion, at the truth.

Discussion Questions for Chapter 3

For Timothy Snyder

1. Look up the definition of the word *tyranny*. Write it out. Is tyranny at work in our "free society"? If so, where? If not, how and why can you be sure? Explain your stance.
2. Is the internet "one great, bloody accident" as Snyder describes it? Be specific in your agreement or disagreement with his assessment. How do you safeguard the truth for yourself and for others on the internet, particularly in your use of social media—*Facebook, Twitter, Instagram, TikTok,* and *Snapchat*?
3. Is journalism a protected profession? If so, why? Identify a *print* journalist who respects this privilege and one who violates it. Be specific.
4. Snyder wrote this piece during the Trump Administration. What is the primary argument that Snyder presents? Have you observed or heard of other elected leaders who have behaved in the way Snyder describes? Offer examples. What methods of organization does Snyder use in his support of his argument? Point out his specific examples.
5. Snyder discusses the importance of engaging in conversations along with conducting individual research to learn more about issues. In your opinion, is this valuable advice? How do you learn about an issue? Would you be willing to investigate to write a "proper article" about an issue that interests you? See the strategies for reporting included in chapter five.

For Mark Twain

1. Can you think of a task or occupation—in the same way Twain views the river as an experienced riverboat captain—that loses its allure once it is mastered? Is this loss a necessity to completing the job correctly? Can this work conversely: beauty emerging from the mastery of a task or job?

2. What pattern of organization does Twain use: continuous or alternating? Explain what would be gained or lost by employing the other method.
3. Write out three of Twain's most detail-driven sentences. Then rewrite each of the three, twice creating a new end focus.
4. A theme Twain seems to be illustrating is the difference between perception and reality. When have you ever realized that a person, place, or event in your life was not how you had initially perceived it? How did the realization change you?

For S. L. Kelly

1. Kelly's essay appears to be about a process. What process, exactly? What are the obstacles she faces when trying to complete it? Is this a directional or an informational process? How do you know?
2. Around what key event does Kelly organize her essay? What are the causes of this key event? What are the effects? Consider the transitions that she uses to move her reader through her article.
3. Examine the eighth paragraph of Kelly's essay and label each sentence using the five purposes—topic sentence, narrow down, support (description, narration, etc.), explanation, conclusion—given above for sentence-by-sentence organization. Also, examine how the paragraph makes use of the known-new contract.
4. Writers convey their personalities in their work. This piece is the second by Kelly that appears in this textbook. Having read both, what can you deduce about Kelly's relationships with her past, her present, and her bike?
5. Kelly carries her late father's voice with her as she faces her challenges with her bike. What words of advice does he give her? What do her father's words represent to her? Do you reflect on a person's past advice to help you through current challenges? What is that advice, and how does it help you?

For Brooke Workman

1. Workman establishes a causal chain between society's historical treatment of the LGBTQIA+ community, the underground efforts to resist this treatment, RuPaul's media presence, and the growing acceptance of new norms for gender roles. Identify the key event of this chain and the effects of it that she presents in her essay.
2. Like Workman, Ursula K. Le Guin and Dariel Suarez (whose essay appears in chapter four) talk in their essays about masculinity. How do the views of the writers agree on this topic? How do they differ?
3. Workman's essay includes research from several sources. Pick one paragraph in which she uses at least one of those sources and label each sentence using the five purposes—topic sentence, narrow down, quotation, explanation, conclusion. Also, examine how that paragraph makes use of the known-new contract.

For Lucinda Everett

1. Identify a children's film that taught you a lesson or helped you cope with a difficult emotion or experience. How did the film comfort you? What did it teach you about yourself and your experience?
2. Identify an individual or a group that dismisses children's and young adult literature and films as being unimportant. Discuss why you think these individuals hold such a view.
3. In what paragraph does Everett put forward her thesis? Write it out. What organization strategies does she use to arrange her support of it?
4. Everett speaks to film helping children cope with life-changing experiences—death, abuse, racism, etc. What is an important coping strategy that you rely on? Describe it. How has it helped you in your life?
5. Everett traces a connection between American cultural mores and the animation produced by Disney and Pixar. Similarly, the art of anime has a strong connection to the mores and

problems of Japanese culture. Do American and Japanese forms of animation tackle the same issues? Do they tackle those issues in the same manner? Explain.

For Ursula K. Le Guin

1. "Why Are Americans Afraid of Dragons?" was first presented in 1973 as a talk Le Guin gave to the Pacific Northwest Library Association. Does the piece still hold truth? Are Americans today still afraid of dragons? If so, why? If not, how have Americans squelched their fear of dragons? What proof do you have of this?
2. According to Le Guin, the purpose of imaginative fiction is to "deepen your understanding of your world, and your fellow men, and your own feelings, and your destiny." Do you agree with that assertion? Do you think this is the purpose of all art or just literature? Explain.
3. Le Guin utilizes more than one mode of writing. Identify specific types of development (description, definition, cause and effect, classification, narration, etc.). Why is it effective for her to use multiple types? How does her organization frame her development?
4. Some of Le Guin's paragraphs are quite short in length. Is her choice of length due to the work originally being a speech? Or is there another reason? Which paragraphs work well transitioning from one idea to the next? What words does she use to move from idea to idea—both within the paragraphs and between them?
5. Le Guin seems to associate wealth with a lack of imagination, or at least with a disconnection from one's childhood, when imagination is supposedly given freer rein. Do you agree with this claim? Why or why not? Can you identify an adult in your life who has not lost touch with their inner child?
6. Both Le Guin and Everett have something to say about how society responds to works of fantasy and imagination. Compare and contrast their views. How have societal views toward imaginative works changed between the times each writer published her piece?

Chapter 4
Mechanics

Overview of Main Elements

Mechanics are the nuts and bolts of writing and of preparing your manuscript for submission. You must pay special attention to your instructor's requirements for submitting your essays because those requirements will make the writing (and the reading) process easier. In particular, you will have to keep in mind seven areas: **essay format**, **documentation**, **vocabulary**, **spelling**, **punctuation**, **grammar**, and **sentence construction**.

The *format* of the essay includes how you put your name, course, assignment title, and other pertinent information on your manuscript. It also includes settings for margins, paragraph alignment, headings, page numbers, and other details that pertain to the appearance of your text on the page. Many instructors in the humanities will ask you to follow the Modern Language Association (MLA) guidelines explained in most student handbooks. However, many instructors may want you to follow their own method of formatting your assignments. Make sure you understand your instructor's requirements before you sit down to write.

The process of *documentation* applies when your instructor has asked you to write a research paper or a literature essay. In either case, you must follow the rules of documentation set out in a style guide, such as the *MLA Handbook*, the *Publication Manual of the American Psychological Association*, or some other source. These rules will also be set out in most student handbooks. The process of documentation has two main parts: a parenthetical citation that appears in the body paragraphs, and a works cited (or references) list. Make sure that you understand the documentation rules that your instructor requires as you are writing your essay. Please also keep in mind that a failure to format and document your paper according to your instructor's guidelines can result in a significant grade deduction regardless of the quality of the essay's content.

Using the correct *vocabulary* in your writing is also important. Generally, your instructor will be looking for two things: the proper use of **key terms** and appropriate **diction**. A key term is a specific concept in a certain field of study. For example, in a literature class (or elsewhere in this book!), you may learn about concepts such as plot, character, and setting. If you are writing an essay in which you must use one of these concepts, the instructor will determine if you have defined that term correctly and applied it accurately to the material you are covering. Diction, on the other hand, pertains to your choice of words in your writing. In an academic setting, your instructor will probably prefer that you use more formal words. Check with your instructor about any limitations on word choice that an assignment may have.

Checking the *spelling* of unfamiliar words, of important vocabulary words, and of words that you frequently misspell should be one of your final tasks when writing your paper. Your computer's spell checker is a handy tool—but it is not perfect. You may misspell a word that the spell checker may not recognize as an error. For example, if you type *an* when you meant to type *and*, the spell checker will not see your misspelling as an error because *an* is a word. An extra pass through your assignment—or the eyes of a classmate or friend—may help you catch many spelling mistakes. Another handy tool, if you're drafting on a computer, is a text-to-speech reader. Mac users have a text-to-speech reader built into their System Preferences menu under the Accessibility icon (click on Speech); Windows users can use Narrator. With this tool, highlight each paragraph in your text and listen closely as you read along. You may be surprised by how many errors you hear that your eyes do not see. You might even hear some of the other errors described below, an added benefit. A classmate or a friend can help you here as well if he or she is willing to read your work aloud.

Errors of *punctuation, grammar,* and *sentence construction* tend to be the most frustrating for students. You may sense that you have made such an error, but you are not sure what that error might be or how to fix it—until you have the assignment handed back with your instructor's marks. Knowing what your instructor is looking for may help you see which errors you commit. Instructors tend to see errors of punctuation, grammar, and sentence construction as belonging to two groups: **frequency errors** and **status errors**.

Frequency errors are those which your instructor sees most often when grading student assignments. Many of these are as simple as a missing comma, but some are as serious as sentence fragments. Following is a list taken from a study published by Andrea A. Lunsford and Karen J. Lunsford in 2008 showing the twenty most frequent mechanical errors:

1	Wrong word
2	Missing comma after an introductory element (presentence modifier, sentence)
3	Incomplete or missing documentation (source not named in text)
4	Vague pronoun reference
5	Spelling error (including homonyms)
6	Mechanical error with a quotation (missing quotation marks; incorrect placement of commas and periods)
7	Unnecessary comma
8	Unnecessary or missing capitalization
9	Missing word
10	Faulty sentence structure
11	Missing comma with a nonrestrictive element
12	Unnecessary shift in verb tense (past to present or present to past)
13	Missing comma in a compound sentence (independent clause, independent clause)
14	Unnecessary or missing apostrophe (including its/it's)
15	Fused (run-on) sentence
16	Comma splice
17	Lack of pronoun–antecedent agreement
18	Poorly integrated quotation (no signal phrase; no coordination with surrounding text)
19	Unnecessary or missing hyphen
20	Sentence fragment

Focusing your attention on the errors that appear at the top of this frequency list may help you to cut down on the number of errors you commit in your own writing. You may also want to look most closely for comma errors, since they appear six times (counting the comma splice). You may wish, therefore, to consult a handbook to learn more about all of these errors.

Status errors are those that stigmatize the writer and elicit a strong response in a reader. Following is a list taken from a study conducted by Maxine Hairston in 1981 (qtd. in Noguchi 59–60) showing the most serious status-marking punctuation, grammar, and sentence construction errors:

Status Marking
Nonstandard verb forms in past or past participle: *we knowed* instead of *we knew*
Lack of subject-verb agreement: *we was* instead of *we were; he don't think* instead of *he doesn't think*
Double negatives: *I don't want no trouble*
Objective pronoun as subject: *Him and me found the dog*
Very Serious
Sentence fragments (sentence or independent clause)
Run-on sentences
Noncapitalization of proper nouns
Would of instead of *would have*
Lack of subject-verb agreement, nonstatus marking
Insertion of comma between verb and complement: *She is, an engineer*
Nonparallelism: *We enjoy hiking, swimming, and to go to the movies*
Faulty adverb forms: *He treats his men bad*
Use of transitive verb *set* for intransitive *sit: I set down in the chair*

Again, focusing your attention on the errors that appear on this list may help you lower the number of mistakes in your own writing, but you will also be reducing the number that your instructor will see as being the most serious. Comparing this list with the previous one may also give you an idea of which errors you may wish to focus your attention on. As with the previous list, you should consult a handbook to learn more about these errors.

Parts of Speech

Knowing the parts of speech will help you recognize some of the errors listed above and construct your sentences with more ease. The traditional parts of speech are **noun, pronoun, verb, adjective, adverb, conjunction, preposition,** and **interjection**.

Nouns tell us who (*human, Todd*) and what (*dog, Winnie; city, Paris; document, Gettysburg Address*). They are also words that can be changed to show **number** (*dog, dogs*) and **possession** (*dog's, dogs'*).

Pronouns are words that take the place of nouns (John = *he*, Samantha = *she*, Najimi = *they*, dog = *it*, Americans = *they*). They can show number (*she, they*) and possession (*his, hers, its, their,* etc.). They also can show **person**, one's position relative to the speaker of an utterance: **first-person** pronouns stand in for the speaker (*I, me, my, mine*) or the speaker's cohort (*we, us, our, ours*); **second-person** pronouns represent the person or people spoken to (*you, your, yours*); **third-person** pronouns fill in for the people or places or things spoken about (*he, she, it, they,* etc.). Pronouns also change to show the *starting point* (*we* did this) or the *end point* (this happened to *us*) of an action.

Verbs tell us state (the water *is* hot), process (the water *is heating*), or action (the water *is heating* the noodles). They also can be changed to show time (the water *was* hot), potential (the water *will be* hot), progress (the water *has heated,* the water *is heating*), or agreement (the noodle *is* hot, the noodles *are* hot). Verbs often appear in a phrase with **helping verbs** (the water *has* heated) and **main verbs** (the water has *heated*).

Adjectives tell us about size (*large, small*), color (*red, green*), shape (*round, square*), condition (*old, pretty*), number (*six, tenth*), and opinion (*silly, harsh*). They typically appear in front of a noun (*the large* dog), immediately after a noun (the dog, *large* and *fierce*, snarled at us), or after a state verb (the dog is *large*). Adjectives can also show comparison (this dog is *larger* than that one; Winnie is the *sweetest* dog).

Adverbs tell us where (*onward*), when (*yesterday*), how (*quickly*), how often (*never*), and degree (*very*). They typically appear around verbs (they went *onward*), adjectives (she is *very* smart), and other adverbs (she runs *pretty* quickly). Adverbs can also show comparison (she runs *quicker* than Bonnie; she runs *quickest*).

Conjunctions and *prepositions* both connect other words together and show a relationship between those words. Conjunctions join words (this *and* that), phrases (on the table *or* by the desk), and clauses (she won, *so* we cheered; *after* she won, we cheered) to show equality, option, contrast, result, reason, and many other relationships. Prepositions begin **prepositional phrases,** which link nouns or pronouns to other words and show where, when, or how (the book *on* the desk; they close *at* ten o'clock; they ate *with* gusto).

Interjections express emotion and are separated from other utterances with an exclamation point (*hooray!* I found my phone) or a comma (*darn,* I missed my show).

Sentence Construction

With the parts of speech in hand, you may then begin to construct sentences. A **simple sentence** has a subject (one <u>noun</u>) and a predicate (one <u>verb</u>): The <u>boy</u> <u>ate</u> the cake. You can build out from this basic model by adding other parts of speech:

> Adjectives: The *hungry* boy ate the cake. The boy, *happy* and *excited,* ate the cake.
> Adverbs: The boy ate the cake *slowly.* The boy ate the cake *yesterday.*
> Prepositional Phrases: The boy ate the cake *with gusto.* The boy *at the table* ate the cake.

Chapter 4: Mechanics   **119**

You can also use some fancier building blocks: **appositives, participial phrases, infinitive phrases**, and **absolutes**. An appositive is a loose noun, a participle is an -ing or -ed form verb, an infinitive is a to+ form verb, and an absolute is a noun with an -ing or -ed form verb:

> Appositive: The boy, *an excited toddler*, ate the cake.
> Participial Phrase: The boy, *eyeing the mound of presents*, ate the cake.
> Infinitive Phrase: *To hide the evidence*, the boy ate the cake.
> Absolute: *Stomach rumbling*, the boy ate the cake.

With **coordinating conjunctions**—the fanboys *for, and, nor, but, or, yet, so*—you can create **compound sentences**, which are two simple sentences set together with equal importance:

> The boy ate the cake, *and* the girl ate the ice cream.
> The boy ate the cake, *but* the girl ate the ice cream.
> The boy ate the cake, *so* we had no dessert.

With **subordinating conjunctions**—which show place, time, manner, degree, condition, cause, result, concession, and purpose—you can create **complex sentences**, two simple sentences joined by relative importance:

> The boy ate the cake *where* the girl was eating the ice cream.
> *After* the boy ate the cake, the girl ate the ice cream.
> The boy ate the cake *how* a hummingbird sips nectar.
> The boy ate less cake *than* a hummingbird sips nectar.
> *If* the boy eats the cake, the girl will eat the ice cream.
> The boy ate the cake *because* the girl ate the ice cream.
> The boy ate *so* little cake *that* his stomach still rumbled.
> *Though* the boy ate the cake quickly, he did not upset his stomach.
> The boy ate the cake quickly *so that* he could get to the mound of presents.

You can also create complex sentences by using a special group of words called **relative pronouns** (*who, which, that*):

> The boy *who ate the cake* is a fan of birthday parties.
> The cake *which he ate* was made by Freed's Bakery.
> The ice cream *that should have been served with the cake* was eaten by the girl.

You can also create a **compound-complex sentence** by using two or more of the building blocks shown above:

> The boy *who ate the cake* is a fan of birthday parties, *but* the girl *who ate the ice cream* prefers reading a quiet book.
> *After* the boy ate the cake, the girl *who ate the ice cream* read a quiet book, *and* the rest of the guests went home.

Line Editing

With the parts of speech and a knowledge of sentence construction in hand, you should line-edit your essay to make sure that your sentences are grammatically and mechanically clean. The three suggestions below can make the line-editing process smooth and helpful.

1) *Find the subjects and the verbs of your sentences.* Seventy-five percent of all errors can be corrected by following this step. For example, look at the sentence below:

> Different syrups **were lined** up on the counter next to the espresso machine, such as vanilla, amaretto, and coconut.

The subject of the sentence has been underlined, and the verbs have been set in bold. One problem lies in the unnecessary use of the passive voice. To revise the sentence, we might write

> Different syrups **lined** the counter next to the espresso machine, such as vanilla, amaretto, and coconut.

Chapter 4: Mechanics **121**

If you are having trouble finding subjects and verbs in a passage, follow these two steps: one, rewrite the passage, changing plural words into singular words and singular words into plural words, and underline the words changed; and two, take the rewritten passage and shift words showing present time into the past and words showing past time into the present. Set in bold the words changed.

> Different <u>syrup</u> **is** lined up on the <u>counters</u> next to the espresso <u>machines</u>, such as <u>vanillas, amarettos</u>, and <u>coconuts</u>.

The subject noun here is *syrups* because when these words changed spellings, the helping verb *is*, now in present tense, changed to agree with *syrup*.

2) *Make sure the modifiers go where they should.* The sentence we created after step one has a modifier placed in the wrong position. The list beginning with the phrase *such as*—an appositive—should be placed next to the word *syrups*:

> Different <u>syrups</u>, such as vanilla, amaretto, and coconut **lined** the counter next to the espresso machine.

3) *Make sure your punctuation goes where it should.* In the sentence we created after step two, the modifying phrase *such as vanilla, amaretto, and coconut* now comes between the subject *syrups* and the verb *lined*. The phrase must be set off with two commas or no commas:

> Different <u>syrups</u> such as vanilla, amaretto, and coconut **lined** the counter next to the espresso machine.

We can improve the sentence even more by writing

> <u>Bottles</u> of different syrups such as vanilla, amaretto, and coconut **lined** the counter next to the espresso machine.

Because we have neatly placed the syrups within their containers, this version of the sentence can stand, for now, without more revision.

★

We hope that this brief look into the process of essay writing will help you through your drafting stages. As stated at the outset, the first draft of an essay is not the final draft. You should get into the habit of writing multiple drafts of each assignment so that you will give yourself the chance to form and organize your ideas and to proofread for errors. To close this chapter, we've provided four readings that should further illustrate the importance of good mechanics. The first, Roxane Gay's essay "To Scratch, Claw, or Grope Clumsily or Frantically," and the third, a chapter from Lynne Truss's *Eats, Shoots & Leaves*, look amusingly at what happens when spelling and punctuation go wrong. The second, another chapter from Timothy Snyder's *On Tyranny*, and the last, "In Orbit" by Dariel Suarez, show how certain vocabulary can affect political discourse and personal identity.

We've also included exercises you may use to practice your punctuation and sentence construction skills. The first set needs simple punctuation changes, but the second set will require that you follow the three-step line-editing process explained above. (Possible answers come at the end of this chapter as well—don't peek!)

Works Cited

Lunsford, Andrea A., and Karen J. Lunsford. "Mistakes Are a Fact of Life: A National Comparative Study." *College Composition and Communication*, vol. 59, no. 4, 2008, pp. 781–806.

Noguchi, Rei R. *Grammar and the Teaching of Writing: Limits and Possibilities*. NCTE, 1991.

To Scratch, Claw, or Grope Clumsily or Frantically[1]
by Roxane Gay

My third tournament started with a brutal game where I lost by more than 200 points. I was the fifth seed, ranked like tennis with words, and feeling confident—too confident, really. "We Are the Champions" may have been on an infinite loop in my head. And yet. It was also early on a Saturday morning. I am not a morning person. Before the tournament started, people milled around the hotel meeting room, chatting idly about the heat, what we had done since the last time many of us had seen one another (the previous tournament in Illinois), and some of the more amazing plays we had made recently.

Scrabble[2] players love to talk, at length, with some repetition, about their vocabulary triumphs.

There were twenty-one of us with various levels of ability, but really, if you're playing this game at the competitive level, you generally have some skill and can be a contender. The more experienced players, the Dragos to my Rocky, studied word lists and appeared intensely focused on something the rest of us couldn't see. Many wore fanny packs without irony—serious fanny packs bulging with mystery. As I waited for the tournament to begin, I studied the table of game-related accessories—books, a travel set, a towel, a deluxe board, and some milled French soaps clearly taken from someone's closet—all for drawings to be held later in the day.[3]

---

1. This is the definition of the word "scrabble" according to *Merriam-Webster's Collegiate Dictionary*.
2. In all seriousness, Scrabble was invented by a man named Alfred Mosher Butts.
3. Scrabble tournaments are a lot like soccer tournaments for four-year-olds in that, oftentimes, everyone goes home with a little something.

"To Scratch, Claw, or Grope Clumsily or Frantically," pp. 29–43 from *Bad Feminist* by Roxane Gay. Copyright © 2014 by Roxane Gay. Reprinted by permission of HarperCollins Publishers.

124   Chapter 4: Mechanics

At nine o'clock, sharp, the tournament director,[4] Tom, began making announcements, one of which was that his wife had died just days earlier. The tournament was going to go on, he said. It was an awkward, touching moment because grief is so personal and this man was clearly grieving. The room was silent. It was difficult to know what to do. He announced that the first pairings would be posted in a few minutes, so we waited quietly until the pairings were posted around the room. We all hovered around the sheet of paper, quickly writing down the names of our first two opponents. I sat across from my first challenger. She was seeded nineteenth. My confidence swelled vulgarly. She stared at me, smug, almost imperious. I felt an uncomfortable chill. We determined she would go first. She drew her seven tiles. I started her time and fixed her with a hard stare as she began shuffling the seven plastic squares back and forth across her rack. I began drawing my tiles. Beneath the table, my legs were shaking.

This is competitive Scrabble.[5]

You have to understand. I was lonely in a new town where I knew no one. I wanted to be back home, with my boyfriend, in our apartment, complaining about how *SportsCenter* seems to air perpetually or listening to him nag me about my imaginary Internet

---

4. Officially rated tournaments are run by NASPA-approved tournament directors. NASPA is the North American Scrabble Players Association. Tournament directors are generally encyclopedic in their knowledge of Scrabble and can easily clarify any confusion about the rules or negotiate disputes that arise during a tournament. Disputes, they arise.

5. This is how serious competitive Scrabble is: there is a national championship, held annually during the summer. The first national tournament was held in 1978. There are also world competitions (the first world championship was held in 1991), a cottage industry of Scrabble-related merchandise, game timers, boards, tiles, etc., plus books, documentaries, and academic articles on the nuances of competitive Scrabble. There are Scrabble-related apps for your iDevices (I use Zarf, CheckWord, the official Scrabble game, Lexulous, and Words With Friends). There are Scrabble games on Facebook (I play the official Hasbro game and Lexulous). Elsewhere online, there's the Internet Scrabble Club (ISC), where I also play. There is a website, cross-tables.com, dedicated to tracking all the official tournaments in the country with scores and rankings. I am ranked 1,336th in the country. I'm guessing that's out of 1,400 players, given my lowliness.

Chapter 4: Mechanics

friends. My apartment was empty, no furniture, because I left my sad graduate-student furniture behind. After work, I'd sit on my lone chair, a step above sad, purchased at Sofa Mart, wondering how my life had come to this.

When my new colleague invited me to her home to play with her Scrabble club,[6] I was so desperate I would have agreed to just about anything—cleaning her bathrooms, watching the grass grow in her backyard, something smarmy and vaguely illegal involving suburban prostitution, whatever.

I didn't quite know what a Scrabble club was, but I assumed it was a group of people enjoying friendly games of Scrabble on a Saturday afternoon. I told my mother I was going to play Scrabble and she laughed, called me a geek, her accent wrapping around the word strangely. I was roundly mocked by my brothers, who were always the popular kids while I was the shunned nerd, a fact they gleefully reminded me of as they made a series of increasingly absurd Scrabble-related jokes, like, "You sure are going through a *DRY SPELL*." The man I left behind said, "Come home. You're freaking me out." I ignored them all.

My colleague Daiva and her husband, Marty, live in a large home in a wooded neighborhood on the very edge of our very small town. Everything is modern and unique and interesting to look at—slick leather chairs, pottery, African art. In their finished basement, there is enough space for ten to twenty people, sometimes more, to get together once a month to play Scrabble all day.

Marty[7] is a nationally ranked player, top fifteen. He knows every word ever invented as well as each word's meaning. If you give him

---

6. There are more than two hundred Scrabble clubs in the United States. The club in my town meets monthly, while the club in Champaign, Illinois, meets weekly. In bigger cities, some clubs will even meet twice a week.
7. He is my Scrabble sensei. I almost beat him once, where "almost" is "not so much." Early in the match I played TRIPLEX for around 90 points. Then I played another bingo. I was way ahead and deluded myself into thinking I was on easy street. The sweetness of my imagined victory was nearly unbearable. Marty would go on to play ENTOZOAN across two Triple Word Score spaces for 203 points. He was Sub-Zero in *Mortal Kombat* tearing out my Scrabble spine with his bare hands—FATALITY. We have not played since. I have been properly humbled.

Chapter 4: Mechanics

a seven-letter combination, he'll tell you all the possible anagrams. I would not be surprised to learn he thinks in anagrams. There are thirty-nine possible Scrabble words in "anagram."[8]

When you are new to the club, Marty carefully explains the rules of competitive Scrabble, and rules, there are many. You have to keep score. When you have completed your turn, you have to press a button on a game timer. You have to monitor time because there are penalties if you exceed twenty-five total minutes for your plays. There's a proper etiquette for drawing tiles (tile bag held above your eyes, head turned away).[9] There's a procedure if you draw too many tiles. There's a protocol for challenging if you believe your opponent has played a phony, a word that isn't in the Official Tournament and Club Word List.[10]

As Marty told me all these rules that first day, I laughed and rolled my eyes like an asshole and struggled to take any of it seriously. Until that day, my Scrabble playing had mostly involved drinking, friends, crazy made-up words, haphazard score keeping, and never ever any time constraints. It was an innocent time.

People slowly filed in with large round cases. One woman's case was wheeled, like a suitcase. They set their cases on tables and pulled out custom turntable scrabble boards, timers, tile bags, and racks. They got out their scoring sheets and personal tokens. The games started,

---

8. I love anagrams. When I was a kid, my mom would write big words on lined paper and ask me to find all the possible words. Now, finding words is kind of my superpower.

9. In the seventh round of the 2011 World Scrabble Championships, Edward Martin, while playing Chollapat Itthi-Aree, realized a tile was missing. The tournament director came up with a reasonable solution, but Itthi-Aree demanded Martin prove he wasn't hiding the missing tile on his person. Play resumed, and Martin eventually won by a single point. My friend/sensei Marty was totally sitting right next to these guys when this went down. He said, "It was a distraction."

10. There are multiple official word lists. In North America, most Scrabble players use the Official Tournament and Club Word List (OWL). Outside of North America, players use the *Collins English Dictionary*. At some tournaments here in the United States, you will find smaller Collins divisions for those Scrabble players who want to test their skills using the Collins dictionary. The challenge is remembering which words are acceptable for Collins and then remembering which words are acceptable for OWL when returning to traditional play.

and the room hushed. I realized this was no time to crack jokes. I realized Scrabble is very serious business.

I have a Scrabble nemesis. His name is Henry.[11] He has the most gorgeous blue-gray eyes I have ever seen. The beauty of his perfect eyes only makes me hate him more. He has been known to wear a fanny pack and often scowls. Nemeses aren't born. They are made.

Shortly after I started playing with my local Scrabble club, Marty told me about a charity tournament he holds in Danville, said it would be a great experience for me to play. I had nothing to lose so I agreed. I had no idea what to expect as I walked into the main building of the community college in Danville. After I registered, I stood awkwardly, wondering what to do, until my club friends took mercy on me and showed me the lay of tournament land.

Serious Scrabble people study words and remember matches from eight years ago where they played a word for 173 points. They remember when they didn't challenge a phony and lost the match. They remember everything. Some serious Scrabble players are poor losers. I am a good loser. I love Scrabble so much I don't care if I lose. I also have to be a good loser because I lose a lot, so practicality plays a role. Unlike most serious Scrabble players, I don't have the patience to study all the possible three- and four-letter words, for example, but still, I am extremely competitive.[12] It's an awkward combination.

I began the tournament thinking, *I am going to win this tournament.* I approach most things in life with a dangerous level of confidence to balance my generally low self-esteem. This helps me as a writer. Each time I submit a story to fancy magazines like, say, *The New Yorker* or *The Paris Review*, I think, *This story is totally going to get published.*

My heart gets broken more than it should.

---

11. Henry is not his name.
12. I have always enjoyed board games. I love rolling dice and moving small plastic or metal pieces around game boards. I collect Monopoly sets from around the world. I will play any game so long as there is a possibility I can win. I take games seriously. Sometimes I take them too seriously and conflate winning the Game of Life with winning at life.

Chapter 4: Mechanics

After getting all my paperwork and such, I looked around at the other word nerds. I felt like people were checking me out. I was prepared to reenact the beginning of "Beat It" when everyone is silently stalking one another, trying to size up the competition. There were thirty-two players, four groups (based on ranking) with eight players in each. We would play seven rounds to determine the one Scrabble player to rule them all. The tournament director read off the name of each person in each group along with his or her seed. He read my name last, and I understood my place. I was the lowest-ranked (worst) player in the room.[13] I was the last kid who would be picked for dodge ball.

I sat down for my first round with the top seed in my division, and she was pretty cocky. I was too, or I was trying to project cockiness and calm. My hands were shaking under the table I was so nervous. My primary ambition was to not humiliate myself, make any missteps where Scrabble etiquette is concerned,[14] or shame the members of my Scrabble club, several of whom were in attendance.

---

13. Scrabble people are really quite friendly and gracious, but to be clear, they are also intense and serious as hell. I have an imagination. In my head, as we prepared to word rumble, I felt as if we were about to throw down like in the music video for Michael Jackson's "Bad." A lot of my life can be described in terms of Michael Jackson's music. I'd explain the significance of "Man in the Mirror," but then you'd think I was crazy.

14. Players can be very . . . *particular* about how you comport yourself during a Scrabble game. Some players want complete silence during matches, so they won't appreciate your idle chatter. Some players think you're cheating if you play with your phone. Don't take a call should your phone ring, that's for sure. I once got a dirty look for tapping on my phone without muting it. Apparently, the gentle beeps were simply too much for that player. The longer you play, the more you finely hone these particularities. I, for example, have developed several Scrabble-related pet peeves and preferences. I have strong opinions on the type of scoring sheets I use and the kind of pens I use to keep score (Uni-ball .5mm roller ball). I now have a very low tolerance for players who draw their tiles in annoying ways. I am particularly aggravated by players who do a lot of mixing the tiles up before each draw. IT DOES NOT CHANGE THE OUTCOME. I also do not look kindly upon players who tap the tiles on the board as they tally their points. Why are they doing that? What really sets me over the edge, though, is when players recount my word scores after I've announced my score at the end of a turn as if I am incapable of simple math. Certainly, math is not my strong suit, but in general, I have addition under control. When this unnecessary score verification occurs, I sometimes have to sit on my hands to keep from punching a player in the face.

My opponent looked up and said, "I was in the next highest division yesterday." The gauntlet was thrown. She said it with a kind, warm smile, but she was trying to intimidate me. I could tell by the way her upper lip curled. Well played. I wondered if I could purchase adult diapers at the nearest gas station.

The tournament started, and I managed to spell my words and use the timer correctly. I got into a rhythm. I placed a bingo.[15] I was feeling good. My skin flushed warmly with early success. I started thinking I had a chance. Then Number-One Seed proceeded to wipe the board with my ass; the final score was 366-277. I smiled and shook her hand, but a small piece of my soul was destroyed. I thought, *Je suis désoleé*.

When I composed myself, I took stock of what happened. I played decently and had two bingos overall. There was simply nothing I could do. I kept drawing terribly (JVK) and getting outplayed, and she was so damn confident the entire time. Worse yet, Number-One Seed played me better than she played the game.[16] At the beginning of the match, she asked if I was a student.[17] I said, "No, I teach writing," and she said, "Oh, I'm in trouble," pretending to be the weaker prey. Here's the thing. I play poker. I know a bluff when I see one. Once she got going, she kept smirking, letting me know her foot was leaving an ugly mark on my neck.

I was determined to win my second match because I am that competitive and I have pride and winning feels way better than losing. My opponent was really quiet and taciturn. It was not fun playing her. I slaughtered her 403-229 and I wanted to scream I was so happy. I was very tempted to jump on the table and shout, "IN YOUR FACE." For the sake of sportsmanship, I remained quiet and

---

15. A bingo is when you play all seven letters on your rack. This is one of the most coveted Scrabble plays. I am a bingo player. I have no time to learn all the three-letter words and random obscure words, so I spend most of my time going for bingos because, in addition to the points you earn from the board, you also earn a fifty-point bonus. There are twenty-three possible Scrabble words in "bingo."
16. Don't get it twisted. Competitive Scrabble is both word chess and word poker. You need a game face, and you need to wear that game face hard.
17. I choose to believe she asked this because I look so fresh and youthful.

polite and thanked her for the game. She coldly walked away without so much as a by-your-leave. Later, as I drove home, I did gloat. I gloated a lot.

The third match was with a woman I play regularly. She's really nice and we get along well. She always beats me, and that day would be no exception—score: 390-327. My ambitious, delusional goal of winning the tournament was faltering. There were four matches left after the break, so before resuming play, we had lunch and I ate a vegetable sandwich. I told Daiva, the woman who had introduced me to the craziness of competitive Scrabble, "I'm going to win this tournament." She gave me the saddest look, as if to say, *There, there, crazy little Scrabble baby.*

There's something to be said for the delusion of confidence. I won my next four matches (389-312; 424-244; 352-312; 396-366). I was a demon. I had my word mojo. I was seeing bingos everywhere and making smart, tight plays, blocking triple play lanes and tracking perfectly.[18] With each win, I felt increasingly invincible. I wanted to beat my chest. I was also trying to distract myself.

In the middle of the night, hours before the tournament began, I received a frantic call from my mother, the kind of call, as your parents get older, you hope to never receive. My normally healthy father had to be rushed to the hospital—chest pains and shortness of breath. My first instinct was to say, "I am coming home," but fortunately, my youngest brother lives nearby and was able to be there. Throughout the tournament, I was getting updates on my father's condition, trying to reassure my mother that everything would be

---

18. Much like in poker where you try to make an educated guess as to the cards your opponent is holding, great Scrabble players will track the letters played throughout a game. By the end of the game, you should know exactly what your opponent has on his rack. It is also important to track because it allows you to make smarter strategic decisions. It's good to know if high-value letters (J, X, Q, K, V, etc.) are in play because if there are few letters left and you're holding on to a U or an I and you know the Q is still in the bag, you want to be smart about where you play those vowels so your opponent cannot build a word with his Q unless he has the necessary vowels in his own rack.

Chapter 4: Mechanics

fine.[19] I was trying not to lose my shit[20] completely. There are 227 possible Scrabble words in "completely."

In my last match of the day, it became clear the winner of our match would win the entire tournament for our division. This is how my nemesis was born.

Henry with the beautiful, piercing blue-gray eyes was sly like a fox. At the start of the match, he kept playing two-letter words, so I did the same. We were stalking each other around a cage. You know the naked fight scene in *Eastern Promises*? It was like that, only we weren't criminals, naked, or in a Turkish bath, and I was the only one with a number of visible tattoos. He wore a T-shirt that read, "World's Best Scrabble Player." It was the T-shirt that made me extra motivated to win. The level of competition was very strong, and as the game unfolded, my excitement grew.

As the second seed, Henry the Nemesis was confident he would defeat me. I could smell the confidence on him. He reeked of it. I played three bingos during the course of the match. He tried to play TREKING[21] for 81 points, but I knew that was not a word. "Trekking" takes two Ks. I challenged. He rolled his eyes like he couldn't believe I had the nerve to challenge his bad spelling. My hands shook as I typed his word into the computer. I won the challenge. By the end of the match, he was irate and I was giddy. When I won, he realized he wasn't going to win the tournament and had fallen to third place. Because I was seeded so low, his ranking was going to take a hit. He refused to shake my hand and stalked off angrily. I thought he was going to throw the table over. Male anger makes me intensely uncomfortable, so I tried to sit very still and hoped the uncomfortable moment would pass quickly. Henry's bad sportsmanship did not temper my mood for long. I won my first tournament despite being the lowest-seeded[22]

---

19. Everything turned out fine.
20. "Shit" is a valid Scrabble word.
21. There are no bingos with the letters T, R, E, K, I, N, and G. If Henry studied, he would know that.
22. I ended up with an amazing ranking, high enough to almost place me a division up. In the next tournament I played, I would be seeded much higher and I would pay for that, dearly.

player in the field and took home a small cash prize. The size of my ego for the following week was difficult to measure. It would not last, though. What Scrabble giveth, another player, at another tournament, will taketh away.

When you succeed early at an endeavor, you convince yourself you will easily replicate that success. Ask child actors.[23] Three months later, I played in another tournament, the Arden Cup, a twenty-match, two-and-a-half-day affair where I won eight games and lost twelve. I learned a lot. I especially learned that it is insane to believe you will walk into a competitive tournament, among a much larger field, with a fragile and inflated ranking, and somehow win that tournament.

Henry the Nemesis was in attendance, as was a host of equally intriguing and intense players who would get under my skin nearly as much as Henry does. My least favorite player was Donnie,[24] who tried to mansplain Scrabble because he didn't recognize me[25] and took me for a neophyte. As we sat down to start our match, he said, "Now, you just play this the same way you play Scrabble at home." I made it my life's purpose, right then, to destroy him. Another opponent asked if we should play at his board or mine. When I told him I didn't have my own set, he gave me a pitying look.[26] I quickly realized I was swimming with Scrabble sharks. I was the blood in the water.

There was one redemptive moment despite the humiliation of that tournament, one where I lost so many times the matches blended into a depressing blur, where I lost mostly to mansplainers who

---

23. The child actors from *Diff'rent Strokes*, among others, know a little something about this. I was thinking I would pull a Mary-Kate and Ashley. Such was not the case.
24. Also not his name.
25. The Scrabble community is fairly small, and once you start attending tournaments regularly, you will see the same people over and over.
26. I have my own tournament board now as well as a timer (with pink buttons), tiles (pink), and long tile racks (sadly not available in pink). I also have a carrying case with a shoulder strap so I can rock my Scrabble board slung across my shoulders like a boss.

defined words[27] even though I did not ask for definitions, regaled me with tales of their sordid Scrabble histories, and otherwise drove me crazy. I beat Henry the Nemesis again. We played twice during the tournament—he won a game and I won a game. At the end of our second game, the one I won, he stood and pointed at me. He said, "You've won two out of three times. Two. Out. Of. Three." I looked down, bit my lower lip to keep from smiling my face off.

"I wasn't keeping track," I said.[28]

I excused myself and ran to the restroom, where in the privacy of my stall, I whispered, "I beat you, I beat you, I beat you." There was fist pumping.

And so. My third tournament started brutally and the brutality was unrelenting. I ended up winning six matches (one was a bye) and losing six and took fifteenth place. My friends told me that was a good outcome. I'm pretty sure they were just being nice given the increased fragility of my Scrabble ego.

I did not get to play my nemesis, but he was there and he performed well. I took that personally.

A new nemesis was also made early during that tournament. In my first match of the day, I was tired. I had slept for only three hours after a late night in the city with friends. I am not a morning person. I did not have time to find the nearest Starbucks. I could not find any dollar bills to buy a Diet Pepsi. I could not find my Visine. I was hungover—gin, which doesn't settle well with me the day after. My stomach kept turning uncomfortably. I was drowsy. If I closed my eyes, I would simply fall into an uncomfortable sleep. I was a mess.

I was the fifth seed in a field of twenty-one, so I was stupidly pleased with myself to still be seeded so high after the previous

---

27. Qoph is a Hebrew letter. My opponent not only shared the word's meaning, he also explained the origins (something about a sewing needle; frankly, I had tuned him out at that point) and pronunciation. After the exciting word lesson, he started telling me all the possible Q words one can spell without a U. I wondered, *Is there a Q in "motherfucker"?*
28. That was a pretty little lie.

tournament. My opponent was unseeded and had no ranking so I mistakenly assumed she was a novice player.[29] From the outset I was certain I would win the match handily even though I was hungover and barely able to cope with the dryness of my eyeballs.

Toward the end of the match, I played BROASTED and BO for a Triple Word Score. My opponent challenged, and she won. When you challenge multiple words, though, the computer only tells you if the word combination is good or bad. If the combination is bad, it will not tell you if one or all the words in the combination are bad. I thought, because I was mentally incapacitated, that BO must not be a valid word. I may not know my three-letter words, but I do know my two-letter words. I was confused. I was not at my best.

A couple moves later, I played BROASTED and BA in the same location. My opponent's eyes widened. She stared at me like I was the stupidest person alive. In that moment, I hated every last cell in her body.

"You're going to do *that* again?" she asked, but it wasn't quite a question.

It was her tone that totally set me off. I had just laid down the tiles, thereby making it crystal clear I was going to make the same, ridiculous, amateurish mistake twice. What did she fail to understand?

In my defense, I was so convinced BROASTED[30] was a word, because it actually *is* a word, that I remained unwavering in my commitment to play the word. Had I succeeded, I would have earned 87 points. As we walked to the challenge computer, I could feel her laughing at me. I wanted to cry, but my eyes were still so terribly dry, and also there is no crying at a Scrabble tournament unless you're in the bathroom and you have carefully checked all the stalls to make sure you are alone.

The next time I see New Nemesis, I must explain, "I am not the idiot you think I am, or at least I am not an idiot for the reasons you think."

---

29. I willfully ignored the memory of the outcome of my first tournament, where I won as the lowest-seeded player, without a ranking.
30. "Broasting" is a proper noun, and proper nouns are not valid Scrabble words. Broasting is a trademarked method of cooking chicken.

Chapter 4: Mechanics

The match was a massacre. The final score: 500-263. That match set the tone for the tournament. Time and again, lower-ranked players taught me painful lessons. Time and again, I was humbled. At the end of the tournament, after the prizes were handed out and we applauded each of the winners and the players who had played the highest-scoring words, we losers stood in small clumps of failure bemoaning how terribly we had played while those who played well tried not to gloat. Their modesty was good-naturedly false. We packed up our boards, and the excitement of the tournament slowly seeped out of our muscles. We shook hands and bid one another good-bye until the next club meeting or tournament. We were no longer adversaries.

Chapter 4: Mechanics

Excerpt from *On Tyranny*
by Timothy Snyder
Chapter 17, "Listen for Dangerous Words"

Be alert to the use of the words *extremism* and *terrorism*. Be alive to the fatal notions of *emergency* and *exception*. Be angry about the treacherous use of patriotic vocabulary.

The most intelligent of the Nazis, the legal theorist Carl Schmitt, explained in clear language the essence of fascist governance. The way to destroy all rules, he explained, was to focus on the idea of the *exception*. A Nazi leader outmaneuvers his opponents by manufacturing a general conviction that the present moment is exceptional, and then transforming that state of exception into a permanent emergency. Citizens then trade real freedom for fake safety.

When politicians today invoke *terrorism* they are speaking, of course, of an actual danger. But when they try to train us to surrender freedom in the name of safety, we should be on our guard. There is no necessary tradeoff between the two. Sometimes we do indeed gain one by losing the other, and sometimes not. People who assure you that you can *only* gain security at the price of liberty usually want to deny you both.

You can certainly concede freedom without becoming more secure. The feeling of submission to authority might be comforting, but it is not the same thing as actual safety. Likewise, gaining a bit of freedom may be unnerving, but this momentary unease is not dangerous. It is easy to imagine situations where we sacrifice both freedom and safety at the same time: when we enter an abusive relationship or vote for a fascist. Similarly, it is none too difficult to imagine choices that increase both freedom and safety, like leaving an abusive relationship or emigrating from a fascist state. It is the government's job to increase both freedom and security.

"Listen for Dangerous Words" and "Investigate" from *On Tyranny: Twenty Lessons from the Twentieth Century* by Timothy Snyder. Copyright © 2017 by Timothy Snyder. Used by permission of Tim Duggan Books, an imprint of the Crown Publishing Group, a division of Penguin Random House LLC. All rights reserved.

Chapter 4: Mechanics

Extremism certainly sounds bad, and governments often try to make it sound worse by using the word *terrorism* in the same sentence. But the word has little meaning. There is no doctrine called *extremism*. When tyrants speak of *extremists*, they just mean people who are not in the mainstream—as the tyrants themselves are defining that mainstream at that particular moment. Dissidents of the twentieth century, whether they were resisting fascism or communism, were called *extremists*. Modern authoritarian regimes, such as Russia, use laws on *extremism* to punish those who criticize their policies. In this way the notion of *extremism* comes to mean virtually everything except what is, in fact, extreme: tyranny.

Chapter 4: Mechanics

Excerpts from *Eats, Shoots & Leaves*
by Lynne Truss

From "Introduction: The Seventh Sense"

Punctuation has been defined many ways. Some grammarians use the analogy of stitching: punctuation as the basting that holds the fabric of language in shape. Another writer tells us that punctuation marks are the traffic signals of language: they tell us to slow down, notice this, take a detour, and stop. I have even seen a rather fanciful reference to the full stop and comma as "the invisible servants in fairy tales—the ones who bring glasses of water and pillows, not storms of weather or love." But best of all, I think, is the simple advice given by the style book of a national newspaper: that punctuation is "a courtesy designed to help readers to understand a story without stumbling."

Isn't the analogy with good manners perfect? Truly good manners are invisible: they ease the way for others, without drawing attention to themselves. It is no accident that the word "punctilious" ("attention to formality or etiquette") comes from the same original root word as punctuation. As we shall see, the practice of "pointing" our writing has always been offered in a spirit of helpfulness, to underline meaning and prevent awkward misunderstandings between writer and reader. In 1644 a schoolmaster from Southwark, Richard Hodges, wrote in his *The English Primrose* that "great care ought to be had in writing, for the due observing of points: for, the neglect thereof will pervert the sense," and he quoted as an example, "My Son, if sinners intise [entice] thee consent thou, not refraining thy foot from their way." Imagine the difference to the sense, he says, if you place the comma after the word "not": "My Son, if sinners intise thee consent thou not, refraining thy foot from their way." This was the 1644 equivalent of Ronnie Barker in *Porridge*, reading the sign-off from a fellow lag's letter from home, "Now I must go and get on my lover," and then

---

"Introduction: The Seventh Sense" from *Eats, Shoots & Leaves: The Zero Tolerance Approach to Punctuation* by Lynne Truss, Copyright © 2003 by Lynne Truss. Used by permission of Gotham Books, an imprint of Penguin Publishing Group, a division of Penguin Random House LLC. All rights reserved.

pretending to notice a comma, so hastily changing it to, "Now I must go and get on, my lover."

To be fair, many people who couldn't punctuate their way out of a paper bag are still interested in the way punctuation can alter the sense of a string of words. It is the basis of all "I'm sorry, I'll read that again" jokes. Instead of "What would you with the king?" you can have someone say in Marlowe's *Edward II*, "What? Would you? *With the king?*" The consequences of mispunctuation (and re-punctuation) have appealed to both great and little minds, and in the age of the fancy-that email a popular example is the comparison of two sentences:

A woman, without her man, is nothing.
A woman: without her, man is nothing.

Which, I don't know, really makes you *think*, doesn't it? Here is a popular "Dear Jack" letter that works in much the same fundamentally pointless way:

Dear Jack,

I want a man who knows what love is all about. You are generous, kind, thoughtful. People who are not like you admit to being useless and inferior. You have ruined me for other men. I yearn for you. I have no feelings whatsoever when we're apart. I can be forever happy—will you let me be yours?

Jill

Dear Jack,

I want a man who knows what love is. All about you are generous, kind, thoughtful people, who are not like you. Admit to being useless and inferior. You have ruined me. For other men I yearn! For you I have no feelings whatsoever. When we're apart I can be forever happy. Will you let me be?
Yours,

Jill

Chapter 4: Mechanics

But just to show there is nothing very original about all this, five hundred years before email a similarly tiresome puzzle was going round:

> Every Lady in this Land
> Hath 20 Nails on *each* Hand;
> *Five & twenty* on Hands *and Feet*;
> And this is true, without deceit.

(Every lady in this land has twenty nails. On each hand, five; and twenty on hands and feet.)

So all this is quite amusing, but it is noticeable that no one emails the far more interesting example of the fateful mispunctuated telegram that precipitated the Jameson Raid on the Transvaal in 1896—I suppose that's a reflection of modern education for you. Do you know of the Jameson Raid, described as a "fiasco"? Marvellous punctuation story. Throw another log on that fire. The Transvaal was a Boer republic at the time, and it was believed that the British and other settlers around Johannesburg (who were denied civil rights) would rise up if Jameson invaded. But unfortunately, when the settlers sent their telegraphic invitation to Jameson, it included a tragic ambiguity:

> It is under these circumstances that we feel constrained to call upon you to come to our aid should a disturbance arise here the circumstances are so extreme that we cannot but believe that you and the men under you will not fail to come to the rescue of people who are so situated.

As Eric Partridge points out in his *Usage and Abusage*, if you place a full stop after the word "aid" in this passage, the message is unequivocal. It says, "Come at once!" If you put it after "here," however, it says something more like, "We might need you at some later date depending on what happens here, but in the meantime—don't call us, Jameson, old boy; we'll call you." Of course, the message turned up at *The Times* with a full stop after "aid" (no one knows who put it there) and poor old Jameson just sprang to the saddle, without anybody wanting or expecting him to.

All of which substantiates Partridge's own metaphor for punctuation, which is that it's "the line along which the train (composition, style, writing) must travel if it isn't to run away with its driver." In other words, punctuation keeps sense on the rails. [. . .]

★

What happened to punctuation? Why is it so disregarded when it is self-evidently so useful in preventing enormous mix-ups? A headline in today's paper says, "DEAD SONS PHOTOS MAY BE RELEASED"—the story relating to dead sons in the plural, but you would never know. The obvious culprit is the recent history of education practice. We can blame the pedagogues. Until 1960, punctuation was routinely taught in British schools. A child sitting a Country Schools exam in 1937 would be asked to punctuate the following puzzler: "Charles the First walked and talked half an hour after his head was cut off" (answer: "Charles the First walked and talked. Half an hour after, his head was cut off"). Today, thank goodness, the National Curriculum ensures that when children are eight, they are drilled in the use of the comma, even if their understanding of grammar is at such an early age a bit hazy. [. . .] [W]e visited a school in Cheshire where quite small children were being taught that you use commas in the following situations:

1 in a list
2 before dialogue
3 to mark out additional information

Which was very impressive. Identifying "additional information" at the age of eight is quite an achievement, and I know for a fact that I couldn't have done it. But if things are looking faintly more optimistic under the National Curriculum, there remains the awful truth that, for over a quarter of a century, punctuation and English grammar were simply not taught in the majority of schools, with the effect that A-level examiners annually bewailed the condition of examinees' written English, while nothing was done. Candidates

142   Chapter 4: Mechanics

couldn't even *spell* the words "grammar" and "sentence," let alone use them in any well-informed way. [. . .]

But to get back to those dark-side-of-the-moon years in British education when teachers upheld the view that grammar and spelling got in the way of self-expression, it is arguable that the timing of their grammatical apathy could not have been worse. In the 1970s, no educationist would have predicted the explosion in universal written communication caused by the personal computer, the internet and the key-pad of the mobile phone. But now, look what's happened: everyone's a writer! Everyone is posting film reviews on Amazon that go like this:

> I watched this film [*About a Boy*] a few days ago expecting the usual hugh Grant bumbling . . . character Ive come to loathe/expect over the years. I was thoroughly suprised. This film was great, one of the best films i have seen in a long time. The film focuses around one man who starts going to a single parents meeting, to meet women, one problem He doesn't have a child.

Isn't this sad? People who have been taught nothing about their own language are (contrary to educational expectations) spending all their leisure hours attempting to string sentences together for the edification of others. And there is no editing on the internet! Meanwhile, in the world of text messages, ignorance of grammar and punctuation obviously doesn't affect a person's ability to communicate messages such as "C U later." But if you try anything longer, it always seems to turn out much like the writing of the infant Pip in *Great Expectations*:

> MI DEER JO I OPE U R KRWITE WELL I OPE I SHAL SON B HABELL 4 2 TEEDGE U JO AN THEN WE SHORL B SO GLODD AN WEN I M PRENGTD 2 U JO WOT LARX AN BLEVE ME INF XN PIP. [. . .]

Taking our previous analogies for punctuation, what happens when it isn't used? Well, if punctuation is the stitching of language,

Chapter 4: Mechanics

language comes apart, obviously, and all the buttons fall off. If punctuation provides the traffic signals, words bang into each other and everyone ends up in Minehead. If one can bear for a moment to think of punctuation marks as those invisibly beneficent fairies (I'm sorry), our poor deprived language goes parched and pillowless to bed. And if you take the courtesy analogy, a sentence no longer holds the door open for you to walk in, but drops it in your face as you approach.

The reason it's worth standing up for punctuation is not that it's an arbitrary system of notation known only to an over-sensitive elite who have attacks of the vapours when they see it misapplied. The reason to stand up for punctuation is that without it there is no reliable way of communicating meaning. Punctuation herds words together, keeps others apart. Punctuation directs you how to read, in the way musical notation directs a musician how to play. [. . .]

Words strung together without punctuation recall those murky murals Rolf Harris used to paint, where you kept tilting your head and wondering what it was. Then Rolf would dip a small brush into a pot of white and—to the deathless, teasing line, "Can you guess what it is yet?"—add a line here, a dot there, a curly bit, and suddenly all was clear. Good heavens, it looked like just a splodge of colours and all along it was a kangaroo in football boots having a sandwich! Similarly, take a bit of unpunctuated prose, add the dots and flourishes in the right place, stand back, and what have you got?

My dear Joe,

I hope you are quite well. I hope I shall soon be able to teach you, Joe—and then we shall be so glad. And when I am apprenticed to you, Joe: *what larks!* Believe me, in affection,

Pip

Chapter 4: Mechanics

In Orbit
by Dariel Suarez

It must have been in the early nineties, as the Soviet Union's collapse rippled its way to Cuba, that I decided to build a spaceship. The plan was to collect anything made of metal: nuts, bolts, rebar. Also spark plugs, doorknobs, loose cables. I hauled large sheets of tin blown off someone's shoddy roof, rusty steel pipes left behind by the neighborhood plumber, the rim and spokes of a bicycle's wheel. I even found the circuit board of a black-and-white television and the discarded innards of a radio, both of which, to my mind, possessed the dazzling intricacy of a computer. Within a few weeks, I accumulated enough to create an impressive mound of trash in my grandparents' yard. The sheer size of it was promising: no doubt I'd be able to fit inside once I put everything together.

    I can't pinpoint a specific event or reason as the genesis of my idea, other than a general aspiration to explore and the belief that, in time, I could actually pull it off. I do remember being fascinated by space, something I inherited from my grandfather. He introduced me to astronomy and science fiction at an early age. He'd spend hours talking about what to him were the latest discoveries (information usually trickled into Cuba on years-long delay), the possible connections between ancient cultures and aliens, the Soviet Union versus the United States space race. He spoke with an infectious air of wonder about human achievements. He claimed we were on a precipitous path toward time travel and finding other dimensions. Once, he saw a documentary on black holes, and that's all he discussed for weeks. He liked to cite Hawking, Einstein, Newton, though I could never tell if he was doing so accurately. Regardless, he passed on enough of a quasi-scientific vocabulary for me to develop a ravenous curiosity for the astonishing, ruthless world beyond our sky.

    When he saw the initial pile of garbage sprouting up in a corner of his yard, he chuckled and slowly shook his head. I explained my

---

From *The Threepenny Review*, Winter 2020 by Dariel Suarez. Copyright © 2020 by Dariel Suarez. Reprinted by permission.

plan with the hope that he would offer his full support. Luckily, his chuckle had been one of approval. He chose to indulge me—as he would rarely have done for others, for my grandfather was an intransigent man, quick to lose his temper. He was, to put it as he might have, a man not adverse to confrontation. He wasn't physically imposing. He was of average height for a Cuban, muscularly thin, and walked with a cautious, almost reserved manner due to his glass eye. He'd suffered an infection that nearly left him blind and that, for most of my life, I believed I had caused: the only time I saw my grandfather cry was after I accidentally poked his left eye, the functioning one, while horsing around. I must have been four or five years old. I carried this guilt with me until very recently, when my mother explained that my poke forced him to get the surgery he'd been stubbornly dodging, a surgery that, according to her, saved his vision.

Although I loved him and thought of him as a protector, there was a mythological aura about my grandfather, especially when he was trying to impose his will. Despite his unimpressive appearance, his personal history and reputation made him a foot taller and several pounds stronger in my youthful perception. He'd openly challenged a well-respected neighbor to a knife fight over a political argument (the neighbor declined and from then on refused to pass by the front of our house). He'd charged at one of my uncles with a lead pipe after this uncle had drunkenly yelled at my grandmother (my grandfather forbade him from entering the house again, and after separating from my aunt, my uncle never did). To help him build water tanks, he hired a friend of the family who'd been in prison for stabbing someone to death during an altercation, a man everyone in our neighborhood avoided and whom my grandfather—in what he likely saw as a defiant display of masculine empathy—treated as a protégé.

All of this is to say that I, a shy kid whose personality might be described as the direct opposite of my grandfather's, both worshiped and feared him. His approval of my spaceship-building endeavor meant so much because he, more than any other person, could undo it with the simplest of words or gestures.

★

Chapter 4: Mechanics

The typical layout of a Havana suburb is unlike its North American counterpart. There are no white picket fences, no large swaths of lawn or ample driveways, no lines of mailboxes neatly arranged down a noiseless street. Instead, there are compact rows of decaying buildings, old houses whose windows are at arm's length from each other, potholed streets so narrow that two-way traffic becomes a challenge. Living in Santos Suarez—a heavily populated residential area nestled between two of Havana's smallest municipalities—was a confining experience, as though I were sequestered in a tiny corner of the world. Santos Suarez was a place from which even the stars seemed inadequately close, as if, like everything else in Cuba, a specific portion of the sky had been allocated to us, with no access to another. This claustrophobic feeling of isolation made me want to leave.

A child, if sufficiently exposed to it, is capable of understanding the ramifications of abject poverty—the sense that tomorrow and the day after, the struggle will be the same, regardless of your efforts or abilities. I recall a constant tension between the intellectually liberal atmosphere at home and the propaganda-riddled, duplicitous nature of Cuba's strict school system. I recall my family's frustrating interactions with Communist neighbors, all of whom were prospective informants for the state. Back then I also had a vague knowledge that life in other countries—and particularly in the United States—offered a more fruitful future, a knowledge that became more alluring by the mid-1990s, when the Special Period crisis gripped virtually every household and emigrating felt like the best solution to all our economic and socio-ideological woes.

A child is not supposed to be grappling with these sorts of questions, not to the extent that they lead to the thought of abandoning one's country. But when you witness the abrupt absence of friends, and later hear how well they're doing in Miami, New York, Madrid, Toronto, Mexico City; when you see photos of them wearing brand new clothes, living in freshly painted houses, riding in polished cars, smiling with a joy so effusive it can only come from people who know they've escaped a lifetime of hardship and disappointment; then the hand-me-down shirts and crumbling buildings and sputtering old cars and sun-beaten faces and socialist dictums suddenly take on a demoralizing quality. I wanted to leave Cuba because I sensed, very early on, that my adult self would be unhappy otherwise.

I suppose building a spaceship would have been one way to accomplish this. Yet I never made a connection between migration and shooting off past Earth's atmosphere. What I do remember is the thrilling prospect of defying ridiculous odds. I remember picturing myself inside a metallic cocoon with beeping lights, hissing pipes, blinking screens. I remember imagining what it would be like to orbit our planet, to look back at its massive splendor, to drift toward distant stars. I was searching for a larger kind of escape.

Most Cubans know the name Yuri Gagarin. We know he was Russian, the first person to orbit Earth, even if we don't always remember that he did so in 1961, that the name of the flight was Vostok 1, that the spacecraft had a spherical design to protect it from extreme heat on atmospheric reentry, and that the entire mission lasted 108 minutes. Gagarin's trajectory around Earth clocked in at a little over an hour. That's more than sixty minutes in space relying on what is now more than half-a-century-old technology. Picture cars, planes, televisions, or phones from the same era, and it is remarkable that we accomplished such a feat with such rudimentary resources. That alone is worthy of genuine admiration. It should make us, regardless of politics or national affiliation or our personal relationship to science, proud of what humans are capable of achieving, of what a person like Gagarin was willing to do.

Unsurprisingly, he was turned into an international spectacle. Gagarin was a symbol not just of the Soviet Union's power, but of its purported superiority over the United States. He was presented to Cubans as a hero, *our* hero. He was an example of Communism's ability—through collaboration, ingenuity, and sacrifice—to attain the impossible. Most of my generation clumped his name alongside Laika (the first animal to orbit Earth) and *Sputnik* (the first man-made satellite to be launched into space), words that, in their sound and relevancy, evoked a sense of artificiality and imposition: a relationship between expansive, cold Russia and small, tropical Cuba that now feels like some historian's cruel idea of a joke. It's no wonder these words, like *tovarish* (Russian for "comrade") or *koniec* ("end"), became a subject of mockery in our vernacular, the first for its obvious Communist connotation, the latter for appearing at the end of many a Soviet film with unresolved plot lines. *Koniec* stood for inexplicable, illogical, absurd—for the almost comical, improbable tragedy of what it meant to live in a Russian-dependent Cuban society.

Sputnik, however, holds greater significance for me. My grandfather referenced it often when I was a child. He wasn't referring to the satellite, but to the magazine. The Soviet Union's version of *Reader's Digest*, poorly written and even more egregiously translated, *Sputnik* was one of the scarce access points we had to anything resembling international pop culture—science and literary news, political discussions, and thematic articles, all aesthetically mushed through a Soviet filter. Like others of his and my parents' generation, Grandpa used it a source of information, particularly when it came to science.

But the irony of living under a despotic, propaganda-driven regime is that, once the idealist portion of the process has dried up and only the disappointment and poverty and oppression remain, the disenchanted youth gravitate toward what has been forbidden. In my generation's case, it was American mythology and products. We consumed Hollywood movies and longed for a refreshing Coke while Fidel Castro spoke of socialist principles and our island's defiance of imperialist threats. I was more fascinated by Neil Armstrong and NASA than by any of the Soviet stories we were told. I don't remember seeing what Gagarin looked like, or memorizing the dates of the Soviet Union's space exploits, but I could close my eyes and picture the iconic images of the moon landing. I could recognize the NASA logo from afar and knew the *Challenger* disaster had occurred on the year of my birth; I had vivid images in my mind of the heartbreaking footage, the dense trail of smoke expanding behind the disintegrating spacecraft as fire consumed it.

Recently I stumbled upon what felt like an important question: What if I stripped away the politically marred layers of my memory, and allowed myself to explore this Soviet space history?

I learned that Yuri Gagarin was born into a peasant family in a Russian village near a town that would later be renamed after him.

Chapter 4: Mechanics   149

His father was a carpenter and bricklayer, his mother a milkmaid. During the Nazi occupation, the family was forced to live in a mud hut behind their home for nearly two years, while his two older brothers performed forced labor in Poland until the end of the war. As a young man, Gagarin volunteered as an air cadet at a local flying club and, after being drafted into the army, became a pilot. In 1950 the Soviet space program selected him as part of an elite training group. He was subjected to extensive training and tests designed to measure physical and psychological endurance. Because of his distinction in performance compared to the other pilots, and because of his diminutive stature (Gagarin was only five feet two inches tall!), he was deemed the perfect candidate to fly into space.

By April 1961 he was aboard the Vostok spacecraft. There's a recording of his voice at the exact instant he was receiving final instructions for the launch. One can hear static and then Gagarin shouting *Poyekhali!*, which translates to "Let's go!"—a phrase that essentially marked the beginning of the Space Age. It's the informal nature of what Gagarin chose to say, though, that intrigued me. Communism has a way of making even the mundane or empty sound laboriously grand. While Americans dress power and exceptionalism in colorful television commercials and romanticized views of democracy, there's a crushingly bureaucratic and militaristic attitude behind the entire Communist enterprise, including the language. At such a pivotal moment for the Soviets, I'd expect Gagarin to sound official, stiff, contrived. Coming across his impatient "Let's go!" stirred something in me. I hit play, again and again, and listened: *Poyekhali! Poyekhali! Poyekhali!*

The hairs on my arms rose. I skipped a breath. I was genuinely moved. Although all of this had taken place in Eastern Europe almost sixty years ago, I felt connected to it. It was as if my history—or, more accurately, a history that is and isn't mine, but to which I'm irrevocably attached—was echoing from somewhere remote and shaking my present self. How do we define what's ours? I wondered. Why did I have such a strong response to Gagarin's voice? Why do I feel compelled to share both his story and my personal reaction, to explore them further? What am I, a Cuban-born American citizen caught between opposing mythologies, really trying to figure out?

There's a danger that, as we get older, our world, instead of becoming larger and more connected, will remain relatively narrow and fractured. I've rarely encountered anyone in the United States, and this includes many writers and intellectuals, who knows about Neil Armstrong *and* Yuri Gagarin, who knows the details of the moon landing *and* Vostok 1, who can speak about American and Soviet events with a comparable level of interest, skepticism, or passion. We've been made to believe that another place's history is someone else's history, to the extent that extraordinary amounts of curiosity and empathy are needed to break through the barrier. Then there are the narratives imposed on us, the single-layered distortions meant to fuel our sense of pride and belonging. Whether we reject or internalize them, these narratives inevitably become entangled with our identity. I am Cuban, but the Soviet influences on my sensibilities, my cynicism and humor, my sense of the past and formative education are undeniable. They linger in my conscience in ways that American acculturation has failed to erase. How much say do we really have in what we discard or accept? How does a Cuban-born individual living in America reconcile the feeling of personal recognition—of a strange but visceral link—to the sound of a Russian astronaut he's always associated with Communist indoctrination?

Maybe we're just at the mercy of our instinctive reactions. Maybe what resonates for us as authentic, as somehow ours, is all that matters. But I can't shake the suspicion that even in moments of recognition, I must continue to prod and question if I want to arrive at anything resembling a unified sense of self. Ultimately, I find solace in the little tokens history gives us. Neil Armstrong and Buzz Aldrin, at the heart of the Cold War in 1969, left a medallion on the moon commemorating Gagarin's contribution to space exploration. Their acknowledgement and appreciation of a fellow astronaut transcended politics. I choose to see this seemingly small gesture as a comforting metaphor for the complex, colliding realities that make up my immigrant life.

★

Chapter 4: Mechanics

It wasn't a simple word or sweep of the hand that extinguished my spaceship-building hopes. My grandfather paced in front of all the parts I'd spent weeks gathering, and with a menacing tremor in his voice ordered me to throw it all out. He needed to build a water tank, he said, and there was no reason for so much trash to be in the way. He offered no other explanation, no alternatives. He didn't acknowledge all the effort I'd put in. He looked at the pile of metal with disdain and exasperation. His indulgence of my dream had reached its limit.

I pleaded with my mother to reason with him. I remember there being a brief argument. Then I was carrying everything to the dumpster on our street corner. I hid the circuit board somewhere in my home but threw it away soon after, for fear that he would find it.

Defying my grandfather was not an option. When I was in kindergarten, he supposedly saw my best friend, Roli, push me while we were in line waiting to be released from school. I don't recall the push. I can barely recount any instances of animosity between Roli and me. But something must have happened, because on the walk home (my grandfather had permission from Roli's mother to bring him with me), he made us fight. He said something about how I shouldn't allow others to disrespect me, about not going home until Roli and I fought. We mainly grabbed each other and tussled on the ground, holding back tears. A neighbor who was walking by called my grandfather an animal. He told her to mind her business and pulled us apart only when he realized there would be no winner.

Roli and I never talked about the incident. We didn't tell our parents. Our friendship continued until his family moved to a different neighborhood when we were in fourth or fifth grade. I also never spoke of it with my grandfather. He wasn't the type to dwell on the past, at least not in the context of personal growth—admitting a wrong, offering or receiving forgiveness. Vulnerability was counter to what he believed and practiced. What hurt me most was his lack of self-awareness, his inability to grasp how much damage he could do.

Though my interest in science continued even after I realized how foolish the spaceship idea had been, my relationship with my grandfather was never the same. Once I left Cuba, we barely spoke for over a decade. A few years back, he and my grandmother came

Chapter 4: Mechanics

to visit my family in Miami. Time hadn't been kind to him. Wrinkles had conquered the whole of his face. His glass eye had sunk deeper into his skull. His spine had developed a forward bend, his walk a sluggish drag. Following the initial hug and typical exchange between people whose distance has turned them into strangers, he said he had something important to ask me. We walked out to my mother's balcony and shut the sliding door behind us. We sat across from each other, let a pause accentuate the moment—he for gravitas, me because I was expecting an insidious question about my long hair, my decision to become a writer, the lack of phone calls on my end. He moved to the edge of his chair, a surprisingly nervous appearance in his posture, and with a sheepish voice said, "I want you to be honest with me: Do you believe in aliens?"

Science, and particularly anything related to astronomy, slowly faded from my life once I arrived in America. By high school graduation, I'd decided becoming an astronomer and working at NASA were out of the question. I dropped out of college within a semester, turning to heavy metal music as my escape and manual labor as my means of support. When I returned to school in my midtwenties, creative writing had become my passion. Science reappeared only in the form of brief affairs with magazine subscriptions. A few *Scientific American*s still sit unread on my bookshelf.

I've done a fair amount of online research, but I've failed to find any copies in Spanish of *Sputnik*. Perhaps in a future trip to Havana I'll come across one, since these kinds of Communist memorabilia have a way of never completely disappearing. Perhaps I just need to reconnect with the person who, before getting on a plane in 1997, would look at the stars and wonder how it was possible for some of them to have died so long ago, how we're able to see something that isn't actually there.

I don't believe my grandfather will ever be that pathway for me. If anything, my relationship with him has deteriorated further. I've learned things about him: the way he betrayed my grandmother with other women, the years of psychological abuse, the disparaging comments he made about my now-deceased father's struggle with alcoholism. Suffice it to say, I don't respect him as I did in my younger days; I now wish to be the opposite of him. My mother tells me he asks about me often, about my personal and professional achievements. She says he loves me. Still, my default emotion toward my grandfather is anger. In moments I'm not proud of, I wish my connection to science had nothing to do with him. I'm glad that leaving Cuba released me from his influence.

But migration isn't only about escape. It's also about irreparable loss. I know that who I am today is not just what I've become, but what is no longer with me. One learns to cope. The knowledge that something cannot be regained eventually moves past grief and nostalgia into a more indefinable state, a state in which hope begins working its way back—in my case to childhood, to what will always be the most authentic version of oneself. There, I find myself having built that spaceship. And unlike Gagarin, with his certainty of return, soon I'm truly in orbit, on an almost endless threshold between the known and unknown, beyond it the entire cosmos and its delightful abundance of possibilities.

Discussion Questions for Chapter 4

For Roxane Gay

1. In her essay, Gay expresses her love of Scrabble and of words. List and define your five favorite words (look up each in a dictionary) and identify their parts of speech. Why do you enjoy these words? Their sounds? Their meanings? The associations they have for you?
2. When facing her nemesis Henry during a Scrabble match, Gay challenges him when he tries to play TREKING. Why isn't this the spelling of the word? What is the rule that makes TREKKING the proper spelling?
3. At the end of her essay, Gay makes a point of explaining that a proper noun is not acceptable as a Scrabble word. What is a proper noun? What other kinds of nouns are there? Which are acceptable for a Scrabble game?

For Timothy Snyder

1. As discussed by Snyder, fear is often the mechanism by which politicians coerce individuals to trade freedom for safety. Discuss other examples of specific language used by a politician or a political party that demonstrate this same technique.
2. Snyder talks about how certain words have become dangerous through misuse. What words in our current cultural discourse, because of how they have been used or by whom they have been used, have lost their original meaning and become similarly dangerous?
3. Words can have both denotative and connotative meanings (please look for definitions of these terms in the glossary at the end of the book), and Snyder is trying to distinguish both kinds in his discussion of the word *extremism*. Look up this word for yourself in the dictionary and then decide what a connotative meaning for this word might be.

For Lynne Truss

1. Truss relates how grammar and punctuation were not widely taught in Great Britain after 1960. Looking over some of the terms used in this chapter (noun, subject, participle, comma, etc.), reflect on your own early education in these skills.
2. The lack of education has also, in Truss's opinion, led to problems today in popular forms of communication such as websites and text messages. What problems have you seen in these media? Truss seems to be exasperated at some of the punctuation errors she sees in these media. What errors do you see that exasperate you? In contrast, what funny or clever examples of effective wording and punctuation have you seen?
3. Truss, in her example "A woman without her man is nothing," shows how the meaning of the sentence is drastically changed by punctuation. Find a similar sentence and practice adding punctuation to come up with different meanings for the word group.

For Dariel Suarez

1. Suarez talks in one passage about the effect that Yuri Gagarin's interjection *Poyekhali!* has upon him when he experiences the footage sixty years after the event. Can you recall a time when such a spoken word or phrase had the same effect on you? What was the language, and what were the circumstances when and where you heard it?
2. Suarez, like Snyder, makes note of how fear is used by a government to manipulate people. What vocabulary does he use in order to express this fear? What analogies does he create to express the restrictions to his freedom he and his fellow Cubans experienced while he was a child?
3. As a child, Suarez embraces his imagination. What image in the essay symbolizes his imagination most strongly? As an adult, his views about his childhood dreams change. What exactly has changed for him, what symbolizes this change, and why did it change?

156   Chapter 4: Mechanics

4. Suarez and Lopez (in chapter two) both write about one's relationship to one's landscape and how that relationship evolves. Write out descriptive passages from both pieces that illustrate this relationship.

Chapter 4: Mechanics   157

Exercises — Set One

Add the correct punctuation to the following sentences.

Example:
Original: John is going to the store but Cindy is going to the mall
Revision: John is going to the store, but Cindy is going to the mall.

1. On Tuesday John is going to break the world record for eating donuts.
2. Wow Did that really just happen
3. When I come back he said lets go out to a movie.
4. You my friend just made a big big mistake.
5. Davy Smith we shouldnt consider anyone else should be our next leader.
6. After school lets out Charlie who is a game junkie is going to sit all night at his Xbox.
7. Computers TVs and cameras are all on sale today at Leftys Electronics
8. Candy is drinking a latté Sylvia is drinking a chai tea
9. She said Ill see you tomorrow
10. Here are the things youll need for the trip a polar jacket which will keep you warm mittens which will save your fingers from frostbite and earmuffs which will keep your ears from freezing off.

Exercises—Set Two

Using the three-step line-editing process, fix the punctuation and sentence-construction errors in the following sentences.

Example:
> Original: Laughing and giggling the elevator took us to the seventh floor.
> Revision: Laughing and giggling, we took the elevator to the seventh floor.

1. Various creatures could be seen out of the corner of the eye scurrying away.
2. Tomatoes, corn, cucumbers, and the sweet scent of watermelon permeate the air.
3. Large teardrops dampened the edge of the glasses as they ran down her face and fell to her lap in a small puddle.
4. The volume of each radio raised to highest level, canceled each other, creating an incoherent babbling of words and sounds.

Chapter 4: Mechanics

Answers to Set One

1. On Tuesday, John is going to break the world record for eating donuts.
2. Wow! Did that really just happen?
3. "When I come back," he said, "let's go out to a movie."
4. You, my friend, just made a big, big mistake.
5. Davy Smith—we shouldn't consider anyone else—should be our next leader.
6. After school lets out, Charlie, who is a game junkie, is going to sit all night at his Xbox.
7. Computers, TVs, and cameras are all on sale today at Lefty's Electronics.
8. Candy is drinking a latté; Sylvia is drinking a chai tea.
9. She said, "I'll see you tomorrow."
10. Here are the things you'll need for the trip: a polar jacket, which will keep you warm; mittens, which will save your fingers from frostbite; and earmuffs, which will keep your ears from freezing off.

Answers to Set Two

1. Out of the corner of his eye, he saw various creatures scurrying away.
2. The sweet scent of tomatoes, corn, cucumbers, and watermelon permeates the air.
3. Large teardrops ran down her face, dampened the edge of her glasses, and fell into a small puddle in her lap.
4. The volume of each radio, raised to the highest level, created a babble of words and sounds.

Chapter 5
Strategies for Advanced Essays and for Research

Introduction

In this chapter and the next, you'll find advanced essays you may encounter in your composition class. In short, the essays are the **informative essay**, the **argumentative essay**, the **problem-solution analysis**, the **cost-benefit analysis**, **reporting**, and the **literary analysis**. This last essay, because it is specialized, and because it requires more explanation about its process and purpose, will appear by itself in chapter six. Be aware that the tasks these essays ask you to complete are not designed simply to get you through English courses or other college classes. Whatever you learn about these tasks can apply to other fields.

All college courses are unique, so the exact nature of the essay will vary depending on the class and the assignment. Whatever essay you write, however, you should begin by prewriting: choosing a method of invention (brainstorming, clustering, thesis triangles, etc.) named in chapter one. The next step should be to create an outline to visualize how the pieces of the essay will fit together. A scratch outline with bullet points will help get the process started, but later, you should move to a formal outline, which uses a system of Roman numerals, capital letters, and Arabic numbers to organize and rank the material. Each subdivision has one thought, and giving equal thoughts equal rank keeps the paper mechanically and linguistically parallel. Additionally, if you cite the sources of your research in the outline, you lessen the chance of plagiarism. If you are not familiar with the process of outlining, outline templates—word and sentence—can be found online at *Purdue University OWL*. You will find that once the outline is completed, the paper is ready to be written.

All these essays have two other necessary elements. First, remember that when you use research, it must be documented. Second, a good research paper uses the discovered material to support the writer's thesis. The paper is not driven by research but by analysis. The writer's voice, not the voice of the research, must guide the paper. A section of this chapter, "Research Strategies," was contributed by Deborah Moore, a research librarian at Highline College, to help you discover source and support materials.

The last section of this chapter, before the sample essays, will cover some final drafting tips. Remember that if you have difficulties at any stage of the writing process, you should ask questions of your instructor. Let's start.

Informative Essay

The purpose of the informative essay is to present one's findings about a topic to an audience. Depending on the topic and on your audience, your readers may know about your issue but not about the research you have uncovered, or they may know nothing about your issue. In either case, you have a secondary purpose: to teach as well as to inform.

Typically, a professor assigns this essay either to ask students to sum up research, lab work, or assignments completed during the term, or to prompt students to explore more deeply an idea presented in the materials. If the topic has two or more lines of thought, two or more varieties, two or more sides, each should be presented accurately and completely. Unless asked for in the assignment directions, the writer should maintain a neutral persona, not choosing a side, not adopting a tone toward the topic or the audience, not stepping in to offer any judgments or criticism.

When writing the informative essay, it's best to use a simple organizational plan so your readers can follow the stages of your research and the progression of your ideas. Here is a template you can use to organize the essay:

- *Introduction:* Present the issue you will be exploring in the body paragraphs, and engage your audience.

Chapter 5: Strategies for Advanced Essays and for Research   163

- *Background:* Present what you know about how the issue originated and how it may have developed over time. When did it begin, and in what circumstances? Who started or invented it? What was the original intent behind its creation? What effect did it have when it appeared? If your issue has two or more sides or lines of thought, you will need to look at the origins of all. Each of these questions may need separate paragraphs of development.
- *Current State:* Present what you know about the issue in its current state. What does it do now? Who is associated with it? Does it still follow its original intent? What effect does it have? If there are two or more sides or lines of thought, consider comparing and contrasting them. Again, each of these questions may need separate paragraphs of development.
- *Conclusion:* What is the outlook for the issue?

As you can see, you have several questions to consider, all of which will require research, before you decide on a final plan. Aside from the template above, the three main plans set out in chapter three—chronological, relative importance, and subordination-coordination—will work for most informative essays. If you are presenting two or more sides, varieties, or lines of thought, then you will have to decide which ideas to present in which order. The continuous or alternating patterns listed for comparison and contrast in chapter three might also be part of your plan.

Argumentative Essay

The purpose of the argumentative essay (also called a **position paper**) is for the writer to take a stance on an issue and to convince her audience of the validity of her stance. As part of the assignment, the writer will present the information she knows about the issue as well as the reasons for and against her position. The audience for this essay should generally be opposed to—or at best neutral toward—the writer's stance. Writing to an audience who agrees with you won't convince them because they are already on your side. You will therefore have to take the audience's attitude into consideration as you present your argument.

Two common forms of argument, induction and deduction, are described in chapter two. There are other forms that have been used over the centuries by influential writers and speakers: *logos* (factual appeal), *pathos* (emotional appeal), *ethos* (moral appeal), *mythos* (appeal to common culture), and *kairos* (the "do it now" appeal). As long as you make these appeals honestly, you stand a reasonable chance of convincing your audience and raising your credibility.

But if you misuse these appeals, you risk creating **logical fallacies** that a careful audience will detect and use to dismiss your arguments. Here is a list of widely seen fallacies:

1. *False Analogy:* consists of making a claim that two different things are similar (e.g., The old governor declared a state of emergency to close businesses when COVID hit, so why can't the new one do the same thing to tamp down violence in our schools?).
2. *Argument in a Circle:* consists of offering a conclusion that simply restates the premise (e.g., Joan is popular with all the students because everyone likes her).
3. *Presumed Cause and Effect*, or *Post Hoc ergo Propter Hoc:* consists of claiming that because one event happened first, it caused the next event (e.g., Young people joined the Bernie Sanders campaign because they were brought up in permissive households).
4. *Non Sequitur* ("It does not follow"): consists of a conclusion that has no relation to its premises (e.g., If gay marriage becomes law, then more children will lose health benefits).
5. *Begging the Question:* consists of asserting a premise as true when in actuality it has yet to be proven. For example, the stance that the president's socialist healthcare plan will cost the nation billions of dollars builds on the unproven claim that the plan is indeed socialistic.
6. *Argumentum ad Hominem:* consists of slamming one's opponent rather than speaking to the issue. For example, a legislator

Chapter 5: Strategies for Advanced Essays and for Research 165

attacks a colleague's mental competence instead of debating a bill for reducing government spending.
7. *Argument by Extension* or *Red Herring:* consists of extending an argument by adding distractions until the argument is about another issue entirely (e.g., Commissioner Sue Jones can't be convicted of embezzlement because the district attorney who is prosecuting her is a wife-beater and hates all women; the DA is therefore unqualified to handle this case).
8. *Either-Or,* or *False Dilemma:* consists of falsely reducing the issue to two alternatives, which in turn may or may not be valid (e.g., The immigration issue is a choice between granting citizenship to everyone who sets foot in our country or deporting them at once).
9. *Hasty Generalization:* consists of making a general assumption without considering enough facts (e.g., All Vroom-Vroom cars are worthless junk because one Vroom-Vroom car blew a tire).
10. *Argumentum ad Populum,* or *Argument by Consensus:* rests on the assumption that a policy should be enacted or a statement is true because a majority of people want it or believe it (e.g., We should watch *The Best TV Show Ever!* because it's the most popular show on television).
11. *Straw Man:* attributes a position or trait to a person that he or she does not actually hold. For example, a newspaper accuses John Smith of sympathizing with terrorists when he has never taken such a position.
12. *Slippery Slope* or *"The Next Thing You Know . . ." Fallacy:* asserts that an action, usually harmless in itself, will invariably lead to other actions that will end in a dangerous consequence (e.g., If we allow sports betting in Calbrasia, then people will spend more of their income on betting, which will lead to bankruptcies, and the next thing you know, the entire state of Calbrasia will fall into ruin).
13. *Tu Quoque* or *Whataboutism:* consists of deflecting an accusation by pointing out a similar or worse offense committed by one's accuser (e.g., You accuse me of cheating on my taxes,

but what about how you skimmed money from the Hoying account?).

Your arguments will also appeal to your audience if you organize them clearly. A common paradigm for the argumentative essay looks like this:

- *Introduction:* The introduction contains the essay's thesis: an issue, and the writer's stance on the issue. The writer may also choose a strategy by which to engage the reader: present a personal experience, establish a mood, pose a problem, describe a relevant person or place.
- *Background Information/History of the Issue:* This section of the essay explores the evolution of the issue to its present condition. A portion of your research must complete this timeline. The questions posed above for the same section of the informative essay will help you begin this process. Some of the modes described elsewhere—description, process, definition, etc.—may help you complete this stage. This section may take more than one paragraph to complete.
- *Opposing Viewpoint:* In at least one paragraph, present the strongest argument for the other side (or sides) and a case for why it (or they) may be valid. This step is necessary to show that you have considered the other side (or sides) of the issue. In a separate paragraph, you may also present a rebuttal to this viewpoint (or these viewpoints) to show why it is (or they are) not as strong as your stance. Again, remember the modes. You will also need research to flesh out this counterargument and your rebuttal.
- *Body of Proofs:* Present your support for your stance. As a rule of thumb, your stance should have at least three good arguments, organized so that the best and strongest comes last. Each should appear in at least one separate paragraph, and each should be well documented by the research you gather. As part of this discussion, you should acknowledge any criticisms of your stance or of your arguments and show why they

Chapter 5: Strategies for Advanced Essays and for Research 167

do not invalidate your thesis. The modes can help you build your arguments, too.
- *Conclusion:* This section brings closure to the essay. Depending on the requirements of the assignment, the conclusion may restate the thesis in fresh language, present a call to action, or speculate on the issue's outlook.

The following frame may help you to create your thesis: Although (some say) ___, in actuality, ___. In the first blank, put the opposing viewpoint you will examine in the essay. In the second blank, put your own stance. This thesis provides a quick preview of the arguments and satisfies the reader that you will be considering more than one side of your chosen issue. Presenting yourself as informed and balanced will go a long way toward raising your credibility in front of a hostile, or neutral, audience.

Further, by following the paradigm, you will know what kind of research you will need to complete each of the sections, and you will have a ready-made plan for presenting that research.

Problem-Solution Analysis

A writing task often performed beyond the academic setting, the problem-solution analysis identifies a problem and proposes a solution to it. The analysis may look at a problem currently faced by a person, an organization, a business, or a government, or it may anticipate a problem looming in the future. The audience for the essay therefore should have a stake in the analysis being presented. Since the problem may be one they are facing or may potentially face, they may be looking for the best solution to put into place. They may even have asked for the analysis to be performed.

Research done for this analysis will underscore two purposes. In terms of exploring the problem, the research should be as complete, as accurate, and as neutral as possible. The writer's tone should be neutral as well, not magnifying or ignoring any harm caused by the problem, and the purpose should be informative. In terms of the solution, the research should also be complete and accurate, but the purpose will be different. Because you are offering your audience a course of action, or a choice of actions, your purpose will be persuasive as well as informative.

The organization plan for a basic problem-solution is a four-step paradigm. The introduction should present the problem you have been assigned (or that you wish to explore). The following paragraphs should present your research about the problem: How, where, and why did it start? How has it changed since its emergence? What is its current status? Who does it affect the most? What harm does it cause? The next paragraphs should propose your solution: What is it? How does it solve the problem? Are there other solutions? What are they, and why are they not as effective as the one you are proposing? You should then conclude your analysis by stating what it will take to implement your solution.

For a more involved analysis, you should consider using Monroe's Motivated Sequence. Developed by Alan H. Monroe at Purdue University in the 1930s, this sequence is a plan by which a writer may alert the audience to a need, identify a solution to that need, and then convince the audience to adopt the solution. The sequence is both a process and an organizational blueprint and is a common strategy used in advertising.

The first step of the sequence is *Attention*: In your introduction, you should grab the attention of your audience. The strategies of *pathos*—humor, a vivid story, an unusual or shocking fact—work best here. (In a commercial, an appealing or eye-catching image is often presented.)

The second step is *Need*: You must alert your audience to a problem that needs their attention. The strategies of *logos*—statistics, data from credible sources—will work best to establish that this problem actually exists and that it truly affects the audience. (In a commercial, the actor is often stuck in some desperate, humorous, or humiliating situation.)

The third step is *Satisfaction*: You must set out the solution to the problem. Again, the strategies of *logos*—credible testimony, solutions researched from authoritative sources, rebuttal of counterarguments—will work best here. (In a commercial, this step introduces the product being sold.)

The fourth step is *Visualization*: You must make the audience see either how the future will be worse if they do not take action (or don't buy the product) or how the future will be better if they adopt your solution (or buy the product). The strategies of *pathos*—emotional appeals to the audience's fears or optimism—may work best here.

The final step is *Actuation*: You must present a reasonable course of action that your audience can immediately take to enact your solution. (In a commercial, this step tells the audience how and where to buy the product.)

This sequence is persuasive in purpose and works best if the writer clearly presents the problem, offers a simple solution, and proposes an easy method for adopting the solution. To learn more about Monroe's Motivated Sequence, you can consult the following resources:

www.changingminds.org/techniques/general/overall/monroe_sequence.htm

www.mindtools.com/pages/article/MonroeMotivatedSequence.htm

Cost-Benefit Analysis

A cost-benefit analysis is designed to consider the pros and the cons of enacting a policy. For example, if you want to buy five new desktop computers for your company, you must weigh the costs of the computers, the software, the internet hookups, the retraining time of employees, etc., against the benefits of higher productivity, fewer software problems, faster internet connection speeds, etc., to decide if purchasing the computers will be worth the investment. If the costs are higher, then you will not likely purchase the computers. If the benefits are higher, then you may consider buying the computers. As you can see, this form of writing is important to making personal and financial decisions.

Generally, the cost-benefit analysis has two purposes: to inform and to persuade. Your audience may know of the policy you are considering, but they may not know of the costs and the benefits you have discovered; that's where you will inform them. At the end of your analysis, you will decide whether the costs outweigh the benefits, or whether the benefits are worth the costs; that's where you will be at your most persuasive. Choose one side and support your reasons for that choice. Again, as with the essays above, be complete and accurate in gathering and presenting your research. And again, as with the problem-solution paper, your audience should have a clear stake in the analysis you are making.

The best way to begin writing this analysis is to brainstorm a list of costs and benefits. How much time and energy will it take to pursue this policy? What are the financial, material, and emotional benefits to be gained by enacting this policy? What are the financial, material, and emotional costs? Who benefits, either directly or indirectly, from this policy? Who gets hurt? What would be gained or lost by not taking any action at all? Don't just use the first two costs and the first two benefits that come to mind. They may not be the best that you can think of. Create a list of as many as you can. Be even-handed in your approach. Don't leave out choices because you have already made up your mind one way or another and you don't want to consider the best points from the other side.

Your next step is to weigh the costs and benefits in the list you have created. You might even assign a point or dollar value to each cost and benefit—for example, ten points to the most serious, zero to the least. Once you've weighed all the points, pick the two of each that score the highest (these scores will not be used in the essay; they are simply meant to help you choose).

For your next step, compare the costs and the benefits. Look at the scores you gave to each. Are the numbers higher for the costs or for the benefits? Whichever side scores higher should determine whether to enact the policy or not.

Once you have a list of costs and benefits, you're ready to present them. One paradigm for organizing the cost-benefit analysis is as follows:

- Begin with an introduction that engages your audience and sets out the policy and your reasons for considering it.

- Set out, in separate paragraphs, the two strongest benefits of enacting the policy. Following the principle of relative importance, you should present the best benefit second.
- Set out, in separate paragraphs, the two biggest costs. As with the benefits, you should present the largest cost second.
- Finish the analysis with your conclusion: Which outweigh the other, the costs or the benefits?

For an example of an essay that follows this paradigm, please read Kassity Higgins's *"Othello: Three Deaths and a Promotion"* in chapter six.

You can, if the assignment calls for it, generate more than two benefits and two costs. Again, though, as noted above, the best of the benefits and the most extreme of the costs should be presented last in each stage.

The research you perform will help you identify the costs and the benefits and substantiate them with statistics, data from credible sources, and testimony from experts. By doing careful research and creating reasoned arguments for both sides, you as the writer will gain credibility, and your final decision will appear well informed.

Reporting

The most general function of reporting is to gather facts and observations and shape them into a coherent whole. You will see as you begin your own reporting that many of the modes—description, narration, process, etc.—will come into play. Reporters cannot give us a picture of a war without describing a battle zone, or recounting a country's history, or narrating the life story of one of the fighters involved, or showing us step by step how an embattled city was captured. Movie reviewers like Justin Chang, who writes for the *Los Angeles Times*, and Rebecca Rubin, who writes for *Variety*, cannot judge a film without describing one of its key scenes, giving us a glance at an actor's background, or telling us how the writing, the directing, the costuming, and so on were carried out.

At all times, however, the writer must remember the audience. The main purpose of reporting is to present the facts and observations in such a way that readers can become more informed and capable of making their own judgments about current events, world leaders, sports, business, entertainment, and other interests.

Reporting consists of several different tasks. Although by no means complete, the list provided for you below should help you to understand the tasks both as a reader and as a writer.

Eyewitnessing: The reporter goes into the field for a firsthand look at the battle, the disaster, the movie premier, the World Series game. The reporter relies upon her own impressions to record the events, the facts, and the significant details. To aid the reporter, a photographer or camera operator may provide pictures or video coverage. Together, the text and the images give the reader a sense of what it was like to be there with the reporter.

Interviewing: A reporter may also interview someone who is closely associated with what is transpiring. After a battle, for example, the reporter might talk to a soldier who was in combat, a resident whose house was captured, or a government leader who is running the campaign. These interviews give readers more insight into the events and put a human face upon them.

Research: To give a broader view of an issue, a reporter will follow an investigative process. An investigative reporter will interview experts, but just as importantly, research books, journals, magazine and newspaper articles, biographies, government or company records, transcripts of prior interviews, and other sources to discover and to substantiate the facts that relate to the issue.

Interpretation: When interviews and research turn up facts, the reporter may discern a connection between them. For example, if a reporter is writing about a new highway project in her hometown, but if she finds records from three different companies that show financial links between the county transportation board and the contractor that was awarded the job, then she will likely interpret those findings as a possible conflict of interest. Be aware, however, that an ethical reporter will make an interpretation that fits the facts. The reporter should not arrange, alter, or spin the facts to support a preconceived or faulty opinion.

Chapter 5: Strategies for Advanced Essays and for Research

Critical Commentary: Much of what we read in a reputable media outlet comes from a professional commentator or critic. Newspaper editorials, sports analyses, advice columns, and movie and product reviews are some of the common topics of the critic. These specialists are considered knowledgeable in a field because they have researched and reported on it for many years or because they have extensive training or work experience in the field itself. Professional commentators therefore often have insights, facts, or opinions worth listening to—even if you disagree with them—because of their expertise.

Editorial Bias: You will often notice that a media outlet has a slant toward a particular political, religious, or socioeconomic viewpoint. What is said, by whom it is said, and how it is said will give you a feel for the outlet's viewpoint. A competent reporter will balance positive and negative influences so that an article will appear unbiased and fair. Although opinion has its place in reporting, deliberately misleading the reader on the basis of that opinion pushes the writing into the realm of propaganda.

Because the process of reporting can lead to a news article, an editorial, a review, a commentary, an advice column, a feature, or one of many other forms, setting forth a single paradigm is not possible. At best, we can offer you some general advice about where certain information is likely to fall:

- *Introduction:* Relate key event—who, what, when, where, how, or why.
- *Body:* Give relevant facts, events, interviews, statistics, opinions, judgments. The three basic organizational patterns found in chapter three—chronology, relative importance, and subordination-coordination—may help you arrange the body paragraphs.
- *Conclusion:* Close the report by offering a lasting image, judgment, fact, or quote.

Again, reporting is based upon facts and observations. At all times, you should appear unbiased when reporting facts or thoughtful when presenting opinions. You should also remember that your chief purpose is to inform your audience, presenting them with enough details so that they can form their own opinions.

Research Strategies

Research begins the way an essay begins—by understanding the assignment, or by asking questions to eliminate confusion. Basic questions to ask yourself or the instructor are as follows:

- What is the question I want to explore?
- What information has already been discussed or researched on my topic?
- What is the best search strategy, and what challenges can be foreseen at this point?

Although these questions may seem overwhelming, finding the answers to them allows you to understand the topic fully and, in turn, plan a search strategy that will discover a trove of sources to help write the essay.

Just as writing requires prewriting, research requires pre-research. Pre-research is done in the early stages of the writing and research process to help you learn the background of your topic, discover how much information is out there, and determine what types of information there are. If you're researching a topic like the electoral college for an informative essay, there will be plenty of research materials. But if you're researching a more recent or narrow topic, like irregularities in the latest election in your state, there will be less information.

Because pre-research helps you learn more about the topic before you begin the process of writing the essay itself, it will ideally come between identifying a topic and prewriting. It will be easier to use one of the methods of invention to brainstorm or cluster information about the topic once you have gained some knowledge about your topic through pre-research. Likewise, creating an outline that includes the sources for your research will also be easier if you've

Chapter 5: Strategies for Advanced Essays and for Research 175

already done some pre-research. Writing an outline after pre-research and before more extended research will help ensure that you don't string together a bunch of sources to build your essay.

Both research and writing are processes, so doing an hour or so of pre-research will not be enough. It gets you started, but you will continue to research throughout the writing process because it's quite common to need additional research later. For example, your pre-research may provide information to support your position in an argumentative essay, but you also need to acknowledge and refute the opposition. You may also discover that you're missing some evidence to support one of your arguments. When this occurs, you will need to pause the writing process and do more research.

As discussed earlier in this chapter, the informative essay, the argumentative essay, the problem-solution analysis, the cost-benefit analysis, and reporting will each require different types of research. If we look at the essay at the end of this chapter, "A Flawed Law" by Michele Olson, this idea becomes more evident. "A Flawed Law" is an argumentative essay that presents three supporting arguments for why Las Vegas City Ordinance 6710 is a flawed law. Because it's an argumentative essay, Olson also acknowledges the opposition's point of view, and then refutes it (see the fifth paragraph). If Olson had written an informative essay instead of an argumentative one, she would simply have included research about what Las Vegas City Ordinance 6710 is, when and why it was created, who it affects, etc. However, because she wrote an argumentative essay, she also included research that supported her argument as well as at least one point from the opposition.

To begin the research process, the student should find a combination of primary and secondary sources. Primary sources such as autobiographies, letters, diaries, and personal interviews provide information that comes directly from the source. Secondary sources such as biographies, articles, books, and printed or broadcast interviews have an intermediary between the source and the information.

In considering these possible sources, it is a good idea to keep the information cycle in mind. Doing this will help you know what types of sources you might want to use. The information cycle tells us that after an event occurs, information appears within minutes on social media. News sites, TV, and newspapers will report information about the event on the same or the following days. Next come reports in weekly and monthly magazines. Usually, you won't find information in scholarly journals until at least three months after the event, and in books until at least a year. This is because it takes time for authors to write the content, submit it for publication, and go through the editing and peer-review process, which is followed by the time it takes to get the scholarly article or book into publication.

Students typically begin their research by going to the internet. When you use websites, evaluate them to be sure they're credible. One recommended technique for evaluating websites is to go to the online site *Ad Fontes*, which measures bias and reliability in several major news outlets. Type the name of an outlet into the search box, and a graph will appear to show where that source stands politically (left, middle, or right) and whether that source objectively reports facts or presents misleading information. Another website is the *Center for Media Literacy (CML)*, whose purpose, according to their vision statement, is to teach how to "communicate competently in all media forms." The site presents tools so that visitors can evaluate not just online media but also print, TV, radio, and other news sources.

Another technique for evaluating websites is to do lateral reading. This involves opening multiple tabs or windows so you can research the claims and credentials of a website and its author by checking what other websites say before deciding to incorporate it into your essay. For example, if you're researching election irregularities in your state and you find a website written by someone who claims to know about many fraudulent ballots submitted during the most recent election, you should take time to research both the credentials of the author and their claims. This is where lateral reading comes in handy.

First, open a new browser tab or window and search for information on the author. You're looking for credentials that show they have reliable access to the information they're claiming to have. Are they an elected official or do they work in a government or other type of position that would have firsthand knowledge about election fraud?

Chapter 5: Strategies for Advanced Essays and for Research

Next, open another browser window or tab and research the claims made on the website. Can you find any other websites stating the same or similar information? If not, you should be concerned about the accuracy of the original website. If you do find other websites that have similar information, then you need to research the authors of these new websites to see what their credentials are.

When using websites for research, it can be helpful to look at the website extensions (.com, .gov, .edu, .org, etc.) to know which domain the information is coming from (commercial, government, educational, organizational, etc.). There is stricter control for who can publish information on a government or education website, so these can sometimes be more trustworthy. However, there are also informational and trustworthy commercial and organizational websites, so ultimately you must make the decision about the trustworthiness of the website you want to use. Remember, if you find some amazing claim on a website and you haven't seen it anywhere else, there's reason to be cautious in accepting it as truth. Doing lateral research takes time, but every researcher is expected to take these steps to ensure that they're using valid resources.

The web is an easy place to start, but you should also look beyond the world of the internet. One of the best means of help with your research is your campus library staff. Librarians are research experts, and their job is to support students in finding the information they need. Plus, they really like anything related to research and information. Even if you are an experienced researcher from previous classes, you may run into a topic that is more challenging. If you've spent ten to fifteen minutes looking for information on a topic and aren't finding anything, ask a librarian. They may have just the thing to get you unstuck.

Librarians will likely point you to an underused resource that's available to all students on your campus—the library's online databases. Some of the most commonly used databases, *EBSCO Complete*, *ProQuest*, *Gale Virtual Reference Library*, and *Opposing Viewpoints in Context*, can find thousands of journal, magazine, and newspaper articles in thousands of vetted, substantive sources. Databases also give you access to research, often organized by format (books and e-books, streaming videos, scholarly and popular articles, etc.) and/or by topic (databases with general information, with psychology articles, with science articles, with art images, etc.). You can save or print copies of these resources for use during your research project. Databases such as *EBSCO*, *ProQuest*, and *Gale* also allow you to listen to an article or translate it into another language. In addition, many databases provide you with the citation for the resource, usually in multiple citation styles (APA, MLA, AMA, etc.).

As you may have already noticed, you cannot find all of the information that's in library databases for free on the web. Copyright laws keep much information, like that in databases, behind paywalls. However, if you're a student at a college or university, you automatically have access to the library databases that your campus subscribes to, so make use of this resource. You can also get access to library databases through your local public library.

Ideally, as you work through your essay, you will use a combination of research from library databases and the web. Research that relies solely on websites will not be as robust and accurate because you'll be missing an entire section of the scholarly conversation taking place on that topic. Not surprisingly, scholarly conversation in a discipline is usually published in scholarly articles. Scholarly articles are written by subject experts for other experts, researchers, and students. Some scholarly articles follow a specific format: Introduction, Methods, Results, Discussion, Conclusion, References. Because scholarly articles are written by subject experts, they can be difficult to understand to those outside the discipline. A useful tip for reading these types of articles is to skim the Introduction, and then the Discussion and/or Conclusion, where the authors will tell you what they learned when conducting their research. This efficient skimming is part of being a smart researcher. Many times, you will eventually read the entire article, but starting with this method can help you determine if the article is useful enough to read all the way through.

As you do your research, keep track of the sources you're finding. This is a critical step to ensure that you don't fall victim to unintentional plagiarism, which happens when you get information from a source but forget to document it, and then use it in your paper as if it were your original thought. As mentioned above, you can get citations from library databases, and you can store them in your outline alongside the thoughts that they support. Another method of storing citations along the way is to use a free, online tool like *MyBib*. Once you're ready to create your bibliography, works cited, or references page, you can download all of your citations from the tool. After downloading, double-check your citations to make sure that you have entered the relevant information about your sources and that you are following the assigned documentation guidelines.

When using MLA guidelines, you will need to cite your sources twice: once at the end of the paper on the works cited page, and again in the body of the paper immediately after you use the source. When presenting the source in the paper, be sure to use signal phrases—or narrow-down language—to let the reader know that the information about to be presented is from an outside source. Finish your quotation with a parenthetical citation. This citation allows the reader to go to the works cited page, find the source, and, if the reader desires, read the source in its entirety. Some readers, especially instructors who question the writer's use of her research, will seek the original to determine if the writer has used the source material correctly.

Research is a part of scholarship, and competent research skills should promote honesty. When students enter college, they become part of a community that must follow certain academic standards. Throughout the research process, all writers must become critical thinkers. Writers must have the ability to look at the information they are gathering with a rational eye. Facts must be examined and crosschecked against other sources. Sources must be unbiased and substantive. A variety of sources ensures that the paper is credible. Keep in mind that the writer's opinion is only as valid as the research she is using to support it.

Final Notes on Drafting

The introduction of the paper should engage the reader. As noted earlier in the book, using a lead (or lede) is a good way to begin. Common leads are direct statement, surprising or unusual detail, mood, anecdote, problem, and description. However, you may find that the strategy you start with may not be suitable for the content of the essay. You won't know the essay that you want to introduce until *after* you have written it. Revise the introduction (and the conclusion, for that matter) after the body paragraphs are completed.

The body itself presents the writer's thoughts and arguments in a clear manner. Again, the basic organization plans of chronology, relative importance, and subordination-coordination will help you decide on the order of paragraphs, and the paradigms set out above will provide a shape for your entire essay. Always make sure that you understand the research you have chosen to support your claims.

An additional priority is to review arguments for logical fallacies. Fallacies can be found in defective evidence, defective proofs, or defective designs. It is vital to convince, stimulate, or actuate the reader with arguments that use facts, observations, and policies (where applicable) and the principles of *logos, pathos, ethos, mythos,* and *kairos* without the intent to manipulate or mislead.

The conclusion should signal the end of your communication with your audience. It may bring a narrative to a close, summarize the main points of the essay, restate the thesis, call the audience to action, suggest avenues for further thinking, make a prediction about the future, offer a lesson the audience should learn, or state a personal judgment on the issue. Your conclusion should not introduce an idea not discussed elsewhere in the essay.

We've included two student essays to show you what some finished products look like. In the first, "Jane Err," Kassity Higgins adopts the persona of a television critic and follows the principles of research and interpretation set out in the reporting section above. In the second, "A Flawed Law," Michele Olson presents an argumentative essay about a Las Vegas city ordinance that affects the homeless.

Chapter 5: Strategies for Advanced Essays and for Research

Kassity Higgins
Professor Moffett
English 100
10 December 2021

Jane Err

    This is Connie "McWeatherpants" Fian, speaking to you live from the Cemetery of Forgotten Books for this edition of *Stormy Scandals*. We'll be ruminating over chapters 11 "Investigate" and 17 "Listen for Dangerous Words" of Timothy Snyder's *On Tyranny*, which read with all the cynical simplicity of a *For Dummies* manual tailored to the blissfully inert citizens of a democracy in peril. We are reminded of the enduring power of truth in journalism, the moral accountability of the messenger, and the consequences as they are shaped by the dogged apathy of bystanders in national politics. Snyder challenges us, as both citizens of a democratic society and consumers of mass media, to hold ourselves accountable not only for the ideas we choose to subscribe to but also for the ancillary falsehoods we perpetuate in support of those ideas. *On Tyranny* exposes us to the cognitive dissonance of the common man and our habitual suspension of disbelief to escape the uncomfortable truths that threaten a storm of change. We are mankind: old enough to see, young enough to err.

© Kassity Higgins

In chapter 11, "Investigate," Snyder harkens back to the wisdom of Leszek Kolakowski, suggesting the Polish philosopher and historian's words recorded in the book's opening epigraph are far more than the inspired ornamentation of an accomplished author; they are the cardinal message of the entire work. The epigraph reads, "In politics, being deceived is no excuse." This simple seven-word statement illustrates contemporary man's ability to wield as well as weaponize, without forethought, powerful media like the internet, a privilege Kolakowski was not yet afforded during the German occupation of Poland. Snyder, through the words of Kolakowski, stresses the importance of our making, as individuals, the active decision to certify the information to which we expose ourselves on a near-daily basis, adding that "we tend to be drawn in by the logic of spectacle" (88). He is also at pains to remind us, "Since in the age of the internet we are all publishers, each of us bears some private responsibility for the public's sense of truth" (90). Words, being the harbinger to action, will always precede the moral and political movements of man. We must not only choose our words carefully but repress the innate desire to scuffle over *shiny* rhetoric like a murder of crows.

Snyder's *On Tyranny*, not unlike other works analyzing the dangers of human naivete and cultlike mentalities, discusses foremost the unbridled importance of an individual's impact on

Chapter 5: Strategies for Advanced Essays and for Research   **183**

greater society and the absolute necessity of reason in the application of belief. In the Age of Information, where the truth is discovered five pages back or three refined Google searches later, there is no sufficient excuse to be an agent of misinformation. Steven Hassan in *The Cult of Trump* digs even deeper into what he calls the "dark forest" of human behavior that makes us susceptible to a metaphorical ant mill, or death spiral, in which innumerable people hold fast to the convictions that threaten to harm the societal structures they celebrate. Hassan, a behavioral psychologist and outspoken former cult member of Sun Myung Moon's Unification Church, says, "When a leader gains psychological sway over his followers and also over other politicians--members of Congress, the cabinet, and even the judiciary--the checks and balances of healthy democracy can be stripped away" (9). In "Listen for Dangerous Words," Snyder cites Nazi legal theorist Carl Schmitt's revelation about the subconscious appeal of fascist governments to the uncritical individual, stating, "A Nazi leader outmaneuvers his opponents by manufacturing a general conviction that the present moment is exceptional, and then transforming that state of exception into a permanent emergency" (122). Hassan's illustration of an acquiescent democracy infatuated by the *exceptional* leader spearheading an *exceptional* cause--yes, like a murder of crows squabbling over a scrap of metal--is nearly indistinguishable from Schmitt's Nazi playbook. Humans are, after all, the poster child for exceptionalist thought.

    Of course, Snyder's talk of individuality is not to be restricted to the average man or woman. Authoritarians such as Adolf Hitler and Vladimir Putin, and critics of authoritarianism such as Hannah Arendt, Victor Klemperer, and Leszek Kolakowski, are all individuals like the next. They wielded or weaponized media in various forms of which the aftershocks can still be felt today by those of us willing to peer back at the great failures and feats of men and women in once democratic societies. Snyder is at pains to remind us that "[w]e do not see the minds that we hurt when we publish falsehoods, but that does not mean we do no harm" (90). Michal Bilewicz and Wiktor Soral, political psychologists at the University of Warsaw, similarly discuss the power of words, saying, "Historically, the derogatory comments and speeches preceding genocide often portrayed outgroup members as lacking warmth and competence and deprived of basic human features. The posters hung in Nazi-occupied Poland portrayed Jews as vermin, rats, and lice and connected them to typhus and other diseases" (27). According to Bilewicz and Soral's research, it is the normalization of terms that ultimately leads to the psychological desensitization of hate-based action, or a human psyche safety feature turned hazardous. Picture the ant death spiral in which the momentary

Chapter 5: Strategies for Advanced Essays and for Research   **185**

confusion of a single ant ultimately leads to the mass death of its colony-mates.

    Snyder's piece addresses the human condition for the perfectly imperfect construct that it is, by acknowledging that even the highly distinguished *homo sapiens* species is susceptible to lies so fantastical, hundreds of Americans were once fooled into believing that the History Channel's *Mermaids* mockumentary captured authentic footage of a mer-primate. People, intelligent as we are, have perfected the art of outsourcing tedious activities like math to calculators and research to bespectacled geniuses named Clark Kent. We trust that "news" is synonymous with "truth" and that every headline is carefully formulated by a well-intentioned whistleblower--and sometimes a headline is all we need to form an opinion that threatens to change the course of democracy as we know it. We are credulous animals with a superiority complex, and we are experts at deluding ourselves otherwise. Snyder's *On Tyranny* is in itself the tacit admission of humanity's reoccurring self-destructive naivete--of our need for a manual to tell us when to be critical thinkers in the first place. Snyder addresses us human beings not as the embodiment of intelligence but rather as the hopeful potential for intelligence.

    I'm your host, Connie "McWeatherpants" Fian, and you're watching *Stormy Scandals*. Back to you, Poppy Cox.

Works Cited

Bilewicz, Michal, and Wiktor Soral. "Hate Speech Epidemic: The Dynamic Effects of Derogatory Language on Intergroup Relations and Political Radicalization." *Political Psychology*, vol. 41, no. S1, 2020, pp. 3-33. *EBSCOhost*, web-p-ebscohost-com.ezproxy.library.csn.edu/ehost/detail/detail?vid=0&sid=27ca989d-50c2-4277-93b5-418f0cfe375c%40redis&bdata=JnNpdGU9ZWhvc3QtbGl2ZQ%3d%3d#AN=145319837&db=aph. Accessed 28 Nov. 2021.

Hassan, Steven. *The Cult of Trump*. Free Press, 2019, pp. 7-9. *ProQuest Ebook Central*, ebookcentral.proquest.com/lib/csn/reader.action?docID=5917074&ppg=8. Accessed 28 Nov. 2021.

Snyder, Timothy. "Chapter 11: Investigate." *Anatomy of an Essay*, edited by Tina D. Eliopulos and Todd Moffett, Kendall Hunt, 2019, pp. 87-90.

---. "Chapter 17: Listen for Dangerous Words." *Anatomy of an Essay*, edited by Tina D. Eliopulos and Todd Moffett, Kendall Hunt, 2019, pp. 122-23.

Michele Olson

Ms. Eliopulos

English 101-1801

13 March 2022

A Flawed Law

  The issue of homelessness has plagued America for centuries, even though the country is among the world's greatest economies. Much effort has been made to solve the problem of homelessness to the point that states and cities have passed laws aimed to help the homeless population in any way possible. One such effort was Las Vegas City Ordinance 6710, formally named Camping, Lodging, And Similar Activities Within Public Right-Of-Way At Specified Locations, making it illegal for people to sleep or camp on the streets or sidewalks. While this may seem cruel, the intent behind this act was to force the homeless populace into seeking shelter. However, this ordinance cannot be successful in achieving said goal. Although Las Vegas City Ordinance 6710 was passed to help steer homeless persons to needed services, in actuality, it criminalizes and perpetuates stigma connected with being homeless, making their situations worse.

  To begin with, one must look at how this ordinance is responsible for criminalizing and perpetuating the stigma connected with being homeless. According to the European Union Agency for Fundamental Rights, homelessness results in "pervasive discrimination, stigmatization and negative stereotyping which can lead to the refusal of, or unequal access to, the same quality of education and healthcare as others, as well as the denial of or unequal access to public places" ("Committee"). As such, there is no denying that homelessness directly leads to the stigmatization of an individual, mainly because these people occupy spaces that are generally constrained for public use. The American Bar Association has acknowledged this factor as they state that "Homelessness is often considered more disruptive than other forms of poverty because homeless individuals occupy public spaces and have an inability to groom and clean themselves regularly" ("Stigma" 1). By banning homeless individuals from occupying public spaces, this ordinance perpetuates the stereotype that homeless people are disruptive or do not deserve to occupy public spaces due to them being unclean. While this may not have been the intention while the ordinance was being passed, this ordinance will most certainly have a negative impact on the homeless community, particularly in terms of their mental health, which will make their situation worse.

    Secondly, it is important to look at how this ordinance will make the situation of the homeless community worse and how mental health plays a massive role in this arena. It is no secret that the homeless community has been linked with mental

Chapter 5: Strategies for Advanced Essays and for Research   189

health issues such as depression and anxiety. According to Cilia Mejia-Lancheros and her colleagues, many homeless individuals have to live through mental health problems due to their financial status. However, stigma plays a significant role in making their mental health problems even worse. They say, "[H]igher levels of internalized stigma are associated with worse mental health symptoms, such as depressive and psychotic symptoms, and suicidal ideation" (Mejia-Lancheros et al., "Trajectories"). When a particular homeless individual suffers from mental health issues, the stigma associated with being homeless will lead them to have depressive episodes, symptoms of psychosis, and even suicidal tendencies. Therefore, it is clear that the stigma associated with homelessness can prove fatal for homeless individuals. This stigma is why there is a need to accept homeless individuals in society. However, banning them from public spaces does the opposite as it shows a lack of acceptance, which leads to the stigmatization that, in turn, leads to mental health problems.

  Lastly, this ordinance does not help push homeless people into seeking help services and is thus highly unnecessary. It must be noted that when the state passes such acts or ordinances, they only help internalize the stigma around the homeless population. Instead of helping homeless individuals, this ordinance makes sure that homeless individuals think of themselves as unworthy of occupying public spaces. Mejia-Lancheros and her colleagues support this argument as they mention that "Stigma and discrimination are often internalized by persons with low income and those experiencing homelessness and mental illness" ("Longitudinal"). Because the majority of the homeless population suffers from one mental disorder or another, it can be believed that most of the population internalizes this stigma. This type of internalization "leads to hopelessness, low self-esteem and the lack of empowerment" (Mejia-Lancheros et al., "Longitudinal"), resulting in the homeless person being unable to ask for help when they need it. All of the factors mentioned above act as barriers to the homeless populace seeking services as they consider themselves unworthy of receiving help, even from organizations designed to help them. Thus, this ordinance only pushes them away from seeking services, making their situation worse.

However, despite the criticism against the ordinance, many intellectuals support it. According to these individuals, this particular ordinance was designed to ensure that the homeless community would not occupy public spaces and would seek the services that exist to help them (Mejia-Lancheros et al., "Trajectories"). As such, according to the supporters, the ordinance is created with good intentions, and it has the added benefit of pushing the homeless community into the arms of those who wish to help them (Mejia-Lancheros et al., "Trajectories"). However, despite the argument that the intention behind the act's creation was pure, the act exists to force the homeless community into a situation that they do not wish to be a part of. It is rather obvious that if a homeless person wished to access services that would help them, then they would do so themselves; as a result, there is no need to force them into seeking help. Moreover, it must also be said that it is not ethical or morally correct to force or manipulate people into doing something that they do not wish to do. Also, since the ordinance only helps to worsen the problems of the homeless community, it can be said that it only acts as a barrier for them to seek help from others.

Since Las Vegas City Ordinance 6710 only helps to make the situation of the homeless community worse, it is important to repeal this law and think about the creation of constructive solutions for the problem of homelessness. Furthermore, since there is a stigma in certain communities linked with homelessness, an ordinance passed by public officials banning this population from settling in public spaces helps cement the opinion that homeless individuals do not deserve to occupy public spaces. Moreover, such ordinances tend to harm the mental health of these individuals as stigma is linked with mental health problems. Lastly, this ordinance only pushes the homeless population away from the services they need as it helps internalize public stigma for the homeless community. Collectively, these factors combine to ensure that the situation of homeless individuals is worsened rather than improved.

Chapter 5: Strategies for Advanced Essays and for Research **193**

Works Cited

"Committee on Economic, Social and Cultural Rights, General Comment No. 20 Non-Discrimination in Economic, Social and Cultural Rights (Art. 2, Para. 2, of the International Covenant on Economic, Social and Cultural Rights)." *European Union Agency for Fundamental Rights*, 30 Apr. 2020, fra.europa.eu/en/law-reference/committee-economic-social-and-cultural-rights-general-comment-no-20-non.

Mejia-Lancheros, Cilia, et al. "Longitudinal Interrelationships of Mental Health Discrimination and Stigma with Housing and Well-Being Outcomes in Adults with Mental Illness and Recent Experience of Homelessness." *Social Science & Medicine*, vol. 268, Jan. 2021, www.sciencedirect.com/science/article/pii/S0277953620306821?via%3Dihub.

---. "Trajectories and Mental Health-Related Predictors of Perceived Discrimination and Stigma among Homeless Adults with Mental Illness." *PloS One*, vol. 15, no. 2, 27 Feb. 2020, doi.org/10.1371/journal.pone.0229385.

"Stigma and Lack of Personal Dignity." *ABA*, American Bar Association, 2019, www.americanbar.org/content/dam/aba/administrative/homelessness_poverty/blueprints/blueprint-9.pdf.

Chapter 6
The Literature Essay

One task you may perform in your English class is the writing of a literature essay. For this task, you will read (or view) a work such as a play, poem, novel, movie, or short story; then you will write an essay in which you discuss how that work was put together. Ideally, this task will give you a better appreciation of the work. Practically, the task will prepare you for times in your career when you might provide an analysis of a financial report, or a business proposal, or a patient's evaluation, or a witness's testimony in court. Below you will find the points a literature essay may cover and directions for how to write it.

The Basic Tools of Storytelling

If you are experiencing a work that is telling a story, such as a play, novel, movie, or short story, then you will need to look for the following six elements: **setting**, **character**, **plot**, **point of view**, **symbolism**, and **theme**.

Setting

The setting is the time and place during which a story occurs. Few authors will tell you this information directly. You will have to look closely at how places and people are described to find the clues you will need. For example, if a group of people is sitting in a cave around a fire, wearing animal skins, and using tools of stone and bone, then the story might be set in prehistoric times. If a group of people is escaping in a spaceship from hostile aliens firing at them with laser cannons, then the story might be set in the future or in an alternate universe.

Setting is important because it limits how characters can act and thus creates expectations in the reader. If in the opening pages of a story a man is riding a horse and wearing a ten-gallon hat, a gingham shirt, leather chaps, and a gun belt circled by bullets, then the reader will expect the story to be a Western, or at the least a story set in the American West. The reader will also expect this man to act and think the way people acted and thought during that time—though the reader will also want the writer to somehow upset the conventions of the genre to avoid clichés or to create surprise. In a fantastical setting like that of *The Lord of the Rings* or *Star Wars*, looking at the details will be even more important. As viewers, we will not know the rules for how these worlds work until we see how the characters interact with their settings.

Even in a setting that isn't quite so far, far away as Middle-earth or Tatooine, this interaction between setting and character not only sets limitations but also helps to establish a mood. In Sherwood Anderson's story "Brothers," for example, the setting not only establishes the time and place—an October day somewhere outside Chicago—but also, with the description of the rain and the fog, creates a gloomy atmosphere that both mirrors the indistinct presence of the narrator and foreshadows the somber account of the murder. On the other hand, in Robert Frost's poem "Mending Wall," the spring New England day contrasts the attitudes that the speaker and his neighbor have for the wall separating their properties. Also, in Kate Chopin's short story "The Story of an Hour," the promise of life-giving spring outside Louise Mallard's window prepares the ground for the irony surrounding the protagonist's fate.

Two important motifs arise from the setting, the first being the *conflict between City and Wilderness*. The City, since ancient times, has represented human laws, cultures, technology, art, and above all, safety and protection from the forces of nature. Psychologically speaking, the City also represents the orderly, the rational, the superego, the conscious mind. On the other hand, the Wilderness represents untamed nature, the forces of which can arise without warning to destroy humans and their settlements. It is also the abode of monsters and of outlaws who cannot or will not live within the laws of the human community. Psychologically, the Wilderness represents the dangerous, the irrational or emotional, the id, the unconscious mind. Despite its dangers, the Wilderness is frequently the landscape in which characters test themselves or quest for new sources of power. In countless stories, a character leaves the safety of home for an adventure in a forest, desert, underground cavern, or some other faraway locale to explore the unknown, rescue a comrade or loved one, endure a rite of passage, or find a meaningful landmark or potent talisman.

A countervailing trend that originated with Roman pastoral poetry and strengthened in the time of William Wordsworth is that the City, instead of being a place of safety and the glowing product of human industry, is rather the cause of human misery and corruption. The Wilderness, in the form of idyllic nature, becomes the means by which humans slough off the taint of the City and renew their spiritual connection to the universe. Wordsworth himself, in his poem "The World Is Too Much with Us," makes such a connection, and modern nature writers like Barry Lopez, whose essay "Love in a Time of Terror" appears in chapter two, can even argue that the Wilderness, far from being psychologically dangerous, is a place of sustenance, a source of love and comfort, and the home we must defend against both corporate greed and climate calamity.

The second motif is the *Cosmic Center*. This Center is the origin or birth point of the universe and the axis between the three cosmic zones: Upper, Middle, and Lower. The Center is thus the location of a power source from which the brave can extract a stepped-down supply to use against a difficulty they are facing. The principal landmarks of the Center are the Sacred Mountain, the World Tree, the Magic Pool, and the Hearth. If you can imagine Mount Sinai (where Moses received the Ten Commandments), Yggdrasil, the Fountain of Youth, or the fiery heart of Mount Doom in *The Lord of the Rings*, you are seeing only four forms out of the thousands that represent the Center. The City described above has its own version of the Center: the Celestial City, often represented by a palace, ziggurat, or temple— think of the Emerald City to which Dorothy journeys in *The Wizard of Oz*. But sometimes, the Center is located in the middle of the most dangerous part of the Wilderness. Access to the Center is frequently barred by a guardian, a labyrinth, a body of water, or another feature known as the Narrow Bridge—like the rickety bridge Shrek and Donkey cross to rescue Princess Fiona, or the marigold-petal bridge that Miguel crosses to enter the Land of the Dead in the movie *Coco*. Numerous quests to the Center have appeared in stories through the ages, and the Center itself is a major element in religions and mythologies worldwide.

Character

A character is any agent that exhibits a distinct personality and affects the outcome of the story. A character can be human, animal, machine, or some other imaginative form. Again, as readers (and viewers), we must pay attention to how characters are described so that we can determine how they fit into the story, how they may act, and how we should respond to them (Is this person likable? Should I be sympathetic?).

The most important character in a story is the *hero* or *protagonist*. This is the character that the story seems to be about, the one who has the most effect on the outcome. Other characters can be ranked as *major* or *minor* based on how much influence they have. The protagonist is typically surrounded by *secondary characters*: love interests, family, allies, or rivals (the main rival being the story's *antagonist* or *villain*). Some of these secondaries also will have a large influence over the plot and thus be major characters. Other characters met in passing during the course of the story are usually minor characters.

Characters can also be classified by the amount of change they undergo and by the complexity of their personalities. If characters change a lot—if they become better or worse, richer or poorer, more powerful or less—then they are *dynamic*. If characters show little or no change, they are *static*. If characters show a complex personality—several or even opposing traits—then they are *round*. If they show only one strong trait—or none at all—then they are *flat*. A simple but productive literary analysis may choose one character from a story and demonstrate whether she is major or minor, dynamic or static, round or flat.

We can classify characters in other ways, too. A *foil*, for example, is a character who provides a sharp contrast to another, typically a major character. The foil thus sets the other character in relief, much like polished gold enhances the brightness of the precious jewel set within it. A related character, the *sidekick*, accompanies the hero on her adventures, providing help and companionship as necessary. Another character, the *stock*, is one with predetermined traits. The femme fatale, the mad scientist, and the straight-shooting law officer are all variations of this type. *Atmosphere* characters do more to set the mood than to advance the plot: for instance, scarred, tattooed bruisers who fill a barroom with an air of menace; or a jokester who provides comic relief with wisecracks; or a killjoy who rails at the other characters—or the world in general. We can also distinguish characters by how they tend to face the problems before them. The *bull* character typically relies on strength, whereas the *fox* relies on wits or dexterity.

Two other aspects of the major characters to consider are their *motivations* and *goals*. A motivation is the cause of a character's action; a goal is a character's desired outcome. Sometimes these two are the same, but sometimes they are not. If all we know about a character is that she hopes to run her own bakery someday, then her motivation and goal are the same. But if we know that the character wants to run the bakery because her mother used to own one, then motivation and goal are different. Something in her past provides a reason for something she wants in the future.

It's important to know the characters' motivations and goals because they often shape the action and the outcome of a story. For instance, if two rival characters hope to find a buried treasure, we immediately sense a conflict between them. We must weigh the reasons each has for finding the treasure, and examine the actions they take, to determine whom we should root for, and we should have a sense of what would happen if our chosen character should fail. The moment when our character is closest to achieving or losing his goal is typically the moment of highest tension in the story. Our enjoyment of the story may well hinge on his success or failure and on the circumstances surrounding this outcome.

Plot

The basics of plot have already been laid out for you in chapter three (in the discussion of the relative importance organizational strategy). But because of the plot's importance in storytelling, we have provided more information here.

Plot and story are not the same. A story is a chronological series of actions, and an *action* is a movement, gesture, or utterance made by a character. An *event*, in turn, is an action that changes the course of a character's life. If a woman chooses to leave her betrothed at the altar, for example, or if she learns her partner has been unfaithful, or if her house is robbed, or if her bakery suddenly goes bankrupt, then we have an action important to her life—and to the direction of the story. These examples, by the way, illustrate four of the most important actions to look for: *decision* (a character makes a significant choice), *discovery* (a character learns new information), *injury* (a character causes or suffers harm), and *reversal* (a character's action brings about an unexpected effect). Sometimes, however, an action is simply a random happening that the universe may interpose at a crucial moment. If, for example, two characters need to climb to the top of a mountain and it suddenly begins to snow, the universe has thrown an obstacle in their path. Here, too, we have an action becoming an event.

A plot is the structure behind these events, and the writer creates a plot by manipulating how the events are presented. She chooses which event opens a story, which event closes it, and which events make up its contents. She also chooses the order in which the events occur: sometimes in chronological order, but sometimes not. A *loop plot*, for example, will pose a mystery or problem in the opening and then lead us into the past to show how the characters have reached this point. Such a plot shapes the disaster film *Titanic* and the Japanese anime *Your Name*. *Flashbacks*, like loops, return us to the past, but only for a moment or for a scene before the plot resumes its normal flow of time. (Beware! Time travel to the past—as when Taki finally meets Mitsuha on the mountaintop in *Your Name*—is not the same as a loop or a flashback!) A story with *subplots*—storylines featuring characters other than the protagonist—may have many events occurring at the same time as the events in the main plot.

Plots usually are shaped by three types of conflict: *internal, personal,* and *extrapersonal*. Internal conflicts typically happen inside a character's mind, body, or heart. A woman may be torn, for example, between her feelings for her lover and her obligations toward her sickly parents. Or she may be battling a drinking problem caused by her sense of inadequacy. Or she may think that her life in general is lacking purpose. Personal conflicts happen between two (or more) characters. The characters may be at odds over a job opening, or a parking space, or a rare artifact. Or perhaps one character causes an injury to a second, and the second seeks reparation. Or perhaps the characters are engaged in a power struggle in their relationship. An extrapersonal conflict sets the characters against a large impersonal force such as nature, or big government, or a heartless corporation, or the universe itself. Extrapersonal conflicts may also occur between countries or corporations or other forces and serve as part of the setting against which the characters operate.

As you can see in these conflicts, plot is heavily influenced by character. In a good story, neither exists without the other. The number of characters in a story often governs the type of conflict within it. If the story has a single character, for example, then the conflict is usually internal or extrapersonal, and the plot forms around a struggle the character has with his inner demons, with a lack she perceives in her life, or with the universe around him. Three common plots that result from these conflicts are the *identity plot*, the *repression plot*, and the *survival plot*. In the first, the character struggles through an *identity crisis*: a change in how she sees herself or in how others see her. In the second, the character must deal with the resurfacing of a repressed memory, feeling, or trauma that is causing physical or psychological distress. The resurfacing trauma often bears little or no resemblance to that which was initially repressed, thus making a cure difficult. In the third, the character faces a one-on-one struggle against the universe for her very survival. Often, it's the resurfacing of a repressed trauma or a struggle against extrapersonal forces that causes an identity crisis, and both sources of conflict must be solved.

With two major characters, we can add the personal level of conflict to the internal and the extrapersonal, and the plot frequently takes one of five forms: *romance, rivalry, revenge, raise,* or *repel.* The events of a romance plot are several, any of which can be the turning points or the climax of the story—unrequited love (X expresses, Y ignores or rejects), unexpressed love (neither X nor Y expresses), X loses Y, X finds Y, X achieves Y. A rivalry plot revolves around the contest between two characters, either in a power struggle against each other, or in a race where they both seek the same goal, or in a battle where one character blocks another from reaching her goal. A special rivalry plot, the *X-plot,* begins with one character superior to another, but their positions gradually converge until a crossover point midway through the story. The X-plot ends with the second character now superior to the first. A revenge plot, at its simplest, begins with an injury—a theft, a wounding, a murder, an abduction, etc.—that one character causes another, and ends with the injured character gaining revenge. The story may grow into a long cycle of injury and revenge, as in a vendetta, that doesn't end until all of the characters die. A raise plot sees one character lift or improve another, as in the relationship between a mentor and a student or initiate. The lifted character thus enters a new, and typically better, life station (though not always! Look at what happens to Anakin Skywalker in the *Star Wars* movies). In the repel plot, an augmentation of the one-character survival plot, the two characters must learn to team up to fight characters or extrapersonal forces outside their duo. The five plots are not mutually exclusive; any and all of them may happen in a single narrative. Furthermore, a two-character plot can also include the conflicts that occur in a one-character plot.

With three major characters, the plot can include the conflicts that arise with one or two characters, but it may also spring from a whole new set based upon the triads that the characters form. One is *two against one*, in which two characters team up against the third. Another is *good angel-bad angel*, in which a character is faced with two choices, sometimes life altering, each represented by an angel; if you've ever seen an angel and a devil pop onto the shoulders of a character to influence her actions, then you've seen this plot form.

Chapter 6: The Literature Essay   203

Flesh and blood characters can also serve as the good angel and the bad angel as in the play *Othello*, where Othello must choose to believe either in the fidelity of his wife Desdemona or in the accusations made by his ensign Iago. A different option is the *power trio*, in which, like the two-character repel plot, the three characters must learn to team up against forces outside their group. Three more triads, derived from older classical models, arise from the romance of the two-character plot: the *rivals*, the *ladies of duty and pleasure*, and the *love chain*. In the first, two suitors strive to win the hand of a woman, who ultimately chooses one over the other; she may reject a suitor even if he is already her significant other. In the second, a man must choose between his expectant bride (the lady of duty) awaiting him at home or the exotic beauty (the lady of pleasure) he meets on a journey. In the last, the first character loves the second, but the second loves the third; this third character may love the first, love another character entirely, or love no one at all. In stories with more than three characters, we usually see extensions or modifications of these basic conflicts.

A plot begins with an event that knocks the hero's life, or the universe around him, out of its usual path. This event may be called the *inducer* (in the Aristotelian plot, the *initial conflict*). Kate Chopin's "The Story of an Hour" opens with Louise Mallard learning of her husband's sudden death by train accident. Any action that precedes the inducer is the *exposition*, often setting the scene and describing the hero's circumstances. The story may form a loop, or use flashbacks, to show us the events that led to the inducer or to take us back to the inducer itself. Aside from its being near the start, there is no set moment when the inducer occurs.

Another kind of inducer arises when at the story's outset the universe of the hero is already off track and the hero has not yet been affected. Alternatively, the hero may be in a state of paralysis created by his universe's disorder, unable to act. (In many legends, the hero has yet to be born.) The inducer either occurs when the disorder touches the hero's life or causes the hero to break out of his paralysis (as at his birth). The inducer in Meron Hadero's story "The Suitcase" may be of the first kind: Saba, the protagonist, already feels out of place in the land of her birth, but the chaos of Addis Ababa touches her directly when she tries, and fails, to assert her self-reliance by crossing an intersection. The inducer in Edgar Allan Poe's story "The Cask of Amontillado" may be of the second kind: Montresor has not taken action against his rival Fortunato—despite the "thousand injuries" done to him by the latter—but finally does so when they meet in the street during Carnival. Again, the story may take the form of a loop, or use flashbacks, to show the events that led to the inducer or to take us back to the moment when the inducer occurred.

The hero has three responses to the inducer. First, the hero can react immediately. Second, the hero can delay reaction. For example, the inducer may occur at some time or place away from the hero and the hero may not learn of it until later. Or the hero may be prevented from immediate action. Or the hero is not ready to act. And third, the hero may resist reaction or deny the inducer has occurred; in this case, a second event will force the hero (who is often, by this time, somehow cornered) to react. The heroes in Chopin's story and in Poe's both react immediately, Mrs. Mallard weeping and retreating to her room, and Montresor baiting Fortunato with his talk about wine. The hero in Hadero's story is clearly not ready to act and does not break out of her paralysis until her final encounter with her relatives.

The middle section of the plot is formed by the protagonist's struggle to resolve the disorder caused by the inducer (in the Aristotelian plot, the *complications* or the *rise in tension*). Tension is created in the audience by the uncertainty of whether the protagonist will succeed or fail. This section is the longest in the plot and relies on the four events named above—decision, discovery, injury, and reversal—to keep that tension high even as the hero moves closer to deciding her fate.

A plot ends when one of three events—called the *climax*—occurs. First, the hero restores order to his life or to the universe. Second, the hero assimilates to the new conditions brought by the inducer. Or third, the hero succumbs to the new conditions brought by the inducer. These events are permanent changes that no further action by the characters or the universe can affect (though in a sequel . . .). Any further action beyond the climax—called the *denouement*—wraps up loose ends and brings the narrative to a close.

Point of View

Point of view is the perspective through which the story is told. Of course, the author is ultimately the person who wrote the story. However, a persona, the *narrator*, actually gives the story its voice. Thus, when you see the I-pronoun used, you must never assume that it's the author behind the I.

We label the narrator by his distance from the story and by the pronouns used to identify him. A *first-person narrator* is one who frequently appears as a character in the story, referred to with the I-pronouns. The first-person narrator can be *central* or *peripheral*. If central, the narrator is also the story's protagonist, as is the narrator of Poe's "Cask." If peripheral, the narrator is either one character chronicling another character's story (as the narrator does in Sherwood Anderson's "Brothers") or else someone telling the story to a waiting audience. In the latter case, the action of the story is often already complete, and the narrator is telling it in retrospect.

A first-person narrator can be also classified by how close she is to the time of the story. A *first-person processional* narrator is telling the story as she experiences it. This narrator typically does not know the outcome of the story and will learn it along with the audience. On the other hand, the *first-person confessional* narrator is telling the story after it has happened and already knows the outcome. This narrator is often telling this story to someone else—either to another character in the story or to the audience directly—as a way of explaining or describing a past occurrence.

A *second-person narrator* stands somewhat outside the story and addresses the protagonist—or the reader herself—as *you*. The effect of this narration is to create a story that reads like an extended one-sided dialogue or else a series of challenges to the character or to the audience.

A *third-person narrator* stands completely outside the story and addresses all characters as *he*, *she*, or *they*. The third-person narrator is further categorized by the control she has over the characters and their environment. An *omniscient* narrator can enter the thoughts of any of the characters, offer judgment on them and their actions, move the story backward and forward through time, or transport the setting to any place in the universe. A *limited omniscient* narrator allows the reader access to the thoughts of only one character (who thus becomes our point-of-view character) and narrows our perceptions of the universe to those of that character. This narrator offers no judgments except those made by the character. Time and place change only if the character changes position. An *objective* narrator stays completely out of the thoughts of the characters and simply records the surface details of their appearances and actions. In this mode, the narrator is like a camera that follows the characters.

The discussion of time and action in first-person point of view may reveal two different modes of time that appear in all forms of narration: *past-focused* and *future-focused*. Past-focused time means that the action of the past determines the action in the present. What has happened already in the story—what has already happened in the history of the world presented in the story—leads by probability and necessity (borrowing from Aristotle) to what the characters are doing as the story unfolds. In the Disney animated film *Moana*, why does Moana leave home to look for Maui? Because, as established by the story, her island is falling to the dark powers prophesied by her grandmother. However, we don't know how her quest will proceed. In this realm of time, the characters have a wider range of choice, and the outcome of the story is uncertain—often to the narrator as well as to the audience.

On the other hand, future-focused time means that the action of the present is determined by the future. Certain stories—such as the epic *Aeneid*, the movie *Planet of the Apes*, or the middle trilogy of the *Star Wars* series—have an inevitability to them because the future has already been established in advance. We know, for example, that Aeneas is going to found Rome, that apes are going to overrun human civilization, and that Anakin Skywalker is going to become Darth Vader; the only question is how. The range of character action is limited because the outcome of the story is already known (often by the audience as well as by the narrator), and events in the narration thus tend to be much less spontaneous.

Whatever the time, action, or point of view, readers must judge what is known as the *reliability* of the narrator. Since every new story is for the audience a venture into the unknown, a place where we can quickly get lost in an unfamiliar world, we rely on the narrator of that story to give us an accurate portrayal of that world. If, once we get our bearing, we find that our experience of that world matches how the narrator portrays it, then we have little cause to question the narrator's reliability.

An unreliable narrator, however, is one who, for one reason or another, cannot be trusted. As we get to know the world inhabited by the narrator and the characters, we begin to perceive how that world works, and we may notice discrepancies between our perception and the narrator's presentation. Some discrepancies are small and explainable: the narrator, for instance, may have limitations that we recognize are preventing her from being accurate. On the other hand, the narrator may tell outright lies, or omit crucial details, and we must judge the severity of those lies and omissions to determine our response to the story.

In some cases, the author, without a word, must let the reader know that an alternate (and more truthful) representation of that world underlies the one which the narrator reveals. In some works, however, the author may impose herself into the story; for example, he may speak to the reader. In such cases, the author will assume a first-person identity.

Symbolism

Symbolism is the use of *symbols*, and symbols in turn are objects or actions that have a meaning beyond themselves. For example, on a first date, a man gives his companion a bird he has folded out of paper. The bird is just that to an outside observer—a bird. However, for the man it might symbolize the effort he is willing to make to please his date. For the recipient, the bird might represent that first date and the beginning of their relationship. If, later in the story, the recipient encases the bird in glass, or throws it into a fire, then that action, too, becomes symbolic: an acknowledgment or a rejection of the man's efforts, or an expression of feeling about the relationship itself.

Symbols grow out of the meanings that the characters, the narrator, and we as readers attach to those objects and actions. They may create a web that stretches under the surface of the story. When that web is discovered, it may help our understanding of the characters' motivations and goals, of the shape of the plot, and of the theme of the story.

Theme

A theme is a broad conclusion that the work as a whole draws about the characters and their actions. Typically, a theme starts with an idea such as love, time, fate, or some other cultural or universal concept and then says something original and important about that idea. Thus, if in a story a couple grows to love each other but must endure separations, temptations, struggles, and other obstacles before they can unite happily at the end, a theme of the story might be that love is worth the difficulties one might face.

Because of its scope, a theme depends upon the other elements described above. Setting, character, plot, and the rest will all have something to contribute to the building of a theme, so you will have to pay close attention to them. Rarely will a modern storyteller simply lay out a theme in the introduction or in the conclusion the way a fable might, or the way we present a controlling idea when writing expository essays.

Since stories are individual creations with their own settings, characters, plots, and so on, they will each have a unique vision in their themes even if they tackle the same ideas. It's also possible that a well-crafted story has more than one theme. If two or more ideas are in play in the characters' actions, then the story will say something about each. Themes, too, rely on the reader's ability to perceive how the author is using the tools of storytelling. Two readers of the same story, because of their distinct life experiences, may see a completely different set of themes.

You can trace the creation of a work's themes by studying two strategies: *repetition* and *emphasis*. Repetition is the reoccurrence of an idea in a word, an image, a spoken exchange, an action, a thought, a narrative judgment, or some other element. Usually the idea arises within several different elements placed throughout the work. Authors use the strategy of repetition to signal to the reader that an important idea has been presented, and an alert reader will catch the signal and study the repetitions closely. For example, in Poe's "The Cask of Amontillado," you will notice that although both characters discuss wine and consume wine throughout the story, only one of the characters (Fortunato) gets drunk. Because of what happens to Fortunato, the story may thus have something to say about how people can be exploited in a moment of weakness. In Chopin's "The Story of an Hour," the word *free* and the idea of freedom are linked strongly to the marital and emotional state of Louise Mallard. From her situation arises the theme that for women, marriage is a trap and a burden they would gladly be free of.

Emphasis is the appearance of an idea during a key moment in the story or poem. In a story, this key moment often advances the plot; therefore, looking at a story's inducer, its complications, its crossovers or changes, and its climax may help the reader determine the story's important ideas. In Meron Hadero's "The Suitcase," the climax arrives when Saba decides to empty her own suitcase of her belongings and fill it with her relative's gifts. What we learn in that moment is how important those gifts are in establishing and preserving family ties and identity across far distances.

In any work, whether fiction, drama, or poetry, the key moments tend to be those of decision, discovery, injury, reversal, or image-making on the part of the narrator or protagonist. As noted above, Saba's visit to her relatives in Ethiopia turns on a decision. In Chopin's story, Louise Mallard's reaction to the final reversal—her missing husband's return home—is the last piece of the theme being built about women and marriage. In Poe's story, the images of the trowel—which foreshadows Fortunato's fate—and of the wall Montresor builds with it take us back to the repression plot. Montresor has gained his revenge, but the wall shows us how hard one must struggle to repress the memory of such a heinous act—and how, despite one's effort, the memory will resurface, even after fifty years.

Theme may also be shaped by another element: *irony*. We frequently use *verbal irony* when we say things we don't really mean:

"Oh, sure, I like sushi," we may say to a friend even though we really don't like sushi at all. Theme, however, usually springs from more complex forms of irony. *Dramatic irony* may arise when we, the audience, know things that the characters or the narrator does not. Such irony shapes Poe's story: Through details such as his false smile, his calling Fortunato his "poor friend," and his disclosure of the trowel, we know that Montresor is leading Fortunato to his death though the latter does not realize it until too late. *Situational irony* is at work when appearance and reality, expectation and fulfillment are at odds. A key moment in Hadero's story comes when, as noted above, Saba, having stolen away from her relatives on her last day to walk through Addis Ababa and prove her independence, can't cross a busy intersection. Finally, *cosmic irony* comes into play when it seems like the universe itself is working against the characters. This form of irony gives us the catastrophic ending of Chopin's story, when Louise Mallard's expectation of a life of freedom, occasioned by the news of her husband's death, is dashed when the universe returns her husband to her safe and sound.

The Basic Tools of Poetry

When you experience a poem, you will need to use all of the elements described above. However, you will also have four others to consider.

Narrative or Lyric

All poems can be broadly categorized as *narrative* or *lyric*. A narrative poem is one that tells a story. It can be long or short, but it will have a clearly defined plot based on the model described above. To understand the narrative poem, then, you must closely follow the events of the plot. Certain types of poems, like the epic or the ballad, will almost always be narratives. Thus, poems such as Homer's *Iliad* and *Odyssey* (both epics) and Samuel Coleridge's "The Rime of the Ancient Mariner" (a ballad) fall into this category.

A lyric poem is one that surrounds a central image or series of images. An *image* is a picture, though in poetry (and in storytelling) images must be created using words rather than paint or clay or film. Typically, the lyric poem is short, no more than a page or two, though some can run longer. The image at the heart of the poem will likely have a symbolic meaning that will be central to its theme; identifying the image, then, is paramount to understanding the poem.

Closed Form or Open Form

In form, all poems distinguish themselves from prose by the use of line breaks and stanzas. A *line break* is the poet's conscious ending of a line before the margin of the page. In prose forms such as the short story, novel, or essay, the lines run to the margin, breaking only at the ends of paragraphs. Poems, on the other hand, have internal rules, determined by the poet or by the poem itself, as to when lines end. The result is that a poem looks quite different from a short story or a novel when printed.

A *stanza* is a series of lines set together as a unit. It is roughly equal to the paragraph in prose writing. Usually, stanzas are separated from one another by an extra blank line, though there are other methods. Stanzas, too, have internal rules governed by the poet or by the type of poem; thus, a poem could have stanzas of equal length, or it could have stanzas of different lengths, or it could have no stanzas at all, just one continuous stream of lines.

Beyond these similarities, though, all poems can further be categorized as *closed form* or *open form*. A closed-form poem has strict rules for the length of lines and stanzas, the use of rhymes and repetition, and the pattern of stressed and unstressed syllables (called a *foot*). A sonnet, for example, has fourteen lines of ten syllables each, the syllables generally in an unstressed-stressed pattern (an *iambic* foot). It also has two rhyme schemes that affect the organization of the poem. A ballad usually relies on four-line stanzas following an 8-6-8-6 or a 4-4-6, 4-4-6 syllable count and an alternating rhyme scheme. Villanelles, pantoums, and sestinas have a set pattern of repeated lines (or words) and stanza lengths. The poet, however, may create her own closed form by following an original pattern of rhymes, syllables, and stanza lengths.

An open-form poem follows no strict patterns of rhyme, syllable count, repetition, or stanza length. Hence, most open-form poems are called *free verse*. Open-form poems, however, aren't simply poems without rules, and they aren't prose passages forced into a poetic form with arbitrary line breaks. The poet's use of stanzas and line breaks still follows a conscious design, and we as readers must determine the nature of that design. Further, the poet uses other resources of language to distinguish his work as a poem. Some of those resources are described below.

Concrete and Specific versus General and Abstract

As you learned earlier, description is the most basic mode of essay writing. However, all writers, no matter what they are writing, must use details to make an effective impression upon the reader. Essays use details to support a thesis or tell a narrative. Fiction uses details to bring settings, characters, and symbols to life. But poetry, in particular lyric poetry, is largely defined by the skill with which writers create and use details that appeal to the senses.

Sensory details must be *concrete* and *specific* rather than *general* or *abstract*. We have touched upon this difference, and the importance of concreteness, before, but this concept bears repeating. A concrete detail such as *red 1966 Mustang convertible* makes a far bigger impression than does the general term *vehicle*. Not just one but all readers will be able to visualize the same car, a necessary step in creating images. Poems that repeat vague abstractions like *love, sorrow, death*, or *joy* will never make the experience of these concepts personal to the reader.

Some poets, like Christine Boyka Kluge in her "Inventing New Bodies," will load a series of images with sensory details to lead us to a greater awareness about the subject of the poem. Done correctly, these images will change how we view the world around us. Hence, Kluge, by taking such great pains to describe the snails' music, the garden in which they live, and their unexpectedly vivid anger toward humans, has changed our appreciation of their simple existence.

Compression

All writers may use *figures of speech* to make their language musical, meaningful, or memorable. Speechwriters use these figures so that listeners will retain the key themes of the speech. Fiction writers use figures to subtly underscore dramatic moments in a story. But again, however, poets go a step further. Poetry might be described as the art of using concentrated figures to squeeze the greatest amount of meaning into the fewest number of words. This art is also known as *compression*.

The fundamental figures are widely known: *simile*, *metaphor*, *metonymy*, *synecdoche*. These can be classified as figures of comparison. There are also figures of opposition such as *litotes*, *paradox*, and *antithesis*. Others, such as *parallelism*, *anaphora*, and *epistrophe*, create pleasing forms of repetition. *Ellipsis* drops unneeded words so that sentences are more compact. *Function shift* lets poets turn nouns into verbs, or verbs into adjectives, and so on, to create colorful descriptions that arrest the eyes. *Personification* gives human traits to animals and non-human objects, whereas *zoomorphism* gives animal traits to humans. The *rule of three* can create harmonies of sound, sense, and structure that reinforce the connection between a poem's form and its content. Definitions for most of these terms can be found in the glossary.

Essay Model

When writing a literature essay, start by stating the name of the author (if known) and the title of the work. In the same sentence and into the next, set forth the work's *premise*—that is, a very brief summary of what happens or what major ideas are in play. You can usually assume that the reader of your essay is familiar with the work you are analyzing, so your premise should have just enough detail to show that you've read and understood the work. The next one or two sentences should present the element you will be analyzing in your paper (setting, plot, theme, compression, etc.) and your thesis. Much like the argument paper, a literature essay requires that you take a stand. Your thesis must clearly state how your chosen element appears in your work, how it affects that work, or what greater meaning it may hold.

A series of frame sentences might help you create your introduction:

- In (his/her/their) book/story/poem _____, (name of author) tells the story of _____.
- An interesting feature of this story/poem is _____ because _____.
- The development of _____ reveals _____.

In the first frame, select the proper pronoun for the author and the type of work. Fill in the first blank with the title of the work, italicized if it's a book, play, or movie, or set in quotation marks if it's a poem, an essay, or a short story. Then put the name of the author and finish by filling in the second blank with the premise of the work. In the second frame, identify the type of work again and then, in the first blank, the feature you will be writing about (plot, compression, theme, etc.); in the second blank, explain why that feature is notable. In the third frame, set out your stance by identifying the feature again in the first blank and explaining how it affects the work in the second blank.

The body of the literature essay then supports the stance you take in your thesis. The structure of the body paragraphs should follow the five-step model set forth in chapter three: topic sentence, narrow down, quotation, explanation, and conclusion. Each body paragraph should start with a topic sentence that, piece by piece, restates your stance. The rest of the paragraph then develops and explains your stance. The main source of support is the work itself. You must be able to show where in the work your chosen feature appears and why you think it functions as it does. For example, if you are analyzing the plot of a story, you must be able to name the events you think are the inducer, the hero's reaction, the main complications, and the climax (or alternately, the initial conflict, rise in tension, and climax) and explain how those events fulfill the definitions supplied above.

To point out where your feature appears in the work, you must use and cite quotations, much like you do in a researched essay. Quotations can be direct (word for word from the text and enclosed in quotation marks) or indirect (rewritten in your own words and not enclosed). To cite your sources, you will typically use MLA format, again as you did for your researched essay. For works of prose (novel, short story), you will cite by author's last name and the page number on which the quoted passage appears in your printed source. Poems are cited by author's last name and line number. Plays, if they are divided into act, scene, and line numbers (as Shakespeare's are), should be cited by those numbers; if not, then by page number.

However, the literature essay is not simply an exercise in stringing quotes together. Never assume your reader sees the same meanings in the passages that you do. You will have to take the time to introduce your quotations to your reader (much like you would handle introductions at a party) and then, perhaps most importantly, take the time to explain how and why the passages support your stance.

The final paragraph of your essay should clearly signal that you have finished your analysis. As with the other essay types, you can simply restate your thesis and summarize your main points. However, depending on your instructor's guidelines, you also have the option of judging the effectiveness of your chosen element, relating your essay topic to a broader concept, or deciding whether the work as a whole deserves its reputation (in other words, is it as good as everyone says it is?). You may also, if allowed, raise and refute an alternative interpretation of your chosen feature.

Here are two examples of how to use the frame sentences for the introductory paragraph and the five-step model for a body paragraph. The first example begins an essay about William Shakespeare's play *Othello*:

Introductory Paragraph

<u>Author-Title + Premise</u>: In his play *The Tragedy of Othello*, William Shakespeare tells the story of how the treachery of one character, Iago, leads to the murder-suicide of two others, Desdemona and Othello.

Introduction of Literary Element: An interesting feature of the play is Iago's plan for revenge because often, after viewing the final scene, the audience will ask itself, Why did Iago do it?

Thesis: The development of Iago's plan reveals that he is motivated by his jealousy of Othello and by his ambition to rise through the ranks of the Venetian army.

Body Paragraph

Topic Sentence: The first of Iago's motivations is jealousy for Othello.

Narrow Down: He first expresses this jealousy when he relates a rumor concerning his wife, Emilia, and Othello:

Quotation: "It is thought abroad that 'twixt my sheets / H'as done my office" (1.3.360-1).

Explanation of Key Term: The "office" he refers to is the duty of a husband to maintain sexual relations with his wife, so he is stating his belief that Othello has slept with Emilia.

Conclusion: This belief, denied later by Emilia herself, is nevertheless a major reason why Iago seeks revenge against Othello.

The second example offers the first two paragraphs of an essay on Kate Chopin's "The Story of an Hour":

Introductory Paragraph

Author-Title + Premise: In the short story "The Story of an Hour," Kate Chopin describes how Louise Mallard, when an acquaintance brings news of her husband's death, sees a chance to escape her limitations and experience the world beyond her house.

Introduction of Literary Element: An interesting feature of the story is the window of Louise's room because it seems to symbolize the freedom that beckons her forward to a new life.

Thesis: The development of Louise's desire, however, reveals that her excitement for her prospects leads her to false hopes and ultimately to a fatal reunion with her husband.

Body Paragraph

Topic Sentence: The attention given to Louise's sensory awareness of the world outside her window emphasizes her strong desire to break free of her repressed life.

Narrow Down: For example, when she sits in the chair facing the window,

Quotation: her body is "haunted" by a "physical exhaustion" that reaches "into her soul" (226).

Explanation of Key Term: These signs mark the fatigue that her current life with her husband has brought her.

Narrow Down: Immediately contrasted with this exhaustion, however, is the description of the first impressions that reach her through the window,

Quotation: the trees "all aquiver with the new spring life," the "delicious breath of rain," and the "twittering" of "countless sparrows" (226).

Explanation of Key Term: In this short passage it is clear that her senses are awake and that these impressions have already begun to renew her energies.

Conclusion: Soon, her body will physically respond to these new stimuli.

The body paragraph in the Chopin essay is more complex, repeating steps two, three, and four to examine the relevant details surrounding Louise Mallard's window. Note, however, that all quotations used are carefully introduced, cited, and explained so that the author has clearly located and documented her sources.

Summary

The literature essay examines the elements that make up plays, poems, novels, movies, and short stories. In part, this essay works like a division essay, breaking an object (in this case a story or a poem) into its parts, but it usually focuses on the use of just one or two of the parts. This essay is also like an argumentative essay: you take a stance by presenting your interpretation of how your chosen feature is used. It's also like a research paper in that you must use and cite quotations in support of your stance. Much of what you learned about the narrative essay—initial conflict, rise in tension, climax, etc.—applies to literary works as well. If you enjoy learning how things work and have ever taken apart a toy or a gadget to see what it looks like inside, then the literature essay should appeal to your sense of discovery.

Below, you will find a collection of short stories and poems, including the complete version of Chopin's "The Story of an Hour," that build upon the literary elements described above. At the end, you will also find Kassity Higgins's analysis of Shakespeare's *Othello*, written in the form of a cost-benefit analysis, and Joshua Dycus's paper about *The Fifth Season*, N. K. Jemisin's Hugo Award-winning novel, so that you can see how the entire literature essay is put together.

The Cask of Amontillado
by Edgar Allan Poe

The thousand injuries of Fortunato I had borne as I best could, but when he ventured upon insult, I vowed revenge. You, who so well know the nature of my soul, will not suppose, however, that I gave utterance to a threat. *At length* I would be avenged; this was a point definitely settled—but the very definitiveness with which it was resolved precluded the idea of risk. I must not only punish, but punish with impunity. A wrong is unredressed when retribution overtakes its redresser. It is equally unredressed when the avenger fails to make himself felt as such to him who has done the wrong.

It must be understood that neither by word nor deed had I given Fortunato cause to doubt my good will. I continued, as was my wont, to smile in his face, and he did not perceive that my smile *now* was at the thought of his immolation.

He had a weak point—this Fortunato—although in other regards he was a man to be respected and even feared. He prided himself on his connoisseurship in wine. Few Italians have the true virtuoso spirit. For the most part their enthusiasm is adopted to suit the time and opportunity to practice imposture upon the British and Austrian *millionaires*. In painting and gemmary Fortunato, like his countrymen, was a quack, but in the matter of old wines he was sincere. In this respect I did not differ from him materially: I was skillful in the Italian vintages myself, and bought largely whenever I could.

It was about dusk, one evening during the supreme madness of the carnival season, that I encountered my friend. He accosted me with excessive warmth, for he had been drinking much. The man wore motley. He had on a tight-fitting parti-striped dress, and his head was surmounted by the conical cap and bells. I was so pleased to see him, that I thought I should never have done wringing his hand.

I said to him—"My dear Fortunato, you are luckily met. How remarkably well you are looking to-day! But I have received a pipe of what passes for Amontillado, and I have my doubts."

"The Cask of Amontillado" by Edgar Allan Poe, 1846

"How?" said he. "Amontillado? A pipe? Impossible! And in the middle of the carnival!"

"I have my doubts," I replied; "and I was silly enough to pay the full Amontillado price without consulting you in the matter. You were not to be found, and I was fearful of losing a bargain."

"Amontillado!"

"I have my doubts."

"Amontillado!"

"And I must satisfy them."

"Amontillado!"

"As you are engaged, I am on my way to Luchesi. If any one has a critical turn it is he. He will tell me—"

"Luchesi cannot tell Amontillado from Sherry."

"And yet some fools will have it that his taste is a match for your own."

"Come, let us go."

"Whither?"

"To your vaults."

"My friend, no; I will not impose upon your good nature. I perceive you have an engagement. Luchesi—"

"I have no engagement; come."

"My friend, no. It is not the engagement, but the severe cold with which I perceive you are afflicted. The vaults are insufferably damp. They are encrusted with niter."

"Let us go, nevertheless. The cold is merely nothing. Amontillado! You have been imposed upon; and as for Luchesi, he cannot distinguish Sherry from Amontillado."

Thus speaking, Fortunato possessed himself of my arm. Putting on a mask of black silk, and drawing a *roquelaure*[1] closely about my person, I suffered him to hurry me to my palazzo.

There were no attendants at home; they had absconded to make merry in honor of the time. I had told them that I should not return until the morning, and had given them explicit orders not to stir from

---

1. A knee-length cloak.

the house. These orders were sufficient, I well knew, to insure their immediate disappearance, one and all, as soon as my back was turned.

I took from their sources two flambeaux, and giving one to Fortunato, bowed him through several suites of rooms to the archway that led into the vaults. I passed down a long and winding staircase, requesting him to be cautious as he followed. We came at length to the foot of the descent, and stood together on the damp ground of the catacombs of the Montresors.

The gait of my friend was unsteady, and the bells upon his cap jingled as he strode.

"The pipe," said he.

"It is farther on," said I; "but observe the white web-work which gleams from these cavern walls."

He turned towards me, and looked into my eyes with two filmy orbs that distilled the rheum of intoxication.

"Niter?" he asked, at length.

"Niter," I replied. "How long have you had that cough?"

"Ugh! ugh! ugh!—ugh! ugh! ugh!—ugh! ugh! ugh!—ugh! ugh! ugh!—ugh! ugh! ugh!"

My poor friend found it impossible to reply for many moments.

"It is nothing," he said, at last.

"Come," I said, with decision, "we will go back; your health is precious. You are rich, respected, admired, beloved; you are happy, as once I was. You are a man to be missed. For me it is no matter. We will go back; you will be ill, and I cannot be responsible. Besides, there is Luchesi—"

"Enough," he said; "the cough is a mere nothing; it will not kill me. I shall not die of a cough."

"True—true," I replied; "and, indeed, I had no intention of alarming you unnecessarily—but you should use all proper caution. A draught of this Medoc will defend us from the damps."

Here I knocked off the neck of a bottle which I drew from a long row of its fellows that lay upon the mold.

"Drink," I said, presenting him the wine.

He raised it to his lips with a leer. He paused and nodded to me familiarly, while his bells jingled.

"I drink," he said, "to the buried that repose around us."

"And I to your long life."

He again took my arm, and we proceeded.

"These vaults," he said, "are extensive."

"The Montresors," I replied, "were a great and numerous family."

"I forget your arms."

"A huge human foot *d'or*, in a field azure; the foot crushes a serpent rampant whose fangs are imbedded in the heel."

"And the motto?"

"*Nemo me impune lacessit.*"[2]

"Good!" he said.

The wine sparkled in his eyes and the bells jingled. My own fancy grew warm with the Medoc. We had passed through walls of piled bones, with casks and puncheons intermingling, into the inmost recesses of the catacombs. I paused again, and this time I made bold to seize Fortunato by an arm above the elbow.

"The niter!" I said; "see, it increases. It hangs like moss upon the vaults. We are below the river's bed. The drops of moisture trickle among the bones. Come, we will go back ere it is too late. Your cough—"

"It is nothing," he said; "let us go on. But first, another draught of the Medoc."

I broke and reached him a flacon of De Grâve. He emptied it at a breath. His eyes flashed with a fierce light. He laughed and threw the bottle upwards with a gesticulation I did not understand.

I looked at him in surprise. He repeated the movement—a grotesque one.

"You do not comprehend?" he said.

"Not I," I replied.

"Then you are not of the brotherhood."

"How?"

"You are not of the masons."

"Yes, yes," I said, "yes, yes."

"You? Impossible! A mason?"

---

2. "No one provokes me with impunity."

"A mason," I replied.

"A sign," he said.

"It is this," I answered, producing a trowel from beneath the folds of my *roquelaure*.

"You jest," he exclaimed, recoiling a few paces. "But let us proceed to the Amontillado."

"Be it so," I said, replacing the tool beneath the cloak, and again offering him my arm. He leaned upon it heavily. We continued our route in search of the Amontillado. We passed through a range of low arches, descended, passed on, and descending again, arrived at a deep crypt, in which the foulness of the air caused our flambeaux rather to glow than flame.

At the most remote end of the crypt there appeared another less spacious. Its walls had been lined with human remains, piled to the vault overhead, in the fashion of the great catacombs of Paris. Three sides of this interior crypt were still ornamented in this manner. From the fourth the bones had been thrown down, and lay promiscuously upon the earth, forming at one point a mound of some size. Within the wall thus exposed by the displacing of the bones, we perceived a still interior recess, in depth about four feet, in width three, in height six or seven. It seemed to have been constructed for no especial use within itself, but formed merely the interval between two of the colossal supports of the roof of the catacombs, and was backed by one of their circumscribing walls of solid granite.

It was in vain that Fortunato, uplifting his dull torch, endeavored to pry into the depths of the recess. Its termination the feeble light did not enable us to see.

"Proceed," I said; "herein is the Amontillado. As for Luchesi—"

"He is an ignoramus," interrupted my friend, as he stepped unsteadily forward, while I followed immediately at his heels. In an instant he had reached the extremity of the niche, and finding his progress arrested by the rock, stood stupidly bewildered. A moment more and I had fettered him to the granite. In its surface were two iron staples, distant from each other about two feet, horizontally. From one of these depended a short chain, from the other a padlock. Throwing the links about his waist, it was but the work of a few seconds to secure it. He was too much astounded to resist. Withdrawing the key I stepped back from the recess.

"Pass your hand," I said, "over the wall; you cannot help feeling the niter. Indeed it is *very* damp. Once more let me *implore* you to return. No? Then I must positively leave you. But I must first render you all the little attentions in my power."

"The Amontillado!" ejaculated my friend, not yet recovered from his astonishment.

"True," I replied; "the Amontillado."

As I said these words I busied myself among the pile of bones of which I have before spoken. Throwing them aside, I soon uncovered a quantity of building stone and mortar. With these materials and with the aid of my trowel, I began vigorously to wall up the entrance of the niche.

I had scarcely laid the first tier of masonry when I discovered that the intoxication of Fortunato had in a great measure worn off. The earliest indication I had of this was a low moaning cry from the depth of the recess. It was *not* the cry of a drunken man. There was then a long and obstinate silence. I laid the second tier, and the third, and the fourth; and then I heard the furious vibrations of the chain. The noise lasted for several minutes, during which, that I might hearken to it with the more satisfaction, I ceased my labors and sat down upon the bones. When at last the clanking subsided, I resumed the trowel, and finished without interruption the fifth, the sixth, and the seventh tier. The wall was now nearly upon a level with my breast. I again paused, and holding the flambeaux over the mason-work, threw a few feeble rays upon the figure within.

A succession of loud and shrill screams, bursting suddenly from the throat of the chained form, seemed to thrust me violently back. For a brief moment I hesitated—I trembled. Unsheathing my rapier, I began to grope with it about the recess; but the thought of an instant reassured me. I placed my hand upon the solid fabric of the catacombs, and felt satisfied. I reapproached the wall. I replied to the yells of him who clamored. I re-echoed—I aided—I surpassed them in volume and in strength. I did this, and the clamorer grew still.

It was now midnight, and my task was drawing to a close. I had completed the eighth, ninth, and tenth tier. I had finished a portion of the last and the eleventh; there remained but a single stone to be fitted and plastered in. I struggled with its weight; I placed it partially in its destined position. But now there came from out the niche a low laugh that erected the hairs upon my head. It was succeeded by a sad voice which I had difficulty in recognizing as that of the noble Fortunato. The voice said—

"Ha! ha! ha!—he! he! he!—a very good joke indeed—an excellent jest. We will have many a rich laugh about it at the palazzo—he! he! he!—over our wine—he! he! he!"

"The Amontillado!" I said.

"He! he! he!—he! he! he!—yes, the Amontillado. But is it not getting late? Will not they be awaiting us at the palazzo, the Lady Fortunato and the rest? Let us be gone."

"Yes," I said, "let us be gone."

"*For the love of God, Montresor!*"

"Yes," I said, "for the love of God!"

But to these words I hearkened in vain for a reply. I grew impatient. I called aloud:

"Fortunato!"

No answer. I called again—

"Fortunato!"

No answer still. I thrust a torch through the remaining aperture and let it fall within. There came forth in return only a jingling of the bells. My heart grew sick—on account of the dampness of the catacombs. I hastened to make an end of my labor. I forced the last stone into its position; I plastered it up. Against the new masonry I re-erected the old rampart of bones. For the half of a century no mortal has disturbed them. *In pace requiescat!*[3]

---

3. "Rest in peace."

The Story of an Hour
by Kate Chopin

Knowing that Mrs. Mallard was afflicted with a heart trouble, great care was taken to break to her as gently as possible the news of her husband's death.

It was her sister Josephine who told her, in broken sentences; veiled hints that revealed in half concealing. Her husband's friend Richards was there, too, near her. It was he who had been in the newspaper office when intelligence of the railroad disaster was received, with Brently Mallard's name leading the list of "killed." He had only taken the time to assure himself of its truth by a second telegram, and had hastened to forestall any less careful, less tender friend in bearing the sad message.

She did not hear the story as many women have heard the same, with a paralyzed inability to accept its significance. She wept at once, with sudden, wild abandonment, in her sister's arms. When the storm of grief had spent itself she went away to her room alone. She would have no one follow her.

There stood, facing the open window, a comfortable, roomy armchair. Into this she sank, pressed down by a physical exhaustion that haunted her body and seemed to reach into her soul.

She could see in the open square before her house the tops of trees that were all aquiver with the new spring life. The delicious breath of rain was in the air. In the street below a peddler was crying his wares. The notes of a distant song which some one was singing reached her faintly, and countless sparrows were twittering in the eaves.

There were patches of blue sky showing here and there through the clouds that had met and piled one above the other in the west facing her window.

She sat with her head thrown back upon the cushion of the chair, quite motionless, except when a sob came up into her throat and shook her, as a child who has cried itself to sleep continues to sob in its dreams.

"The Story of an Hour" by Kate Chopin, 1894

Chapter 6: The Literature Essay

She was young, with a fair, calm face, whose lines bespoke repression and even a certain strength. But now there was a dull stare in her eyes, whose gaze was fixed away off yonder on one of those patches of blue sky. It was not a glance of reflection, but rather indicated a suspension of intelligent thought.

There was something coming to her and she was waiting for it, fearfully. What was it? She did not know; it was too subtle and elusive to name. But she felt it, creeping out of the sky, reaching toward her through the sounds, the scents, the color that filled the air.

Now her bosom rose and fell tumultuously. She was beginning to recognize this thing that was approaching to possess her, and she was striving to beat it back with her will—as powerless as her two white slender hands would have been.

When she abandoned herself a little whispered word escaped her slightly parted lips. She said it over and over under her breath: "free, free, free!" The vacant stare and the look of terror that had followed it went from her eyes. They stayed keen and bright. Her pulses beat fast, and the coursing blood warmed and relaxed every inch of her body.

She did not stop to ask if it were or were not a monstrous joy that held her. A clear and exalted perception enabled her to dismiss the suggestion as trivial.

She knew that she would weep again when she saw the kind, tender hands folded in death; the face that had never looked save with love upon her, fixed and gray and dead. But she saw beyond that bitter moment a long procession of years to come that would belong to her absolutely. And she opened and spread her arms out to them in welcome.

There would be no one to live for her during those coming years; she would live for herself. There would be no powerful will bending hers in that blind persistence with which men and women believe they have a right to impose a private will upon a fellow-creature. A kind intention or a cruel intention made the act seem no less a crime as she looked upon it in that brief moment of illumination.

And yet she had loved him—sometimes. Often she had not. What did it matter! What could love, the unsolved mystery, count for in the face of this possession of self-assertion which she suddenly recognized as the strongest impulse of her being!

"Free! Body and soul free!" she kept whispering.

Josephine was kneeling before the closed door with her lips to the keyhole, imploring for admission. "Louise, open the door! I beg; open the door—you will make yourself ill. What are you doing, Louise? For heaven's sake open the door."

"Go away. I am not making myself ill." No; she was drinking in a very elixir of life through that open window.

Her fancy was running riot along those days ahead of her. Spring days, and summer days, and all sorts of days that would be her own. She breathed a quick prayer that life might be long. It was only yesterday she had thought with a shudder that life might be long.

She arose at length and opened the door to her sister's importunities. There was a feverish triumph in her eyes, and she carried herself unwittingly like a goddess of Victory. She clasped her sister's waist, and together they descended the stairs. Richards stood waiting for them at the bottom.

Some one was opening the front door with a latchkey. It was Brently Mallard who entered, a little travel-stained, composedly carrying his grip-sack and umbrella. He had been far from the scene of the accident, and did not even know there had been one. He stood amazed at Josephine's piercing cry; at Richards's quick motion to screen him from the view of his wife.

But Richards was too late.

When the doctors came they said she had died of heart disease—of joy that kills.

Brothers
by Sherwood Anderson

I am at my house in the country and it is late October. It rains. Back of my house is a forest and in front there is a road and beyond that open fields. The country is one of low hills, flattening suddenly into plains. Some twenty miles away, across the flat country, lies the huge city, Chicago.

On this rainy day the leaves of the trees that line the road before my window are falling like rain, the yellow, red, and golden leaves fall straight down heavily. The rain beats them brutally down. They are denied a last golden flash across the sky. In October leaves should be carried away, out over the plains, in a wind. They should go dancing away.

Yesterday morning I arose at daybreak and went for a walk. There was a heavy fog and I lost myself in it. I went down into the plains and returned to the hills and everywhere the fog was as a wall before me. Out of it trees sprang suddenly, grotesquely, as in a city street late at night people come suddenly out of the darkness into the circle of light under a street lamp. Above there was the light of day forcing itself slowly into the fog. The fog moved slowly. The tops of trees moved slowly. Under the trees the fog was dense, purple. It was like smoke lying in the streets of a factory town.

An old man came up to me in the fog. I know him well. The people here call him insane. "He is a little cracked," they say. He lives alone in a little house buried deep in the forest and has a small dog he carries always in his arms. On many mornings I have met him walking on the road and he has told me of men and women who were his brothers and sisters, his cousins, aunts, uncles, brothers-in-law. The notion has possession of him. He cannot draw close to people near at hand so he gets hold of a name out of a newspaper and his mind plays with it. One morning he told me he was a cousin to the man named Cox who at the time when I write is a candidate for the presidency. On another morning he told me that Caruso the singer had married

---

Source: *The Bookman*, 1921

a woman who was his sister-in-law. "She is my wife's sister," he said, holding the little dog closely. His gray watery eyes looked appealingly up to me. He wanted me to believe. "My wife was a sweet slim girl," he declared. "We lived together in a big house and in the morning walked about arm in arm. Now her sister has married Caruso the singer. He is of my family now." As some one had told me the old man had never been married I went away wondering.

One morning in early September I came upon him sitting under a tree beside a path near his house. The dog barked at me and then ran and crept into his arms. At that time the Chicago newspapers were filled with the story of a millionaire who had got into trouble with his wife because of an intimacy with an actress. The old man told me the actress was his sister. He is sixty years old and the actress whose story appeared in the newspapers is twenty, but he spoke of their childhood together. "You would not realize it to see us now but we were poor then," he said. "It's true. We lived in a little house on the side of a hill. Once when there was a storm the wind nearly swept our house away. How the wind blew. Our father was a carpenter and he built strong houses for other people but our own house he did not build very strongly." He shook his head sorrowfully. "My sister the actress has got into trouble. Our house is not built very strongly," he said as I went away along the path.

For a month, two months, the Chicago newspapers, that are delivered every morning in our village, have been filled with the story of a murder. A man there has murdered his wife and there seems no reason for the deed. The tale runs something like this—

The man, who is now on trial in the courts and will no doubt be hanged, worked in a bicycle factory where he was a foreman, and lived with his wife and his wife's mother in an apartment in Thirty-Second Street. He loved a girl who worked in the office of the factory where he was employed. She came from a town in Iowa and when she first came to the city lived with her aunt who has since died. To the foreman, a heavy stolid-looking man with gray eyes, she seemed the most beautiful woman in the world. Her desk was by a window at an angle of the factory, a sort of wing of the building, and the foreman, down in the shop, had a desk by another window. He sat at his desk making out sheets containing the record of the work done by each man in his department. When he looked up he could see the girl sitting at work at her desk. The notion got into his head that she was peculiarly lovely. He did not think of trying to draw close to her or of winning her love. He looked at her as one might look at a star or across a country of low hills in October when the leaves of the trees are all red and yellow gold. "She is a pure, virginal thing," he thought vaguely. "What can she be thinking about as she sits there by the window at work?"

In fancy the foreman took the girl from Iowa home with him to his apartment in Thirty-Second Street and into the presence of his wife and his mother-in-law. All day in the shop and during the evening at home he carried her figure about with him in his mind. As he stood by a window in his apartment and looked out toward the Illinois Central railroad tracks and beyond the tracks to the lake, the girl was there beside him. Down below women walked in the street and in every woman he saw there was something of the Iowa girl. One woman walked as she did, another made a gesture with her hand that reminded of her. All the women he saw except only his wife and his mother-in-law were like the girl he had taken inside himself.

The two women in his own house puzzled and confused him. They became suddenly unlovely and commonplace. His wife in particular was like some strange unlovely growth that had attached itself to his body.

In the evening after the day at the factory he went home to his own place and had dinner. He had always been a silent man and when he did not talk no one minded. After dinner he, with his wife, went to a picture show. When they came home his wife's mother sat under an electric light reading. There were two children and his wife expected another. They came into the apartment and sat down. The climb up two flights of stairs had wearied his wife. She sat in a chair beside her mother groaning with weariness.

The mother-in-law was the soul of goodness. She took the place of a servant in the home and got no pay. When her daughter wanted to go to a picture show she waved her hand and smiled. "Go on," she said. "I don't want to go. I'd rather sit here." She got a book and sat reading. The little boy of nine awoke and cried. He wanted to sit on the po-po. The mother-in-law attended to that.

After the man and his wife came home the three people sat in silence for an hour or two before bedtime. The man pretended to read a newspaper. He looked at his hands. Although he had washed them carefully grease from the bicycle frames left dark stains under the nails. He thought of the Iowa girl and of her white quick hands playing over the keys of a typewriter. He felt dirty and uncomfortable.

The girl at the factory knew the foreman had fallen in love with her and the thought excited her a little. Since her aunt's death she had gone to live in a rooming house and had nothing to do in the evening. Although the foreman meant nothing to her she could in a way use him. To her he became a symbol. Sometimes he came into the office and stood for a moment by the door. His large hands were covered with black grease. She looked at him without seeing. In his place in her imagination stood a tall slender young man. Of the foreman she saw only the gray eyes that began to burn with a strange fire. The eyes expressed eagerness, a humble and devout eagerness. In the presence of a man with such eyes she felt she need not be afraid.

She wanted a lover who would come to her with such a look in his eyes. Occasionally, perhaps once in two weeks, she stayed a little late at the office, pretending to have work that must be finished. Through the window she could see the foreman, waiting. When every one had gone she closed her desk and went into the street. At the same moment the foreman came out at the factory door.

They walked together along the street, a half-dozen blocks, to where she got aboard her car. The factory was in a place called South Chicago and as they went along evening was coming on. The streets were lined with small unpainted frame houses and dirty-faced children ran screaming in the dusty roadway. They crossed over a bridge. Two abandoned coal barges lay rotting in the stream.

He went along by her side walking heavily, striving to conceal his hands. He had scrubbed them carefully before leaving the factory but they seemed to him like heavy dirty pieces of waste matter hanging at his side. Their walking together happened but a few times and during one summer. "It's hot," he said. He never spoke to her of anything but the weather. "It's hot," he said; "I think it may rain."

She dreamed of the lover who would some time come, a tall fair young man, a rich man owning houses and lands. The workingman who walked beside her had nothing to do with her conception of love. She walked with him, stayed at the office until the others had gone to walk unobserved with him, because of his eyes, because of the eager thing in his eyes that was at the same time humble, that bowed down to her. In his presence there was no danger, could be no danger. He would never attempt to approach too closely, to touch her with his hands. She was safe with him.

In his apartment in the evening the man sat under the electric light with his wife and his mother-in-law. In the next room his two children were asleep. In a short time his wife would have another child. He had been with her to a picture show and presently they would get into bed together.

He would lie awake thinking, would hear the creaking of the springs of a bed from where, in another room, his mother-in-law was crawling under the sheets. Life was too intimate. He would lie awake eager, expectant—expecting what?

Nothing. Presently one of the children would cry. It wanted to get out of bed and sit on the po-po. Nothing strange or unusual or lovely would or could happen. Life was too close, intimate. Nothing that could happen in the apartment could in any way stir him. The things his wife might say, her occasional half-hearted outbursts of passion, the goodness of his stout mother-in-law who did the work of a servant without pay—

He sat in the apartment under the electric light pretending to read a newspaper—thinking. He looked at his hands. They were large, shapeless, a workingman's hands.

The figure of the girl from Iowa walked about the room. With her he went out of the apartment and walked in silence through miles of streets. It was not necessary to say words. He walked with her by a sea, along the crest of a mountain. The night was clear and silent and the stars shone. She also was a star. It was not necessary to say words.

Her eyes were like stars and her lips were like soft hills rising out of dim, star-lit plains. "She is unattainable, she is far off like the stars," he thought. "She is unattainable like the stars but unlike the stars she breathes, she lives, like myself she has being."

One evening, some six weeks ago, the man who worked as foreman in the bicycle factory killed his wife and he is now in the courts being tried for murder. Every day the newspapers are filled with the story. On the evening of the murder he had taken his wife as usual to a picture show and they started home at nine. In Thirty-Second Street, at a corner near their apartment building, the figure of a man darted suddenly out of an alleyway and then darted back again. That incident may have put the idea of killing his wife into the man's head.

They got to the entrance to the apartment building and stepped into a dark hallway. Then quite suddenly and apparently without thought the man took a knife out of his pocket. "Suppose that man who darted into the alleyway had intended to kill us," he thought. Opening the knife he whirled about and struck his wife. He struck twice, a dozen times—madly. There was a scream and his wife's body fell.

The janitor had neglected to light the gas in the lower hallway. Afterward, the foreman decided that was the reason he did it, that and the fact that the dark slinking figure of a man darted out of an alleyway and then darted back again. "Surely," he told himself, "I could never have done it had the gas been lighted."

He stood in the hallway thinking. His wife was dead and with her had died her unborn child. There was a sound of doors opening in the apartments above. For several minutes nothing happened. His wife and her unborn child were dead—that was all.

He ran upstairs thinking quickly. In the darkness on the lower stairway he had put the knife back into his pocket and, as it turned out later, there was no blood on his hands or on his clothes. The knife he later washed carefully in the bathroom, when the excitement had died down a little. He told everyone the same story. "There has been a holdup," he explained. "A man came slinking out of an alleyway and followed me and my wife home. He followed us into the hallway of the building and there was no light." The janitor had neglected to light the gas. Well there had been a struggle and in the darkness his wife had been killed. He could not tell how it had happened. "There was no light. The janitor had neglected to light the gas," he kept saying.

For a day or two they did not question him specially and he had time to get rid of the knife. He took a long walk and threw it away into the river in South Chicago where the two abandoned coal barges lay rotting under the bridge, the bridge he had crossed when on the summer evenings he walked to the street car with the girl who was virginal and pure, who was far off and unattainable, like a star and yet not like a star.

And then he was arrested and right away he confessed—told everything. He said he did not know why he had killed his wife and was careful to say nothing of the girl at the office. The newspapers tried to discover the motive for the crime. They are still trying. Some one had seen him on the few evenings when he walked with the girl and she was dragged into the affair and had her picture printed in the paper. That has been annoying for her, as of course she has been able to prove she had nothing to do with the man.

Yesterday morning a heavy fog lay over our village here at the edge of the city and I went for a long walk in the early morning. As I returned out of the lowlands into our hill country I met the old man whose family has so many and such strange ramifications. For a time he walked beside me holding the little dog in his arms. It was cold and the dog whined and shivered. In the fog the old man's face was indistinct. It moved slowly back and forth with the fog banks of the upper air and with the tops of trees. He spoke of the man who has killed his wife and whose name is being shouted in the pages of the city newspapers that come to our village each morning. As he walked beside me he launched into a long tale concerning a life he and his brother, who had now become a murderer, had once lived together. "He is my brother," he said over and over, shaking his head. He seemed afraid I would not believe. There was a fact that must be established. "We were boys together, that man and I," he began again.

"You see we played together in a barn back of our father's house. Our father went away to sea in a ship. That is the way our names became confused. You understand that. We have different names but we are brothers. We had the same father. We played together in a barn back of our father's house. All day we lay together in the hay in the barn and it was warm there."

In the fog the slender body of the old man became like a little gnarled tree. Then it became a thing suspended in air. It swung back and forth like a body hanging on the gallows. The face beseeched me to believe the story the lips were trying to tell. In my mind everything concerning the relationship of men and women became confused, a muddle. The spirit of the man who had killed his wife came into the body of the little old man there by the roadside. It was striving to tell me the story it would never be able to tell in the courtroom in the city, in the presence of the judge. The whole story of mankind's loneliness, of the effort to reach out to unattainable beauty tried to get itself expressed from the lips of a mumbling old man, crazed with loneliness, who stood by the side of a country road on a foggy morning holding a little dog in his arms.

The arms of the old man held the dog so closely that it began to whine with pain. A sort of convulsion shook his body. The soul seemed striving to wrench itself out of the body, to fly away through the fog down across the plain to the city, to the singer, the politician, the millionaire, the murderer, to its brothers, cousins, sisters, down in the city. The intensity of the old man's desire was terrible and in sympathy my body began to tremble. His arms tightened about the body of the little dog so that it screamed with pain. I stepped forward and tore the arms away and the dog fell to the ground and lay whining. No doubt it had been injured. Perhaps ribs had been crushed. The old man stared at the dog lying at his feet as in the hallway of the apartment building the worker from the bicycle factory had stared at his dead wife. "We are brothers," he said again. "We have different names but we are brothers. Our father you understand went off to sea."

I am sitting in my house in the country and it rains. Before my eyes the hills fall suddenly away and there are the flat plains and beyond the plains the city. An hour ago the old man of the house in the forest went past my door and the little dog was not with him. It may be that as we talked in the fog he crushed the life out of his companion. It may be that the dog like the workman's wife and her unborn child is now dead. The leaves of the trees that line the road before my window are falling like rain—the yellow, red, and golden leaves fall straight down, heavily. The rain beats them brutally down. They are denied a last golden flash across the sky. In October leaves should be carried away, out over the plains, in a wind. They should go dancing away.

The Suitcase
by Meron Hadero

On Saba's last day in Addis Ababa, she had just one unchecked to-do left on her long and varied list, which was to explore the neighborhood on her own, even though she'd promised her relatives that she would always take someone with her when she left the house. But she was twenty, a grownup, and wanted to know that on her first-ever trip to this city of her birth, she'd gained at least some degree of independence and assimilation. So it happened that Saba had no one to turn to when she got to the intersection around Meskel Square and realized she had seen only one functioning traffic light in all of Addis Ababa, population four million people by official counts, though no one there seemed to trust official counts, and everyone assumed it was much more crowded, certainly too crowded for just one traffic light. That single, solitary, lonely little traffic light in this mushrooming metropolis was near the old National Theater, not too far from the UN offices, the presidential palace, the former African Union—a known, respected part of the city located an unfortunate mile (a disobliging 1.6 kilometers) away from where Saba stood before a sea of cars, contemplating a difficult crossing.

Small, nimble vehicles, Fiats and VW Bugs, skimmed the periphery of the traffic, then seemed to be flung off centrifugally, almost gleefully, in some random direction. The center was a tangled cluster of cars slowly crawling along paths that might take an automobile backward, forward, sideward. In the middle of this jam was a sometimes visible traffic cop whose tense job seemed to be avoiding getting hit while keeping one hand slightly in the air. He was battered by curses, car horns, diesel exhaust as he nervously shifted his body weight and tried to avoid these assaults. Saba quickly saw she couldn't rely on him to help her get across. She dipped her foot from the curb onto the street, and a car raced by, so she retreated. A man walked up next

---

"The Suitcase" by Meron Hadero. Copyright © 2016 by Meron Hadero, used by permission of The Wylie Agency LLC.

to her and said in English, "True story, I know a guy who crossed the street halfway and gave up."

Saba looked at the stranger. "Pardon, what was that?"

"He had been abroad for many years and came back expecting too much," the man said, now speaking as slowly as Saba. "That sad man lives on the median at the ring road. I bring him books sometimes," he said slyly, taking one out of his messenger bag and holding it up. "A little local wisdom: don't start what you can't finish." Saba watched the stranger dangle his toes off the curb, lean forward, backward, forward and back, and then, as if becoming one with the flow of the city, lunge into the traffic and disappear from her sight until he reemerged on the opposite sidewalk. "Miraculous," Saba said to herself as he turned, pointed at her, then held up the book again. Saba tried to follow his lead and set her body to the rhythm of the cars, swaying forward and back, but couldn't find the beat.

As she was running through her options, a line of idling taxis became suddenly visible when a city bus turned the corner. She realized that, as impractical as it seemed, she could hail a cab to get her across the busy street. The trip took ten minutes; the fare cost 15 USD, for she was unable to negotiate a better rate, though at least she'd found a way to the other side. She turned back to see the taxi driver leaning out the window talking to a few people, gesturing at her, laughing, and she knew just how badly she'd fumbled yet another attempt to fit in. All month Saba had failed almost every test she'd faced, and though she'd seized one last chance to see if this trip had changed her, had taught her at least a little of how to live in this culture, she'd only ended up proving her relatives right: she wasn't even equipped to go for a walk on her own. What she thought would be a romantic, monumental reunion with her home country had turned out to be a fiasco; she didn't belong here.

She was late getting back to her uncle Fassil's house, where family and friends of family were waiting for her to say goodbye, to chat and eat and see her one last time, departures being even more momentous than arrivals. Twelve chairs had been moved into the cramped living room. Along with the three couches, they transformed the space into a theater packed with guests, each of whom sat with his or her elbows pulled in toward the torso to make space for all. They came, they said, to offer help, but she sensed it was the kind of help that gave—and took.

It was time to go, and she was relieved when Fassil said—in English, for her benefit—"We are running out of time, so we have already started to fill this one for you." He pointed past the suitcase that Saba had packed before her walk and gestured to a second, stuffed with items and emitting the faint scent of a kitchen after mealtime. At her mother's insistence, Saba had brought one suitcase for her own clothes and personal items and a second that for the trip there was full of gifts from America—new and used clothes, old books, magazines, medicine—to give to family she had never met. For her return, it would be full of gifts to bring to America from those same relatives and family friends.

Saba knew this suitcase wasn't just a suitcase. She'd heard there was no DHL here, no UPS. Someone thought there was FedEx, but that was just for extremely wealthy businessmen. People didn't trust the government post. So Saba's suitcase offered coveted prime real estate on a vessel traveling between here and there. Everyone wanted a piece; everyone fought to stake a claim to their own space. If they couldn't secure a little spot in some luggage belonging to a traveling friend, they'd not send their things at all. The only reasonable alternative would be to have the items sent as freight on a cargo ship, and how reasonable was that? The shipping container would sail from Djibouti on the Red Sea (and with all the talk of Somali pirates, this seemed almost as risky as hurling a box into the ocean and waiting for the fickle tides). After the Red Sea, a cargo ship that made it through the Gulf of Aden would go south on the Indian Ocean, around the Cape of Good Hope, across the Atlantic, through the Panama Canal, to the Pacific, up the American coast to Seattle. An empty suitcase opened up a rare direct link between two worlds, so Saba understood why relatives and friends wanted to fill her bag with carefully wrapped food things, gifts, sundry items, making space, taking space, moving and shifting the bulging contents of the bag.

Fassil placed a scale in front of Saba and set to zeroing it. She leaned over the scale as he nudged the dial to the right. The red needle moved ever so slightly, so incredibly slightly that Saba doubted it worked at all, but then Fassil's hand slipped, the needle flew too far, to the other side of zero. He pushed the dial just a hair to the left now, and the red needle swung back by a full millimeter. He nudged the dial again; now it stuck.

"Fassil, Saba has to go," Lula said, shaking her hands like she was flicking them dry. "Let's get going. Her flight leaves in three hours, and with the traffic at Meskel Square and Bole Road . . ."

Saba leaned toward that wobbly needle as Fassil used his fingernail to gently coax the dial a breath closer. A tap, nearly there. A gentle pull.

"Looks good, Fassil," Saba said kindly but impatiently.

"It has to be precise," Fassil replied, then turned to the gathered crowd. "Look what you're making the poor girl carry." He pointed to that second suitcase.

Saba tried to lift it, but it was as heavy as an ox. Fassil rushed over and helped her pick it up, and when he felt its weight, he said, "There's no way they'll let her take this." The crowd was unhappy to hear that, and so was Saba. The room hummed with disapproval, punctuated with *tsk*s and clicked tongues. "I can just pay the fee," Saba quickly said, but Lula stood again, put up her hands, and boomed, "You will not pay a fee. It's too much money. You are *our* guest, and *our* guest will pay no fee!"

"It's okay," Saba said. "If we must, we must." But now the resistance came from everyone. Saba looked helplessly at Fassil. "Let me pay. I have to go. What else can I do?" she asked. She looked at the others and wondered if this was one of those times when a "No" was supposed to be followed by a "Please, yes!" "No, no." "Really, I insist." "No, we couldn't." "Really, yes, you must." "Okay." "Okay." Was it that kind of conversation? That call and response? Or was it the other kind, the "No, no!" "Really, I insist!" "No, we just couldn't." "Okay, no, then."

"Of course you can't pay. They will never let you," Fassil said, ending Saba's deliberation. He announced, "I'll weigh the suitcase," and there was a general sigh of approval. "But," Fassil continued, "if it's overweight, which it is, we are going to have to make some tough choices." He turned to Saba. "You are going to have to make some tough choices." She nodded and hoped silently that it would come in at weight, please. If she could be granted one earthly wish in this moment, that was what she would wish for. She watched Fassil heave the suitcase onto the scale and winced as the needle that hovered, almost vibrated, above zero shot to the right. Thirty kilos—ten kilos too heavy.

The crowd began to murmur anxiously, and a few shouted out sounds of frustration. Then one by one, the guests began to speak in turns, as if pleading their cases before a judge.

Konjit was the first up. She was old, at least seventy, a verified elder who settled disputes and brokered weddings and divorces, part of that council of respected persons that held a neighborhood together. As Konjit walked toward Saba, Saba bowed a little.

"Norr," Saba said, a sign of respect.

"Bugzer," Konjit replied, acknowledging that the order of things hadn't been completely turned on its head. Konjit lifted the edge of her shawl, flung it around her shoulder, and walked slowly right up to the suitcase and unzipped it. She took out a package of chickpeas and tossed it on the ground, and though someone grumbled at this, Konjit just smoothed her pressed hair behind her ears as if she were calming herself before an important announcement, an orator about to make a speech, an actress set to perform. Konjit held a hand up to the others who sat on the couches and chairs, and waited for total silence. Then she turned to Saba, put her hands on both her hips, which swayed as she stepped closer to Saba, and said in a low voice that filled the small space, "Please, Sabayaye, I haven't seen my grandchildren since they were two years old. How old are you?"

"Twenty," Saba said apologetically.

"Twenty? Ah, in all the time you've been alive in this world I have not seen them. Imagine! I'm old now. Who can even say how old I am? I'm too old to count and getting older. I want to send this bread so they know people here love them."

Most of the others in the room nodded in agreement, but not Rahel. Rahel shook her head as she stood from the couch and walked right up to Konjit, putting a hand on Konjit's arm. "Who can say how old you are, Konjit? Me, I can say how old you are. Not the number of years of course, but I can say for sure that I am older than you. One month, remember."

Rahel brought up that one-month position of seniority often, and Saba had come to expect it. Within just her first week there, Saba learned that Rahel and Konjit had grown up and grown old fighting often about things like which church had the most blessed holy water, Ledeta (Rahel) or Giorgis (Konjit), or whether it was better to use white teff flour (Konjit) or brown teff flour (Rahel), or where you could get the best deals on textiles, Mercato (Konjit) or Sheromeda (Rahel). Without fail, each argument ended with Rahel staking out a win by virtue of being slightly elder.

Rahel bent down and removed one of the three loaves of bread from the suitcase and tried to hand it back to Konjit, who refused to take it. Saba, wanting to hurry things along, reached out for the loaf, but Rahel placed the bread on the floor by her feet. "You can bake a loaf, Konjit, I give you that, but it takes you three hours to make that bread? Eh? I spent two days—two *days*—making this beautiful dorowat for my nephew. The power kept switching off. I had to go to Bole to freeze it in Sintayu's freezer, and she has all those kids and all those in-laws and hardly any space in her house, let alone her freezer, but still, that's what it took to make this beautiful wat. Then I had to wrap the container so tight that, should any melt in transit, it will stay safe and secure—and with these old old old fingers," she said, putting up her index, middle, and ring fingers. "Can you believe it? These old old fingers," she said, now raising her pinky and thumb. "These fingers a month older than yours, Konjit." She pulled Saba over and put her fanned fingers on Saba's left shoulder, leaning on her. "Just take this beautiful wat for me. It will be no problem, right?"

Before Saba could say that this seemed reasonable, Wurro walked up to Saba, and Saba shifted her attention again. "I may not be the oldest, and my hands don't ache like Rahel's, but please, think about this objectively, Saba," said Wurro, whose utilitarian views led her to make obviously questionable decisions, like employing fifteen workers in her small grocery so that fifteen more paychecks went out each month and fifteen more families would be happy, even if it put her one family on the verge of ruin. Wurro never argued her utilitarian views as forcefully, though, as when they matched her own purposes. She cleared her throat, and Saba waited for what she feared would be another well-argued plea. Wurro began, "If you don't send this bread, Konjit, your family will still eat bread. If you don't send this wat, Rahel, your family will still eat wat." Wurro took Saba's hand and said, "My niece had a difficult pregnancy. You have to take this gunfo because if you don't take it, well, there is no way to get gunfo in America, and who has ever heard of a woman not eating gunfo after labor? If you don't bring it, she won't have it. Milk for the baby, gunfo for the mother. It's natural logic. You can't deny it."

"But American women don't eat gunfo. Do they eat gunfo, Saba?" asked Lula.

"She's never been pregnant in America, right? How would she know?" asked Wurro.

"She's never been pregnant here. Does she even know gunfo?" Konjit asked.

Saba said, "I know gunfo," and was met with whispered words of approval, so she refrained from adding how hard she had to swallow to get a spoonful down of the thick paste made from (she'd heard) corn, wheat, barley, or banana root, she wasn't even sure. Whatever gunfo was, she'd rather not bring it, if it was up to her, but she wasn't actually sure of that either. Was it up to her?

"Saba is a smart girl," Lula said. "She probably read *at least* ten books in the four weeks she was here." Saba felt guilty then, because it was true that she had declined as many invitations as she accepted, choosing sometimes to read alone at home. "She must know Americans have high-tech things for women after their pregnancies. They don't need gunfo," Lula said, rearranging the contents of the suitcase to make room for her own package. "But you know what they do need in America? Have you ever tasted American butter?"

Lula looked at the others as if this would end the discussion. She stood up, opened her arms. "Have you had American butter?" No one spoke. Saba kept quiet, for of course she had eaten American butter, but what good would it do to mention that now? Besides, few had the courage to challenge strong-willed Lula, even with the truth.

Chapter 6: The Literature Essay   **245**

"No one here has ever had American butter, so then that settles it." Lula took out another of Konjit's loaves of bread and a bag of roasted grains. "*I* have eaten American butter. *I* have tasted it with my own tongue. *I* can say with certainty that American butter is only the milk part, no spices, no flavor. It just tastes like fat. Please bring this butter to my best friend for her wedding banquet," Lula said with her hands now pressed over her heart and looking pleadingly at Saba. "Ahwe, her wedding! And what a feat to get that man to the altar. His gambling and staying out late and—"

"Aye aye aye," Konjit interrupted, shaking her head and removing Lula's butter and putting a second loaf back into the suitcase. "You want her to bring butter so your friend can marry a bad man? Have you ever heard such nonsense?" Konjit asked Saba. Saba shrugged, and Konjit said, "See, she has never heard such nonsense," and Saba didn't have the heart to correct her and didn't have the heart not to correct her, and she didn't know which would have helped her bring this to the right resolution, so she just made a vague gesture and let them finish.

"He is not a bad man, just a *man* man," Lula said.

"Well, my son is a *good* man raising *good* grandchildren. Lula, my son brought you the stretchy pants you asked for from America when he visited. Wurro, my son brought you a laptop last time he came. Rahel, he brought you cereal with raisins, the kind you always ask for. Fassil, he brought you books, since you have long gone through everything at every library here, I assume. Saba, one day if you live in Ethiopia, he will bring you something too, anything you ask. Name something you miss here."

"Too much talk, Konjit!" Rahel yelled. "The traffic, she has to go!"

Konjit swatted away Rahel's interruption and gestured to Saba.

Saba tried to think of what to say. She didn't want to offend them by making them believe she had lacked for anything. She remembered how hurt Konjit had been when Saba visited after lunchtime, only to find a full meal waiting for her. When Saba refused, Konjit insisted that the dishes were very clean and the food fresh. That wasn't as bad, though, as sitting down to eat "just a little" and passing on the salad, the water, the cheese, the fruit, eating only the lentils and bread, accepting some coffee but not even the milk. "You have all been so kind to me," Saba said, bowing respectfully, pronouncing all her syllables perfectly, precisely, as quickly as she could. "I have not missed a thing. But it's late, and it's true, the traffic is bad . . ."

Konjit dismissed Saba. "She has learned the Ethiopian way. Good girl. Too polite to say you need anything here," Konjit replied, putting an arm on Saba's shoulder. Konjit continued, "Okay, don't tell us, that's okay. But if you visit again to stay a while, and if you find you are homesick for something you grew accustomed to there in America, my son will bring it. He is a good son. I am asking you to take two loaves of bread. Okay, forget about the third, I don't want to ask too much of you, even though I am an old lady who has not seen her grandchildren in, oh, who knows how long. But these two loaves must stay in the suitcase, two loaves for my three grandchildren so they know I am thinking about them. That I have not forgotten them." Saba could see that Konjit was too proud to say what she really meant: she didn't want her grandchildren to forget about her, a fear she must bear, living so far away for so many years with only limited lines of connection.

Konjit's argument hung there in the air until Fikru stood hesitantly and walked over to the suitcase, finding his bags of spices on the floor beside it. He reached into the suitcase and took out three Amharic-English dictionaries and tossed them onto the coffee table. Hanna shouted out, "Aye! Why, Fikru, would you do that?" She ran over and picked up the books, then threw them back in, but Konjit took them out, for they crushed her bread.

Fikru, who kept opening his mouth to speak but found himself overpowered by the more forceful voices, seized his opportunity like a fourth-chair orchestral musician stealing a flourish at the end of a number. He stood next to an overwhelmed Saba and said, "Everyone here has a relative in Seattle, yes? Then why is it that only my son is going to pick Saba up from the airport?" He turned to the others. "You talk about what so-and-so needs or has done, but my son, without asking for anything, has volunteered to get her. He will be carrying this heavy suitcase to his car. Then he will take her to her dorm and bring this heavy suitcase up the stairs, if there are stairs, or down the hall, should there be a hall. What can it hurt to bring a few items for him?" Fikru showed Saba his items. "Just a few bags of spices: corrorima, grain of paradise, berbere. Please, Saba, a humble parcel for my humble son."

Saba turned to her uncle Fassil and discreetly pointed to her watch. "Okay, you all have something to say," Fassil offered, cutting off the remaining guests who gathered around the suitcase, eager to make their appeals. "But the traffic!"

"Yes, the traffic," said Fikru.

"The traffic," Rahel and Konjit said in unison, and Lula nodded.

Fassil turned to Saba. She asked him, "What do you want to do?"

"What do *you* want to do?" Fassil asked her. Though each person in that room had his or her body turned to the suitcase, all eyes were on Saba, who was trying to figure out how to navigate this scene. They looked her over and imagined she looked so . . . what? Different? Just . . . apart with her woven bag, which intermittently glowed with the light from her iPhone or beeped and pinged and vibrated from the sound of her other gadgetry, her American jeans tucked into tall leather boots, a white button-down shirt and gold earrings, while they wore modest clothes and hand-me-downs, some of which she had brought herself.

She had been in the country one whole month and had tried, they must know, to learn the culture, to reacquaint herself with her first home and fit in. And now, here she stood, on the last moments of her last day, still not sure what to do, while they looked at her lovingly and with curiosity too. Saba felt the weight of choosing what should be taken and what should be left behind. She was looking for a way out and a way in, but she realized there really were no shortcuts here.

"You have all been so kind," Saba said. "Rahel, you took me to listen to the Azmaris sing," she said, omitting that she had been too shy to dance such unfamiliar dances no matter how encouraging Rahel had been. A few days later, Rahel came back to take her to one of the fancy new hotels where an American cover band played to a foreign crowd, and Saba pretended to like being there. She imagined Rahel had pretended too.

"Wurro, you took me to the holiday dinner, and we ate that delicious raw meat," Saba said, of course not mentioning that Fassil had to take her to the clinic the next day to get Cipro for her stomach cramps.

"Fikru, you brought me to Mercato to buy a dress," Saba said. But what she most remembered was spending the trip chasing after him through the labyrinthine alleyways; every so often, when Fikru looked back at her, she would wave and smile, and he'd keep going, losing her twice.

She remembered the man with the messenger bag that morning, the one who had crossed the street, and his warning about starting things you can't finish or giving up too soon. Saba walked to the suitcase she had packed herself, filled with her own things, and in one quick gesture opened it, emptied the contents. Her best clothes fell to the floor: her favorite old jeans, most sophisticated dresses, her one polished blazer, a new pair of rain boots, T-shirts collected from concerts and trips and old relationships. She pushed this empty suitcase to the center of the room.

"Dear friends, neighbors, and relatives," she said in forced Amharic, looking at the confused expressions that confronted her, "please, now there is room for it all."

There were gasps, whispers, whistles, an inexplicable loud thud, but no laughter.

"Are you sure?" Fikru asked.

"This is the least I can do," Saba said slowly. "It is the least I can do."

"What about your belongings?" Fassil asked.

"We'll keep them safe for her in case she returns," Konjit said, her voice commanding the space.

"*Until* she returns," Rahel corrected.

"Until you return?" Konjit asked, and Saba said yes.

Fassil got a bag, put Saba's things in, and told her he would store it in his own closet. The two suitcases were packed, weighed (the room applauded when both came in just under the limit), and thrown into the trunk of Fassil's car, which sagged a little in the rear. There were three cars in their little caravan that headed to the airport. The ride was slow. The weight of the overfull cars possibly complicated the trip, as did the rocky side streets and, of course, the congestion at the difficult intersections. They pressed on, and they reached the airport with absolutely no time to spare. Saba said quick, heartfelt goodbyes, thank-yous, made fresh promises, then pulled the two big suitcases onto a luggage cart. Her family and friends of family watched from the waiting area as she moved quickly through the line to get her boarding pass. They looked on as the two suitcases were weighed and thrown on the screening belt, and they saw her pass the main checkpoint. Every time she looked back to the lobby, she could catch glimpses of them on tiptoe, waiting to see if they might connect with her one more time.

Border Lines
by Alberto Ríos

A weight carried by two
Weighs only half as much

The world on a map looks like the drawing of a cow
In a butcher's shop, all those lines showing
Where to cut.

That drawing of the cow is also a jigsaw puzzle,
Showing just as much how very well
All the strange parts fit together.

Which way we look at the drawing
Makes all the difference.
We seem to live in a world of maps:

But in truth we live in a world made
Not of paper and ink but of people.
Those lines are our lives. Together,

Let us turn the map until we see clearly:
The border is what joins us,
Not what separates us.

Alberto Ríos, "Border Lines" from *A Small Story About the Sky*. Copyright © 2015 by Alberto Ríos. Reprinted with permission of The Permissions Company, Inc. on behalf of Copper Canyon Press, www.coppercanyonpress.org.

Mending Wall
by Robert Frost

Something there is that doesn't love a wall,
That sends the frozen-ground-swell under it,
And spills the upper boulders in the sun;
And makes gaps even two can pass abreast.
The work of hunters is another thing:
I have come after them and made repair
Where they have left not one stone on a stone,
But they would have the rabbit out of hiding,
To please the yelping dogs. The gaps I mean,
No one has seen them made or heard them made,
But at spring mending-time we find them there.
I let my neighbor know beyond the hill;
And on a day we meet to walk the line
And set the wall between us once again.
We keep the wall between us as we go.
To each the boulders that have fallen to each.
And some are loaves and some so nearly balls
We have to use a spell to make them balance:
"Stay where you are until our backs are turned!"
We wear our fingers rough with handling them.
Oh, just another kind of out-door game,
One on a side. It comes to little more:
There where it is we do not need the wall:
He is all pine and I am apple orchard.
My apple trees will never get across
And eat the cones under his pines, I tell him.
He only says, "Good fences make good neighbors."
Spring is the mischief in me, and I wonder
If I could put a notion in his head:
"*Why* do they make good neighbors? Isn't it

Source: Robert Frost, 1914

Where there are cows? But here there are no cows.
Before I built a wall I'd ask to know
What I was walling in or walling out,
And to whom I was like to give offense.
Something there is that doesn't love a wall,
That wants it down." I could say "Elves" to him,
But it's not elves exactly, and I'd rather
He said it for himself. I see him there
Bringing a stone grasped firmly by the top
In each hand, like an old-stone savage armed.
He moves in darkness as it seems to me,
Not of woods only and the shade of trees.
He will not go behind his father's saying,
And he likes having thought of it so well
He says again, "Good fences make good neighbors."

Inventing New Bodies
by Christine Boyka Kluge

We become small, we become soft. We turn ourselves inside-out, inventing new bodies. Our skins of oiled silk glide over the beaded grass. For a season, even our ribs disappear. Our hearts expand, ripening like cherries.

Night creatures, we hide from the sun's fierce eye. We fear the feet of heedless humans. We tamp each other into acorn caps, escape beneath fallen branches and moss-haired stones. We sleep for a long time, changing.

In the darkness, only our eyes stay hard. Even dreaming, they never close. They glint like diamond chips at the ends of stalks. Our nights grow infinite, blossoming into secret days. Flowers and leaves are our only lanterns. Veins of roses glow like forked lightning. Maple leaves furl and unfurl, beckoning fingers. We are always hungry. The stars call us to dinner.

Trailing silvery paths across brick walks and patios, we slip into gardens and flowerpots. We paint patterns, leaf to leaf. We fasten our mouths to petals and stems and swallow, knowing nothing but sweetness. We are lost, eating your invisible world.

Come dawn, we disappear. We retreat into tunnels, wrap ourselves in shadows. Swollen with night's offerings, we curl into dreams.

You never hear our slithery music, the sound of molten bronze crawling in rivulets through the lawn. You never look down in search of beauty. Humans rarely do. You only see the holes, the lace made of raspberry and geranium leaves. Angered, you leave us saucers of terrible ale. You sprinkle us with salt like stinging snow. A blind giant, you march across our intricate art, never noticing the glittering graffiti that clings to the soles of your shoes.

"Inventing New Bodies" first appeared in *The Bitter Oleander*, then was published in *Stirring the Mirror*, the author's collection from Bitter Oleander Press. Copyright © by Christine Boyka Kluge. Reprinted by permission.

Black Pearl
by Christine Boyka Kluge

I'm sure she stumbled for miles in high school, that loss cutting into her sole like crushed glass in her shoe, until the drowning dulled and death glowed like a black pearl, pain's accretion of dark luster. She held out the pearl of her father's death like a prize, something we might be tempted to snatch, that kept us in a fascinated circle around her tear-stained face. Teenagers, we were hooked by this mystery and sadness, lured by the story of the tipped boat, the hole in the water he had vanished through.

We all leaned forward when she cried, alarmed by her face, puckered red and ugly as a neglected baby's. But we were drawn to that smoky pearl, grief's sharp-edged grit transformed to strange beauty. We all longed to touch its satin and shiver, but none of us wanted to hold the cold sphere within her own fist.

She looked up at us from our cafeteria table, as if she had dived to the dark bottom of the sea with her father, then alone dared to rise. The pearl of his last breath was cupped in her hands like an iridescent bubble of air, lifting her back to the surface, where light was captured in the water's crazed glass. Beyond that shattered pane, she searched for our soft, blurred faces looking down from their great height, from the safe, sunlit ledge she might never climb back to again.

"Black Pearl" first appeared in *The Bitter Oleander*, then in No Boundaries: Prose Poems by 24 American Poets, an anthology from Tupelo Press; then in *Stirring the Mirror*, the author's collection from Bitter Oleander Press. Copyright © by Christine Boyka Kluge. Reprinted by permission.

The World Is Too Much with Us
by William Wordsworth

The world is too much with us; late and soon,
Getting and spending, we lay waste our powers;—
Little we see in Nature that is ours;
We have given our hearts away, a sordid boon!
This Sea that bares her bosom to the moon;
The winds that will be howling at all hours,
And are up-gathered now like sleeping flowers;
For this, for everything, we are out of tune;
It moves us not. Great God! I'd rather be
A Pagan suckled in a creed outworn;
So might I, standing on this pleasant lea,
Have glimpses that would make me less forlorn;
Have sight of Proteus rising from the sea;
Or hear old Triton blow his wreathèd horn.

Source: Williams Wordsworth, 1807

Leaving Forever
by Denise Levertov

He says the waves in the ship's wake
are like stones rolling away.
I don't see it that way.
But I see the mountain turning,
turning away its face as the ship
takes us away.

By Denise Levertov, from *Poems 1960–1967*, copyright © 1964 by Denise Levertov. Reprinted by permission of New Directions Publishing Corporation.

Chapter 6: The Literature Essay

Higgins 1

Kassity Higgins

Professor Moffett

English 102

8 April 2022

Othello: Three Deaths and a Promotion

Dear Sheryl,

I thought about what you said in the employee bathroom yesterday, about William Shakespeare's hallmark tragedy *Othello* and the cost-benefit analysis of Iago's impromptu revenge plot. We discussed over intermittent flushes the villainous ensign's haphazard scheme to destroy Othello's good standing in the Venetian army and usurp Cassio as a lieutenant, a title Iago believed to be rightfully his. I didn't realize it at the time, as we passed a square of toilet paper beneath the stall partition and paused to eavesdrop on Jennifer's conversation (did you see the travesty she was wearing?), what a brilliant idea it was to tabulate Iago's actions like expenditures on an H&R Block tax sheet. Call it divine providence, but with all this talk of an advancement going around, I think we should ready ourselves with a little preemptive homework. Also, keep your eye on Tiffany. I don't trust her.

As you know, *Othello* kicks off with Iago's petty and seemingly knee-jerk decision to upset Othello's father-in-law, Brabantio, with news of the Venetian general's elopement with

© Kassity Higgins

Brabantio's daughter, Desdemona. Given a vague idea of destroying Othello's marriage, Iago indeterminately weaponizes his colleague Roderigo's unrequited love of Desdemona for later use in Cyprus. By telling Roderigo the lie that Desdemona loves Cassio, he refocuses Roderigo's anguish into a shared ambition to dismiss Cassio by goading the lieutenant's misconduct via drunken fisticuffs. Iago posits that siccing Cassio on Desdemona in an effort to reinstate the former lieutenant's title can, thus, be misconstrued by Othello as a scandal. Iago reinforces the narrative of an extramarital affair by planting Desdemona's handkerchief in Cassio's room. Othello, satisfied with the physical proof, vows to kill Desdemona; Iago, in turn, agrees to kill Cassio. Iago, however, consigns the task to Roderigo by convincing him that *he* must murder Cassio to delay Desdemona's departure from Cyprus. The resultant scuffle leaves both Roderigo and Cassio injured. Othello, spurred into action by the chaos, leaves to murder Desdemona, in whose bedroom he is eventually discovered by Emilia, Iago's wife and Desdemona's attendant. Emilia divulges Iago's subterfuge and is unceremoniously slain by her wrathful husband. At last, Othello kills himself in anguish, and Iago is taken into custody. Fridays, am I right?

    Let's face it, Sheryl, knowing what we do about Shakespearean tragedies, Iago should have counted Cassio's demotion as the ultimate win and pulled the emergency brake. Cassio's voluntary consumption of alcohol, and Othello's apparent promotion of a social alcoholic, achieves something akin to the desired effect. Cassio warns us several times that he is prone to excess: "I have very poor and / unhappy brains for drinking" (Shakespeare 2.3.34-35), and again, "I am (unfortunate) in the infirmity and / dare not task my weakness with any more" (2.3.42-43). Although we may never accurately measure the precipitous fallout of these events, I remain convinced that they would have sufficed in terms of *emotional compensation*. The mantle of lieutenant will have been vacated and Cassio's dismissal on the heels of his promotion would no doubt reflect poorly on the judgment of his superior officer, Othello. Mission, I dare say, accomplished.

Of course, Iago desires far more than the pleasure of watching Othello fall from grace and Cassio lose his station. Iago desires the lieutenancy for himself and achieves as much by feeding into Othello's paranoia that his wife, Desdemona, is being unfaithful. By presenting himself as a support system in Othello's time of need, Iago curries the general's favor with relative ease. Othello expresses his appreciation of Iago's assistance mere moments after granting him the lieutenancy: "I greet thy love / Not with vain thanks but with acceptance bounteous, / And will upon the instant put thee to 't" (3.3.533-

260   **Chapter 6:** The Literature Essay

Higgins 4

36). After Othello mistreats Desdemona in full view of Lodovico, Brabantio's kinsman, Iago again achieves some semblance of his original plan, as we might then assume that Lodovico will forward these events to Desdemona's father.

    Now, take notes, Sheryl, because through Iago's actions I have found a correlation between outsourcing tasks to various pawns and the growing precariousness of a covert operation. That is to say, the more people you involve, the less likely you are to succeed sans casualties. Iago realizes too little too late that Desdemona's handkerchief is not a diamond in the rough but rather fool's gold, tempting the untrained eye into an investment pitfall whence he would never recover. Emilia, Iago's wife, is both the landmine *and* the casualty of her husband's, quite frankly, *amateur* revenge plot. Maybe I'm old-fashioned, but I tally the loss of a spouse as a failed business venture. Iago, who screams, "Villainous whore!" (5.2.273) before cutting down his wife, might disagree on account of Emilia's unwavering loyalty to her mistress. However, I submit to you that a wife lost—loyal or not—is still a loss. With Iago having been branded a conspirator and a murderer, his sexual appeal took a massive hit in the Venetian dating market. His chances of procuring another wife are slim at best.

    Iago's ultimate loss, Sheryl, is his freedom. Lodovico lands the final blow to Iago's scheme when he addresses Cassio of all men, "To you, lord governor, / Remains the censure of this hellish villain" (5.2.430-432). Iago is theretofore doomed to be prosecuted by the very man to whom Othello initially granted the lieutenancy. In one fell swoop, Iago's goal is upended; he loses his reputation and the lieutenancy (again). There is no worse outcome, I believe, than to achieve the exact *opposite* of what you originally planned.

    At long last, Sheryl, we must ask ourselves if the costs of Iago's actions outweigh the benefits. Yes, they do. Unless death was Iago's primary goal, his investment practices fail miserably to produce the desired results. His lieutenancy is short-lived and suffers from a severe shortage of wives. One might total Iago's losses as several, but let's not pretend that Roderigo's injury and Othello's and Desdemona's deaths registered as costs on our villainous ensign. Supposing Emilia's loyalty to her husband had surpassed that to her mistress and she had kept quiet about Iago's schemes, then his plan may have, at a time, been cost-efficient at two deaths and a promotion. Now, Sheryl, I must ask the ultimate question: To whom are you most loyal?

Works Cited

Shakespeare, William. *The Tragedy of Othello, the Moor of Venice.* Edited by Barbara Mowatt and Paul Werstine, Simon and Schuster Paperbacks, 2009.

Chapter 6: The Literature Essay

Joshua Dycus

Professor Moffett

English 223

13 December 2021

Father Earth, the Tyrant

    The novel *The Fifth Season* by N. K. Jemisin tells the story of Essun, also known as Syenite and Damaya, a magical channeler of thermal and kinetic energies known as an orogene or derogatorily as a rogga. It details her struggle for survival on a hostile planet characterized by frequent seismic activity and among a populace that views her and her kind as subhuman monsters to be killed or enslaved. An interesting aspect of the story is the anthropomorphism of Father Earth because it reveals that the people of the Stillness have cast the planet itself in the archetypal role of the Tyrant. Accordingly, they seek to appease him through sacrifice, take from his vast wealth of hoarded resources, and ultimately free themselves of his tyrannical influence through force.

    Before analyzing how the citizens of the Stillness characterize their planet, we should define some key terms. The archetypal role of the Tyrant is embodied in "any figure of abusive power or authority, especially a parental figure" (Moffett 3), who often begins as a beneficent leader. However, "differences in his psychology and behavior" (Moffett 3) lead the

© Joshua Dycus

264 Chapter 6: The Literature Essay

Dycus 2

Tyrant astray and cause him to become greedy, dictatorial, and even abusive towards his subjects. This is in stark contrast to the archetypal role of the Chief who "dispenses justice wisely . . . and liberally rewards his subjects" (Moffett 4). These negative attributes typically manifest in three aspects of the Tyrant: The Predator, characterized by the malevolent Tyrant "[wandering] about the world looking for victims" (Moffett 8); the "passive role" (Moffett 9) of the Holdfast, characterized by a greedy hoarding of valuable resources or life-giving boons; and the violent Avenger who lashes out "[i]f his lair is threatened or violated" (Moffett 10).

    The planet Earth is not literally the king or father of the people living on its surface, but he is characterized as such by the Lorists of the Stillness "who [study] stonelore and lost history" (Jemisin 461) to preserve the wisdom of previous civilizations. They mainly do this in the form of myths and historical legends. In these myths, the planet is cast in the role of an angry and violent father who abandoned his responsibility to shepherd life on his surface after humanity gravely wounded him by destroying the Moon:

> [O]nce upon a time Earth did everything he could to facilitate the strange emergence of life on his surface. . . . He did not create life—that was happenstance—but he was pleased and fascinated by it. . . . Then people

Chapter 6: The Literature Essay   **265**

Dycus 3

began to do horrible things to Father Earth. . . . And at
the height of human hubris and might, it was the orogenes
who did something that even Earth could not forgive: They
destroyed his only child. (Jemisin 379-380)

By anthropomorphizing the planet to have wrathful emotions, the ancient societies who passed these stories down have devised a way to communicate the violent and unstable nature of a moonless Earth without relying on concepts like science which is easy to lose during an apocalyptic event. The myth of Father Earth teaches the inhabitants of the Stillness to expect nothing but pain and greed from their planet and serves as an easy explanation for its tyrannical nature.

    Before he became the Tyrant, Father Earth suffered greatly at the hands of mankind: "They poisoned waters beyond even his ability to cleanse, and killed much of the other life that lived on his surface. They drilled through the crust of his skin, past the blood of his mantle, to get at the sweet marrow of his bones" (Jemisin 379). They also likely killed his mate—"Life had a mother, too. Something terrible happened to Her" (Jemisin 115)—although this may be another allusion to the destruction of the Moon. This violation of his "lair" (Moffett 10) precipitated the shift from generous caretaker to vengeance-seeking Avenger: "Father Earth's surface cracked like an eggshell. Nearly every living thing died as his fury became manifest in the first and most terrible of the Fifth Seasons: The Shattering Season" (Jemisin 380). This retribution marked an end to the halcyon days of consistent, temperate seasons on the planet and instilled in the mythological character of Father Earth an abiding hatred of humanity whom "He has burned with hatred for . . . ever since" (Jemisin 115).

    The people of the Stillness use this trait of Father Earth to explain why the planet "no longer [grants them] the boons of the cosmic source" (Moffett 5) by enabling life to flourish on his surface. This retention of resources is characteristic of the aspect of the Tyrant Joseph Campbell described as the Tyrant Holdfast who hoards "the general benefit" (qtd. in Moffett 5) and "[b]lights [the] lives" (qtd. in Moffett 5) of the orogenes he favors with access to his accumulated wealth of power:

> When Father Earth stirs, he unleashes so much raw power that taking some of it does no harm to you or anyone else. . . . When there is no earth-power nearby, an orogene can still make the earth move, but only by taking the necessary heat and force and motion from the things around her . . . even rocks. And, of course, living things . . . despite all your terrible power. . . . You can be beaten. . . . We learn how orogenic power works, and we find ways to use this knowledge against you. (Jemisin 91-93)

Chapter 6: The Literature Essay   **267**

The institutionalized fear of the Tyrant Earth instilled in the populace of the Stillness through mythological tradition and stonelore has permanently associated the earth-shifting orogenes with the horrific violence of Father Earth. This fear is compounded by the tendency of untrained orogenes to lose control of their powers, resulting in unpredictable surges of destruction that mirror the third aspect of the Tyrant.

    The Predator aspect of the Tyrant is "his active role" (Moffett 8), characterized by the Tyrant seeking out victims and "spreading fear and destruction" (qtd. in Moffett 8) throughout his domain. The Predator is the aspect most predominantly experienced by the citizens of the Stillness as Father Earth's constantly shifting plates ensure that the question on all their minds isn't if the next earthquake will come, but when it will hit and how severe it will be:

> The people of the Stillness live in a perpetual state of disaster preparedness. They've built walls and dug wells and put away food, and they can easily last five, ten, even twenty-five years in a world without a sun. . . . [P]eople here build for the inevitability of shakes. (Jemisin 8-9)

By infusing their stonelore, architecture, and worldview with the fear of Father Earth's predatory destruction, often on an apocalyptic scale, the people of the Stillness have developed an attitude of subsistence even in the best of times. Survival is the best they can manage until the reign of the Tyrant comes to an end.

The end of the Tyrant's story in *The Fifth Season* is the predominant focus of the present-day, Essun sections of the book. Traditionally, the threat represented by the Tyrant resolves when "The source of the Tyrant's power is destroyed. . . . The Tyrant himself is crushed [or]. . . . The Tyrant has a change of heart and is redeemed" (Moffett 11). Crushing their home planet or destroying the geothermal energy that enables their existence is hardly an option for the victims of Father Earth, but Alabaster's destruction of the infrastructure restricting seismic activity and initiation of an especially apocalyptic Fifth Season has begun a process that he believes may redeem the Tyrant:

> His fingers spread and twitch as he feels several reverberating points on the map of his awareness: his fellow slaves. He cannot free them, not in the practical sense. He's tried before and failed. He can, however, make their suffering serve a cause greater than one city's hubris, and one empire's fear. (Jemisin 7)

His belief in the redemption of Father Earth through the destruction of the established order is later adopted by Essun:

> "It was collateral damage, but Yumenes got what it deserved. No, what I want you to do, my Damaya, my Syenite, my Essun, is make it worse. . . ." Then he leans forward. . . . But

Chapter 6: The Literature Essay   **269**

> when he is close enough, he grins again, and suddenly it hits you. Evil, eating, Earth. He's not crazy at all, and he never has been. (Jemisin 449)

While *The Fifth Season* is only the first in a trilogy relating the adventures of Essun and "*the way the world ends*. For the last time" (Jemisin 14), the nature of the story so far makes it clear that Alabaster has no remaining motivation other than the liberation of the orogenes. The only practical way to do that is to eliminate the status quo of dehumanization and fear enforced by the stonelore. Invalidating the stonelore can only be accomplished by rehabilitating the Tyrant whose influence necessitates its adherence.

    By casting Father Earth in the role of the Tyrant, N. K. Jemisin has created a dystopia where one cannot count on the very earth beneath one's feet for stability. The result is a society characterized by a deep-rooted paranoia and a willingness to make horrible sacrifices for peace of mind, however fleeting it may be. That fearful attitude facilitates the exploitation of the orogenes and normalizes hatred of them as avatars of the hated Tyrant. The resulting atmosphere of institutionalized oppression and paranoia is entrenched so firmly that the orogenes have no options available for peaceful change. Alabaster's cataclysm serves as a final act of rebellion and revolution, an attempt to dethrone the Tyrant and the terroristic status quo his domination

                                                                Dycus 8

maintains, or at least to reform Father Earth and in part restore
the boon of life that allows humanity to flourish.

Dycus 9

Works Cited

Jemisin, N. K. *The Fifth Season: The Broken Earth, Book One.* 1st ed., Orbit, 2015.

Moffett, Todd. "The Primal Village-Tyrant." *English 223: Science Fiction Literature*, College of Southern Nevada, csn.instructure.com/courses/1350299/files/63151407?module_item_id=15195934.

Discussion Questions for Chapter 6

For Edgar Allan Poe

1. What is the setting for "The Cask of Amontillado"? How does the setting affect the events of the story?
2. There is strong evidence of a loop plot underneath "The Cask of Amontillado." What is this evidence? Explain.
3. Is Montresor a first-person processional or first-person confessional narrator? What is your evidence?
4. How reliable do you find Montresor as the narrator? What evidence exists to suggest he is not reliable?

For Kate Chopin

1. At what level would you place the conflict faced by Mrs. Mallard: internal, personal, or extrapersonal? Why? Which form of the one-character plot does it follow: the identity, the repression, or the survival? Why?
2. Why does Chopin tell the story from a third-person and not a first-person point of view? What are the benefits and the drawbacks of this choice? Is the story past-focused or future-focused? How can you tell?
3. Chopin uses very little dialogue in the story. Why do you think so little would be used? Do you agree with this decision? If yes, why? If you think the story would benefit from more dialogue, explain why and where dialogue is needed.

For Sherwood Anderson

1. "Brothers" is told in an unconventional fashion: without the usual techniques of plot structure. What exactly is the form of this story? What is one of its major themes?
2. What point of view is this story told through? Who is our narrator? Do you think this narrator is reliable? Why or why not? How would the story, and the point of view, have changed if

the story had been simply about the workingman, his wife, and the young woman from Iowa?
3. Three times the story mentions the colors of the leaves and their fall from the trees. What is the significance of this image? Why is the image placed where it is in the story?
4. The triad of the ladies of duty and pleasure, one of the three-character plots described in the chapter headnotes above, seems to appear in this story. Which characters fill these roles? What is the outcome of this plot as it appears in the story?

For Meron Hadero

1. Even though Saba is visiting Ethiopia, the country of her birth, there are multiple moments in the story when she feels like an outsider. Name five of these moments. How are the moments complicated by her family members' reactions, customs, and treatment of her?
2. During Saba's family's debate about what she should take home with her to Seattle in her second suitcase, Saba appears helpless to mediate the conversation. Have you ever, like Saba, been placed in a situation where your actions were complicated or exploited because of the motives of others? How did you resolve your situation? Be specific.
3. At the opening of the story, Saba meets a stranger who offers her a piece of "wisdom" about crossing the busy intersection in Meskel Square; he tells her in English, "Don't start what you can't finish." How do his words affect the choice she makes at the end of the story? Do you view his words as wise for Saba? Explain.
4. The story contains allusions to ancient mythic conceptions of the journey the soul makes to the land of the dead. What are those conceptions? How do they appear in Hadero's story? How are they relevant to Saba's own journey?

For Alberto Ríos

1. In "Border Lines," what simile opens the poem? How does it set the mood for the rest of the poem?
2. Is Ríos's poem a narrative or a lyric? If the former, what story does it tell? If the latter, what is the central image that shapes the rest of the poem?
3. The first four stanzas of "Border Lines" seem to make assertions: descriptions, observations, statements. The last stanza, however, seems to have a different purpose. What is it? And how is that purpose signaled?

For Robert Frost

1. In "Mending Wall," whom is the speaker addressing, his neighbor or someone else outside the poem? What is his purpose for speaking to this audience?
2. The central image of Frost's poem is a wall. What symbolism surrounds this image? How does it compare to the meaning and the purpose of the border described in Alberto Ríos's poem?
3. "Mending Wall," at first glance, would appear to be an open-form poem. But look at the line lengths and the syllable patterns. Do you see any similarities between the lines?

For Christine Boyka Kluge

1. In "Inventing New Bodies," whose bodies are being invented? What details in the poem give clues to their identity?
2. "Inventing New Bodies" is strongly lyrical, but there is also a conflict at the heart of it. What kind of conflict: internal, personal, or extrapersonal? What makes up this conflict?
3. "Inventing New Bodies" relies on one of the figures of speech, personification, mentioned earlier in this chapter. What is personification, and how is it used in the poem? What other figures of speech can you find?

4. Kluge's poem "Black Pearl" and Violet E. Baldwin's essay "Drowning," which appears in chapter two, speak of a similar event, but with decidedly different outcomes. What happens in the poem that is different from what happens in the essay?
5. Who is the speaker in "Black Pearl"? What do we gain from hearing this speaker that we would not if the poem had been told through the perspective of the unfortunate girl?
6. What is the "ledge" mentioned in the last lines of "Black Pearl"? Why can't the unfortunate girl climb to it? What symbolic meaning might be behind the image?

For William Wordsworth

1. Wordsworth's poem "The World Is Too Much with Us" deals with the conflict between the City and the Wilderness. Which images in the poem represent the City? Which the Wilderness? How does the conflict play out in the poem?
2. Is Wordsworth's poem open form or closed form? How can you tell?
3. Wordsworth makes two allusions to Greek mythology: the names Proteus and Triton. Who are they, and why are they relevant to the poem?

For Denise Levertov

1. What exactly is meant by the title of the poem? Consider the parts of speech of both words and how changing their categories creates different meanings for what happens in the poem. What title would you give this poem if it were yours?
2. What is happening to the speaker and her companion in the poem? What is different about their responses to what is happening?
3. Why do you suppose Levertov repeats the word *away* several times within the poem? What do you make of the repeated *way-way* sounds throughout the poem? Which words carry that sound?

4. Compare the theme of this poem to the theme that Dariel Suarez draws in the final paragraph of his essay "In Orbit" in chapter four. In what ways are the two themes similar?

For Kassity Higgins

1. In "*Othello*: Three Deaths and a Promotion," Higgins follows the model for the cost-benefit analysis given in chapter five. On what is she performing the analysis? What is her inspiration for doing so? What persona is she adopting as the writer, and who is her intended audience?
2. After summarizing the play in the second paragraph, Higgins sets forth two benefits and two costs. What are they? Does she find that the benefits outweigh the costs, or vice versa? For what reasons?
3. Look closely at Higgins's third paragraph. What is the topic sentence? What is (are) her narrow down(s)? What is (are) her quotation(s)? What is (are) her explanation(s)? What is her conclusion? Write them out word for word as done in the examples for Shakespeare and Chopin above.

For Joshua Dycus

1. In "Father Earth, the Tyrant," Dycus follows the model for the literature essay given earlier in this chapter. Who is the author and what is the title of the work to which he is responding? What is the premise of that work? What feature does he choose to discuss? What is his thesis?
2. In his second paragraph, Dycus defines some key terms he uses later in the essay. What are those terms? Why did he define them here before going on to his analysis?
3. Look closely at Dycus's third paragraph. What is the topic sentence? What is (are) his narrow down(s)? What is (are) his quotation(s)? What is (are) his explanation(s)? What is his conclusion? Write them out word for word as done in the examples for Shakespeare and Chopin above.

Glossary of Important Terms

Abstract: An abstract word names a quality instead of a specific object. Abstract words require the reader to assume what the writer means—but the reader's understanding may not align with the writer's intent. A *Camaro* is a specific brand of car, but a Camaro's *appeal* is a quality we will have to describe further for the reader to understand our meaning. Is it the tint of the red paint that appeals to us? Is it the smell of the leather interior? Is it the satisfying rev of the engine we hear when we hit the gas? Words ending in *-ance/-ence, -ism, -ity, -ment, -ness, -ship,* or *-tion* (e.g., *variance, dynamism, enormity, involvement, completeness, friendship, subtraction*), often derived from adjectives and verbs, are typically abstract.

Action: (1) Actions are the movements, gestures, or vocalizations made by the characters in a story. From Kate Chopin's "The Story of an Hour," we find this example: "She sat with her head thrown back upon the cushion of the chair, quite motionless, except when a sob came up into her throat and shook her, as a child who has cried itself to sleep continues to sob in its dreams." The sobs and the manner in which Mrs. Mallard sits—motionless yet weeping—convey her despair. (2) Action is a happening that affects a character in a story. In another passage from Chopin's story, we read, "The delicious breath of rain was in the air. In the street below a peddler was crying his wares. The notes of a distant song that someone was singing reached her faintly, and countless sparrows were twittering in the eaves." In this passage, Mrs. Mallard is affected by the actions of the air, the peddler, the singer, and the birds.

Analogy: An analogy is a special type of comparison. A straight comparison looks for similarities between two objects that are somewhat alike. An analogy makes a comparison between two unlike objects. If you are looking for similarities between the Toyota Camry and the Honda Accord, for example, you are making a comparison between two cars—two like objects. If, however, you are finding similarities between a Toyota Camry and molten lava, you are creating an analogy. A *simile* or a *metaphor* is often the starting point of an analogy. See **Figures of Speech**.

Anaphora: Anaphora, one of the figures of speech considered a *scheme*, is the repetition of a word or words at the start of each word group in a string: "We are young, we are strong, and we are ready to take over the world."

Anecdote: An anecdote is a short narrative often useful in an introductory paragraph to engage the audience or in body paragraphs to provide brief examples that develop and support larger ideas. For instance, to illustrate the water crisis in Nevada, a writer might tell the tale of a boating trip taken on Lake Mead and describe how her party came upon a newly exposed skeleton. Anecdotes often help the writer connect to the reader through shared personal experiences.

Antithesis: Antithesis, a figure of speech considered a *scheme*, sets ideas of contrasting or opposing value in a parallel structure: "She was kind yet vicious, honorable yet cruel, loving yet deadly." Often the antithesis is signaled by words such as *yet*, *but*, or *though*.

Argumentation: In argumentation, writers set forth a position on an issue and try to convince readers to accept their stance. For an argument to take place, this issue must have at least two disputable (and supportable) sides. No one, for example, could ever take the stance that child abuse is a good thing. On social and economic issues, arguments based on policy (whether to adopt one course of action or another on the issue) rather than morality (whether the issue is right or wrong) or fact (whether the issue is true or not true) make for better essay topics. Two common argumentative strategies are *induction* and *deduction*. Often, argumentative essays contain a *body of proofs* that comes from research.

Audience: Your audience is the person or the people with whom you are communicating. As a writer, you must choose your audience before you begin to write or discover that audience in the process of drafting. The audience should not be the same person as the writer (too private and personal), and it should not be the general public (too vague and broad). Someone with a stake in the issue at hand—or someone you can convince has a stake—would be the best choice. Depending on your audience, you will also need to choose how to develop your thesis. For instance, if to an audience of concerned parents you propose that the school week be limited to four days, you will have to address how the four-day week will affect their work schedules and their ability to provide care for their kids. If, on the other hand, you are addressing the local school board, you will have to present case studies showing where a four-day week has been instituted and what benefit it provides to students.

Body: (1) The body of a paragraph is the portion between its topic sentence and its conclusion. In this portion should appear the chosen pattern of development signaled by a transition. (2) The body of an essay is the group of paragraphs between the introduction and the conclusion. In the body, we choose the development and support best suited to our essay's thesis. The required length of your essay and your thesis will guide how many paragraphs you will need in the body of the essay and how much development and support you will need to bring to each body paragraph.

Cause and Effect: *Cause* looks for sources: the reasons why an event happened or why an object exists. *Effect* looks for the consequences or the outcomes of the event or the existence of the object. A *causal chain* creates a series of events or objects, one serving as the cause of the next item in the series, or as the effect of the previous item. Cause and effect typically work together to create a causal chain around a key event or object. If, for instance, you choose the iPhone as your key event or object, one cause might be people's need for a better communication device than the old flip-phones or pagers. An effect of the iPhone, on the other hand, might be the proliferation of personal photos on social media.

Character: A character is an agent in a story who has a distinct personality and influences the outcome of the plot. A *major* character has much influence, and a *minor* character has little or no influence. A *dynamic* character shows change in her personality or circumstances as the story progresses, whereas a *static* character remains relatively the same. A *round* character exhibits several different traits, but a *flat* character has at most one discernible trait. All characters, major or minor, dynamic or static, round or flat, are products of the writer's imagination.

Closed Form: Closed-form poetry strictly adheres to a pattern of rhyme, syllable count, word or line repetition, or stanza length.

Coherence: Coherence is a measure of how well an essay focuses on a single issue. A coherent essay begins with a thesis that governs the topic sentences of the body paragraphs, and those topic sentences in turn govern each sentence within the paragraphs.

Cohesion: Cohesion governs the flow of a sequence of sentences. In the sequence, each sentence should open with information learned in a previous sentence and end with information that is new or unknown to the reader. This information, however, must relate to the essay's issue, or the essay will lack coherence. Consider the following passage: "I like doughnuts. The best doughnuts in town are sold at Connie's Bakery. Connie's Bakery stands on the corner of Main Street and First Avenue. First Avenue was torn up in the recent downtown development. The development took a long time." The sentences are cohesive because each opens with information learned in a previous sentence, but they are incoherent because they do not focus on the issue raised in the first (topic) sentence: the speaker's fondness for doughnuts. In contrast, consider this passage: "I like doughnuts. One doughnut I prefer is the chocolate cake because the sweetness of the chocolate offsets the slightly heavy texture of the cake. My favorite doughnut, though, is glazed because I enjoy the taste of the sweet melted sugar surrounding the springy interior." In this passage, the writer has provided coherence (focus on one issue) as well as cohesion. See also **Known-New Contract**.

Comparison: A comparison finds similarities between two like objects. If you write that a Toyota Camry and a Honda Accord both have 2.5-liter engines, six-speed automatic shifts, and zero-to-sixty times of four seconds, you are creating a comparison. Comparison is frequently done alongside a *contrast* or may verge into *analogy* if two unlike things are examined. See also **Analogy** and **Contrast**.

Conclusion: (1) In a body paragraph, a conclusion should signal that you have finished examining the controlling idea for that particular paragraph. (2) As the final part of an essay, the conclusion should signal the end of your communication with your audience. It may bring a narrative to a close, summarize the main points of the essay, restate the thesis, call the audience to action, suggest avenues for further thinking, make a prediction about the future, offer a lesson the audience should learn, or state a personal judgment on the issue.

Concrete: The term *concrete* refers to nouns that name very specific objects and to those descriptive words and details that stimulate the senses. The word *car* is general; but a Toyota Camry is a specific type of car and thus more concrete. We can also take the abstract description of a car's appeal and make it more concrete: "This Toyota Camry has a wine-red glossy exterior paint, a black leather interior that smells of mint-fresh oil, paddle shifting on the steering wheel, and a zero-to-sixty time of four seconds." Similarly, saying "The flower is pretty" makes a general statement. You leave too much to the interpretation of your reader. Saying "The daffodil has bright yellow petals" or "The daisy has long white petals and an herbaceous scent" prevents your reader from visualizing a different flower entirely.

Connotation: Unlike denotation, a connotation is an associative meaning of a word. For instance, the word *rose* names a flower but may suggest love and romance.

Contrast: A contrast is a study of differences between two like objects. If you point out that the Toyota Camry has an optional 3.0-liter engine, paddle shifting instead of a stick, and a turbo boost—options that the Honda Accord doesn't have—then you are making a contrast between the two cars. Contrast is frequently done alongside *comparison*.

Coordinating Conjunction: The coordinating conjunctions are known best as fanboys: *for*, *and*, *nor*, *but*, *or*, *yet*, *so*. With them, you can create **compound sentences**, which are two simple sentences set together with equal importance.

Cost-Benefit Analysis: A cost-benefit analysis considers both the costs and the benefits of a policy to show which weigh more heavily. Businesses perform this analysis to decide whether a purchase or a change of policy will produce positive results. Individuals think of costs and benefits when making lifestyle choices such as whether to buy a gym membership, LASIK eye surgery, or something similar.

Definition: A definition creates a meaning for a word. Definitions are the reason why dictionaries and lexicons exist, but a writer may choose to apply a word in a new context that calls for redefining the term. A traditional definition has three parts: the *term* being defined, the *class* to which that term belongs, and the *differentiation* that distinguishes that term from others in its class. A frame for creating a definition is "A ___ is a ___ that ___." Put the term in the first blank, the class in the second, and the differentiation in the third: "A <u>trombone</u> is a <u>musical instrument</u> that <u>changes pitch with a large slide</u>."

Denotation: Unlike connotation, denotation is a word's dictionary definition. The word *rose*, according to the *New Oxford American Dictionary*, means "a prickly bush or shrub that typically bears red, pink, yellow, or white fragrant flowers."

Description: Description is a mode of development but is also an important tool by which the other modes can convey concrete details from writer to audience. The best descriptions rely on concrete nouns and details that appeal directly to the five senses. Many consider description to be the most essential type of development and support because all writing requires some level of description.

Development: Development is the use of a strategy (or *mode*) in the body of an essay to support the essay's thesis and convey the writer's experience, purpose, or meaning to the audience. The chapter on development names several modes—description, narration, cause and effect, etc.—that the writer may choose based on her purpose and her audience.

Diction: Diction refers to your choice of words when writing. Your word choice, in turn, will depend on your issue and your audience. Generally speaking, diction can be either formal or informal. See also **Style**.

Ellipsis: (1) Ellipsis, one of the figures of speech considered a *scheme*, drops unneeded words in parallel structures so that sentences are more compact: "I went to the store; she, to the bank." (2) As punctuation marks, the ellipsis dots (. . .) are frequently used in academic writing to indicate where words have been dropped from the original of a quoted source.

Epistrophe: Another figure of speech considered a *scheme*, epistrophe is the repetition of a word or words at the end of consecutive word groups: "I scream, you scream, we all scream for ice cream."

Essay: An essay is a short, nonfiction writing product focused on a single controlling idea. An essay can be categorized by its purpose (expository, argumentative, persuasive, speculative, literary, etc.) or by its dominant mode of development (narrative, descriptive, comparison-contrast, process, etc.). It typically has an introduction, a body, and a conclusion.

Ethos: *Ethos* is a term, based on Aristotle, for a method of persuasion relying on the character of the person making the argument. For example, if the person presenting a case about the dangers of pesticides on cattle is a veterinarian with several years' experience in industrial agriculture, then her credentials will add weight to the argument; the audience is more likely to trust the validity of the argument based on the speaker's expertise and authority in the field. A student writer must bolster her own authority by proving her expertise or by citing credible sources: experts and writers with established credentials, who published in professional forums under the eye of careful editors. By introducing these sources in her paper by name and job title or degree, she will earn the respect and trust of her audience.

Event: In a story or a plot, an event is a significant action taken (or experienced) by a character, one that changes her life.

Evidence: When a writer presents a stance or a claim, she must present evidence (also known as *proof*) to support it. If she argues that electric cars will cause more environmental damage than gas-engine cars, she must support that stance by providing environmental studies, testimony from experts, statistical analyses, eyewitness accounts, or other forms of proof. If she claims that *Star Wars* hero Luke Skywalker fits the model of the Divine Child archetype, then she must present the criteria for the model and show how Luke, in his actions and characterization, meets those criteria. Evidence will appear in the essay's development, after a thesis that sets out the stance or claim.

Figures of Speech: A figure of speech compresses more meaning into our words or creates pleasing patterns in our phrases and clauses. Some figures are *tropes*, which assign novel meanings to words, and some are *schemes*, which change the usual order of words.

One example of a trope, the *metaphor*, is a direct comparison equating two objects of different classes. Shakespeare's famous line "All the world's a stage, and all the men and women merely players" is a metaphor comparing human activity to the action of a stage play. Other metaphors include "All our words are but crumbs that fall down from the feast of the mind" (Khalil Gibran), and "Delia was an overbearing cake with condescending frosting" (Maggie Stiefvater). An *implied metaphor* sets up a comparison by borrowing a trait of one object to describe the other. For example, the sentence "The ship plowed the ocean" compares a ship and a plow. The implied equation is ship/ocean = plow/earth, with the final term (earth) dropped. The trick to understanding metaphors (and similes, described below) is not to take the comparisons literally. A careful reader understands that some trait of one of the objects is being transferred to the other. Thus, the world isn't really a stage, but it may seem so at times when we feel that our lives have been scripted for us—or after we've viewed our umpteenth *TikTok* challenge.

Another trope, the *simile*, also compares two objects in different classes but uses linking terms such as *like*, *as*, and *so*: "The trumpet section was so loud that it sounded like a herd of elephants." This simile likens trumpet players to elephants. Other similes include "She is as in a field a silken tent" (Robert Frost) and "It was Françoise, motionless and erect, framed in the small doorway of the corridor like the statue of a saint in its niche" (Marcel Proust).

Another common trope, *personification*, attributes human qualities to nonhuman objects. The sentence "The wind scolded us through the cracks in the fence" is an example because wind cannot scold. Another example is "Love whispered sweet nothings into her ears." Love, being an abstract quality, cannot whisper into an ear.

Two more tropes are *synecdoche* and *metonymy*, both of which rely on substitution. Synecdoche means a part substitutes for the whole, or a whole for the part: "All hands on deck!" substitutes *hands* (part) for *sailors* (whole); "I bought a new set of wheels" substitutes *wheels* (part) for *car* (whole); "Los Angeles won the World Series" substitutes *Los Angeles* (the entire city) for the *Angels* or *Dodgers* (the baseball team). Metonymy means substituting a term closely associated with another: "The White House issued a statement" substitutes *White House* (residence) for *president* (resident; person making statement); "The fish rose from the deep" substitutes *deep* (attribute) for *ocean* (object with depth; home of fish); "All reports go to the corner office" substitutes *corner office* (workspace of important worker) for *boss* (important worker).

Some common schemes such as *anaphora, epistrophe,* and the *rule of three*, among others, are defined elsewhere in this glossary. Other, lesser-known tropes are defined elsewhere as well.

Function Shift: The figure of speech known as function shift (*anthimeria*), another *trope*, lets writers turn nouns into verbs, or verbs into adjectives, and so on, to create colorful descriptions that arrest the eyes: "Her family summers in the mountains and winters in Florida"; "This drink will hair your chin"; "The kids arted the walls with several drawings."

General: A general word names a whole class of objects or people rather than a specific item or person. Whether or not a word is too general depends on where it stands on the *ladder of abstraction*. For example, the word *instrument* is general and high on the ladder. Even if we limit ourselves to musical instruments, we have several varieties to choose from. The word *trumpet*, however, is more specific and moves us down the ladder; we have now found a particular type of musical instrument. Most specific of all is *Super Olds*, a very special model of trumpet; by naming the model, we move to the more concrete rungs of the ladder.

Helping Verb: Also called *auxiliary verbs*, helping verbs pair with main verbs to create a verb phrase. The helping verbs are the various forms of *have*, *be*, *do*, and the *modals*. See also **Modal**.

Image: An image is a word or a group of words that creates a picture in the mind by appealing to the senses with concrete details or figures of speech. This passage from Christine Boyka Kluge's prose poem "Inventing New Bodies" makes generous use of images (in italics): "*Trailing silvery paths* across *brick walks and patios*, we slip into *gardens* and *flowerpots*. We *paint patterns*, *leaf* to *leaf*. We *fasten our mouths* to *petals* and *stems* and *swallow*, knowing nothing but sweetness."

Induction: Through induction, we move step by step along a series of specific observations until we can discern a general pattern. If, for example, we've heard the neighbor's dog bark every evening at exactly nine o'clock, and we expect the dog to bark tonight at the same time, we use induction to reach that conclusion. The series of observations is often called an *inductive chain*.

Introduction: The introduction is the first part of the essay, the part that greets the audience, establishes the issue, sets the writer's tone, and, in many cases, presents a thesis. Depending on the type of essay you are writing, your introduction can either state a problem, offer an opinion, present a stance on an argument, identify a literary element for analysis, propose an action for your audience to undertake, or have some other purpose. See also **Lead**.

Irony: A widely used figure of speech, *verbal irony* is the expression of one's meaning by using words that have contrasting or opposing value. Its use generates humor, emphasis, or surprise. Thus, in this basic form, irony is considered a *trope*. In contrast, *situational irony*, *dramatic irony*, and *cosmic irony* work at the structural level of storytelling and therefore are *schemes*; they arise from the actions taken by a story's characters or from a difference between the perceptions of the characters and those of the reader. For examples of all these forms of irony, see the discussion of *theme* in chapter six.

Issue: In an academic setting, a writer may be assigned an essay topic or may choose one for herself. In either case, she must narrow the topic down to an issue that fits the subject matter and length requirements of the assignment. To find an issue, the writer must spend time brainstorming, clustering, free writing, researching, or using other means of prewriting and invention. For example, if your instructor asks you to write an essay on controversial legal decisions, you can narrow the topic down to the not-guilty verdict for George Zimmerman in the Trayvon Martin murder trial. Issue, along with writer, audience, and purpose, must be clearly signaled in the essay's thesis.

Kairos: *Kairos* is a form of persuasion based on opportunity. The speaker tries to persuade his audience that a certain moment (usually the present one) is the best for a particular course of action. The famous poetic idiom *carpe diem* ("seize the day") is based on this appeal.

Known-New Contract: This contract is a universal pattern of sentence construction that places information already known to the audience in the subject slot and new information in the predicate. Following this pattern creates cohesion among a group of sentences. See **Cohesion**.

Lead (or Lede): A lead is a means of engaging the audience in the introduction of an essay. One may choose from among several strategies: *direct statement, anecdote, surprise, description, mood, problem,* and others.

Litotes: Litotes, a *trope*, is the use of understatement, usually for emphasis or humor: "Her new yacht cost only three million dollars"; "She is the president of no small company"; "He feels not unlike a fool." Litotes can be signaled, as in the examples above, by the deliberate use of negatives (*no, not un-*) or an ironic use of qualifiers such as *only* or *just*.

Logical Fallacies: Logical fallacies are faulty or misleading lines of reasoning and often appear in arguments, either spoken or written. See the description of the argumentative essay in chapter five.

Logos: *Logos* is a term derived from Aristotle for a method of persuasion based on an appeal to reason. The most basic forms of appeal are those of induction or deduction. This appeal also works when the writer can back up her assertions with statistics, research data, or other hard facts that are relevant to the subject matter at hand. For example, if the writer finds data from the National Transportation Safety Board that establish a link between traffic fatalities and cell phone use while driving, then she has a valid reason to assert a cause-and-effect relationship between the two. By using *logos*, the writer also burnishes her own standing with an audience by appearing knowledgeable about the issue under discussion.

Lyric Poetry: Poetry that centers on an image or series of images is called lyric poetry.

Modal: A modal is a helping verb that shows certainty, probability, possibility, capability, permission, obligation, or condition. The traditional modals are *will, would, shall, should, can, could, may, might,* and *must*. Other words and phrases that can work like modals are *ought to, used to, have to, need,* and *dare*.

Mode: A mode is a form of development: narration, description, etc. See **Development**.

Monroe's Motivated Sequence: Monroe's Motivated Sequence is a writing plan developed by Alan H. Monroe at Purdue University in the 1930s. The plan is persuasive in nature, intended to prompt an audience toward a specific course of action. Initially, the sequence gains the readers' *attention* with an interesting introduction. It then continues by presenting the *need*: alerting the audience of the problem. It moves from the need to the *satisfaction* step: the proposed solution. It then adds a *visualization* step that paints a picture of the world with the implemented solution. Finally, there is an *actuation* step to tell readers what they specifically need to do. Think of modern-day infomercials to understand the effectiveness of the approach. To use Monroe's effectively, the writer must evaluate the research she has found, determine the arguments she is most moved by, and use the most persuasive sequence available.

Mood: (1) A mood is an atmosphere created by a written work that evokes an emotion in the reader. Mood is usually created by a combination of setting and tone. See also **Setting** and **Tone**. (2) Mood also is a grammatical term for how the writer or speaker signals her intent by altering the verb. The three primary moods are *indicative* (the speaker states a fact: I *am leaving* the store), *imperative* (the speaker makes a command or request: *Leave* the store!), and *subjunctive* (the speaker expresses a wish, demand, or hypothetical: I asked that she *leave* the store). A fourth mood, called the *potential* or *conditional*, voices what the speaker thinks may, could, or should happen (but hasn't) and requires a **Modal** (I *will leave* the store, I *could leave* the store, etc.).

Mythos: *Mythos* is a form of persuasion based on a cultural or national tradition the speaker shares with her audience. If, for example, a speaker tries to persuade an audience to support legislation based on a common belief in "government of the people, by the people, for the people" (an allusion to Abraham Lincoln's Gettysburg Address), then she is appealing to a shared sense of patriotism. Lincoln's own speech includes an allusion to Thomas Jefferson's Declaration of Independence—the proposition that "all men are created equal"—and thus also makes an appeal to *mythos*.

Narration: (1) Narration is a mode of development that tells a story, often a personal experience of the writer. However, narration may also appear as part of the development of a definition, a process, an argumentation, or some other essay form. (2) In storytelling and literary analysis, narration is related to point of view. Asking what type of narration is used in a story is roughly equivalent to asking what point of view is used. Narration may include, therefore, raw exposition from the narrator—his or her perceptions of or commentary on events and characters and setting—or may simply record the action of the story, much like a camera, without any narratorial intrusions.

Narrative: A narrative is a story told by a narrator, typically shaped to a plot and colored by the narrator's persona. The narrative can take many forms: a movie, a novel, a short story, an essay, a poem, a fable, and so on.

Narrative Poetry: Poetry that tells a story is called narrative poetry.

Narrator: The narrator is a special persona adopted by an author or writer to be the voice or witness of a story. Depending on the narrator's role, he or she may comment on the action of the story itself. The narrator's distance from the story is measured by the pronouns used to identify the narrator. See **Point of View**.

Open Form: In contrast with closed-form poetry, open-form poetry does not strictly adhere to any patterns; also known as *free verse*.

Paradox: Paradox, a form of *trope*, is a statement containing a contradiction that is nevertheless true: "The deeper you go, the higher you fly / The higher you fly, the deeper you go" (The Beatles).

Paragraph: A paragraph is a series of sentences set off by an indentation of the first line and a break at the end of the last line. In an essay, certain paragraphs fill specific functions: the introduction, the body, and the conclusion. The number of paragraphs in an essay is dictated by the scope of the thesis. A narrow thesis should limit the essay to fewer paragraphs, whereas a broad thesis will demand several paragraphs of development.

Parallelism: A figure of speech we would classify as a *scheme*, parallelism balances word groups by setting them in the same grammatical form. Abraham Lincoln employs a famous example of parallelism (and *anaphora*, too) in the Gettysburg Address when he states, "But, in a larger sense, we can not dedicate—we can not consecrate—we can not hallow—this ground." In his ringing conclusion to the same speech, he employs parallelism again (and this time, *epistrophe*) when he states "that government of the people, by the people, for the people, shall not perish from the earth." If the parallel structures are exactly alike, with the same number of words or syllables, as Lincoln has done in both examples above, then the writer has created an *isocolon*.

Parts of Speech: The parts of speech are the categories by which we sort words according to their form, meaning, or function. The traditional categories are *adjective, adverb, conjunction, interjection, noun, preposition, pronoun*, and *verb*. Adjectives and adverbs describe other words; conjunctions and prepositions connect other words; pronouns substitute for other words; interjections express emotion; nouns identify who or what; verbs identify actions, processes, and states.

Pathos: *Pathos* is a term, based on Aristotle, for a method of persuasion based on an appeal to emotion. The writer has several methods of making such an appeal: vivid or engaging storytelling, striking figures of speech, and humor are three common devices. A writer may try to elicit an audience's sense of optimism, or fear, or any emotion in between in order to establish an emotional connection between himself and his readers. One goal of such an appeal is to make the audience believe that the writer shares their views and their feelings. The *pathos* appeal, because of its power, should never be used to distract the audience from the real issues or to exploit them by driving them into a rage or a panic.

Persona: A persona is an identity the writer adopts within a work—but it is not the writer herself. A writer who refers to herself in an essay or story with first-person pronouns is perhaps the clearest-cut instance of the use of a persona. In many cases, a persona creates humor or satire. For example, Horace Miner adopts the persona of an anthropologist from a superior civilization in his spoof of Americans and of his own profession in "Body Ritual among the Nacirema."

Plot: The structure of events in a story, a plot begins with an *inducer*, which causes disorder in the life of the story's *protagonist*, and ends when the protagonist somehow resolves that disorder. In the Aristotelian model (initial conflict, rise in tension, climax, denouement), the plot saves its most exciting or tension-building event for late in the story, usually the moment when the protagonist is closest to achieving or losing his goal.

Point of View: The perspective through which a story is told, point of view describes the narrator's distance from the story and the pronouns used to label the characters. Point of view is categorized as *first person*, *second person*, or *third person*.

Premise: (1) A premise is the basis of support for an argument. It should be an assumption or an observation (e.g., all humans are mortal) that can be verified. A *syllogism* relies on a major premise and a minor premise to arrive at a conclusion that, if the premises are true, can be accepted as sound. (2) A premise may also be the central conflict that drives a narrative's plot. The premise of the movie *Star Wars: A New Hope*, for example, is that a team of rebels is trying to destroy the Empire's Death Star before the Empire can use it to crush the rebellion.

Problem-Solution Analysis: At its most basic, a problem-solution essay identifies a problem and proposes at least one possible solution to it. The purpose of the essay is typically informative or persuasive. Depending on the requirements of the essay and the complexity of the problem and the solution, the writer may have to do research to describe the breadth of the problem and the feasibility of the solution. One sophisticated version of this essay is the **Monroe's Motivated Sequence** described in chapter five.

Protagonist: The protagonist (often called the *hero*) is the main character in a story. The character who struggles against her is called the *antagonist*. The character next in importance to the protagonist is the *deuteragonist*, often a companion to or helper of the protagonist. The protagonist is often surrounded by *secondary characters* who are typically family, love interests, allies, or rivals.

Purpose: Purpose is the goal of the writer. Essays have at least one of four goals: to teach, to inform, to entertain, or to persuade. The writer decides on a purpose once she has an issue and a target audience in mind.

Reporting: The most general function of reporting is to gather facts and observations and shape them into a coherent whole. The facts and observations can come from many sources, most of which originate outside the writer. The reporter may be a passive observer, simply setting down newsworthy events, or an active interpreter, putting a personal or editorial spin on the material.

Rhetorical Question: Considered a *trope*, a rhetorical question is the use of a question not to ask for information but to make a point: "Is it America's problem when some other country goes bankrupt?"; "Isn't it time we did something about inflation?" Generally, a positive rhetorical question implies a negative statement ("It's not America's problem"), and a negative question implies a positive statement ("It's time we did something"). The rhetorical question can be a persuasive device that can move an audience toward an accord with the speaker. The examples above, if given in a speech to a crowd that does not favor foreign aid or that is concerned about inflation, can influence the listeners to accept more strongly the speaker's stance.

The Rule of Three: The rule of three, or *trebling*, is the deliberate use of three elements to shape a sentence, a passage, or an entire work of art. This figure of speech is one of many examples of a *scheme*. The two examples of **Parallelism** drawn from Lincoln's Gettysburg Address show how the rule of three creates pleasing harmony in sentence construction. Trebling can also raise and release tension, especially in the building of a plot, by delaying resolution or adding a final twist. It takes one of three forms: (1) the *uniform three*, in which all events have similar value, as when Jonah is trapped in the belly of the whale for three days; (2) the *accumulative three*, in which each of the three events is increasingly better (or worse), and in which the sequence leads to a climax, as when Ebenezer Scrooge is visited by three increasingly scary Christmas ghosts; (3) the *contrasting* or *opposite three*, in which the last event overturns or counters the first two, as when the three stepsisters in Cinderella try on the slipper, or when Goldilocks encounters the chairs, the bowls of porridge, and the beds in the house of the Three Bears. In stories, when the rule of three appears (as in the Cinderella story), it often signifies that the hero is about to undergo a transformation.

Satire: Satire is an expression that mocks a specific target—a person, an institution, a trend, an idea. Satire at its mildest can be humorous, but it can also offer sharp criticism with the goal of highlighting or reforming bad behavior. Horace Miner in "Body Ritual among the Nacirema" satirizes both the American obsession with hygiene and the superior tone often taken by the writers of anthropological studies.

Setting: The setting of a story (or of a narrative essay) is the time and place in which the characters (including the narrator) act. The setting is not only a backdrop but also the boundary imposed on the characters: They cannot act in a way not suitable to the setting.

Speaker: A speaker is the persona who gives voice to a poem and is equivalent to the narrator of a story.

Stanza: In a poem, a stanza is a group of lines comparable to a paragraph in prose.

Story: A story is a sequence of actions, usually shaped by a plot and told by a narrator.

Style: Style is how a writer uses language to express herself. Abraham Lincoln's style, for instance, is marked by elevated vocabulary and complex sentence structure:

> It is rather for us to be here dedicated to the great task remaining before us—that from these honored dead we take increased devotion to that cause for which they gave the last full measure of devotion. . . .

Alberto Ríos's style, on the other hand, is much more informal:

> The world on a map looks like the drawing of a cow
> In a butcher's shop, all those lines showing
> Where to cut.

Subordinating Conjunction: Subordinating conjunctions are connecting words that show place (*where, wherever*), time (*when, until, before*), manner (*as if, as though*), degree (*as . . . as, than*), condition (*if, unless*), cause (*because, since*), result (*so . . . that, such . . . that*), concession (*though, although, while*), and purpose (*so that*). With them, you can create **complex sentences**, two simple sentences joined with relative importance.

Syllogism: A form of deduction, the syllogism is a fundamental pattern of argumentation: a major premise, a minor premise, and a conclusion.

> Major premise: All musical instruments produce sound.
> Minor premise: A drum is a musical instrument.
> Conclusion: A drum produces sound.

The predicate of the major premise (*produce sound*) becomes the predicate of the conclusion; the subject of the minor premise (*drum*) becomes the subject of the conclusion. For the syllogism to work, the premises must be valid and the conclusion must logically follow from them.

Symbol: A symbol is an image with a special meaning attached to it. A rose, as an image, may appeal to our sight and our sense of smell (and prick us if we touch a thorn), but a rose given by one lover to another on February 14 may have special romantic associations—and hence, be symbolic.

Theme: A theme is an overall message or impression that arises when certain images or ideas are repeated or emphasized. An action may be repeated by characters in a story, an idea may appear at the climax of a narrative essay, an image may spring from a critical description in a poem, irony may arise out of a difference in how characters (and the audience) perceive events—there are several ways to create repetition or emphasis. Themes, however, are not what the story or essay or poem is about, but what the work says about a certain idea. For instance, in Frankie Mac's essay "Being Good," the idea in the title is not the theme. What her essay says about trying to be good at something—that peer pressure should not lower our self-esteem or prevent us from trying new things— is the theme. In Lisa Bailey's essay "Black and White and Blue All Over," media coverage is not the theme. What her essay says about media coverage—that a community can misapprehend a local newspaper's presentation of events—is the theme. A good piece of writing may contain multiple themes.

Thesis: The thesis sets forth the claim, the idea, the item, the person, the definition, the key event, the story, or poetic element—the main point—that the writer will examine in detail throughout an essay. A thesis should embody *issue, audience, writer's stance*, and *purpose*. An explicit thesis appears in one sentence, whereas in an implied thesis, a series of sentences conveys the essay's intent through images, anecdotes, observations, etc.

Tone: (1) A writer, as part of her persona, may express—openly or covertly—an attitude toward her topic or issue. Thus, H. Lee Barnes in his essay "I Was Young . . ." seems to show exasperation toward what he calls the literary establishment. (2) A writer may also express an attitude toward her audience. In her essay "Why Are Americans Afraid of Dragons?," originally presented as a speech to an audience of librarians, Ursula K. Le Guin gently admonishes her listeners with a brief anecdote about a censorial librarian at the start but politely acknowledges them in the following paragraphs.

Transitions: Transitions signal direction, order, and intent within an essay. They link sentences and bridge paragraphs, and they tell the reader the relationship between the ideas presented in those word groups. There are three kinds of transitions: the repetition of a key word or idea used earlier in the essay, a synonym or a pronoun substituting for that idea, and expressions such as *first*, *however*, *for instance*, *therefore*, and so on. A larger list of these expressions appears in chapter three.

Writer: The writer, the essay's author, can adopt any number of personas, serious or not, to present his issue to his audience. You have many roles to fill in your life, and you can use any of them as an essay writer. You could be a concerned parent, an angry taxpayer, an avid anime fan. You can also pretend to be someone else entirely. Whatever persona you adopt, it should have a vested interest in the issue being discussed and should demonstrate a credible understanding of that issue. In part, your essay's merit will be judged by how well you present your voice and your knowledge in the essay. Be aware, however, that creating a persona for an essay does not mean you are writing a short story for a creative writing class. The persona you craft (and the essay itself) still has the purpose of conveying a truth to your audience.

Printed in the USA
CPSIA information can be obtained
at www.ICGtesting.com
JSHW010846270824
68799JS00001B/1